LAW AT THE FRONTIERS OF [illegible]E

How should judges and legislators address challenges arising at the frontiers of biomedicine? What if it became possible to edit the DNA of embryos for enhanced traits, gestate a fetus in an artificial womb, self-modify brain implants to provide new skills or bring a frozen human back to life?

This book presents an innovative legal theory and applies it to future developments in biomedicine. This legal theory reconceptualises the role of legal officials in terms of moral principle and contextual constraints: 'contextual legal idealism'. It is applied by asking how a political leader or appeal court judge could address technological developments for which the current law of England and Wales would be ill-equipped to respond.

The book's central thesis is that the regulation of human conduct requires moral reasoning directed to the context in which it operates. The link between abstract theory and practical application is articulated using future developments within four areas of biomedicine. Developments in heritable genome editing and cybernetic biohacking are addressed using Explanatory Notes to hypothetical UK Parliamentary Bills. Developments in ectogestation and cryonic reanimation are addressed using hypothetical appeal court judgments.

The book will be of great interest to scholars and students of medical/health law, criminal law, bioethics, biolaw, legal theory and moral philosophy.

Law at the Frontiers of Biomedicine

Creating, Enhancing and Extending Human Life

Shaun D Pattinson

•HART•
OXFORD • LONDON • NEW YORK • NEW DELHI • SYDNEY

HART PUBLISHING

Bloomsbury Publishing Plc

Kemp House, Chawley Park, Cumnor Hill, Oxford, OX2 9PH, UK

1385 Broadway, New York, NY 10018, USA

29 Earlsfort Terrace, Dublin 2, Ireland

HART PUBLISHING, the Hart/Stag logo, BLOOMSBURY and the Diana logo are trademarks of Bloomsbury Publishing Plc

First published in Great Britain 2023

First published in hardback, 2023

Paperback edition, 2024

A catalogue record for this book is available from the British Library.

A catalogue record for this book is available from the Library of Congress.

Library of Congress Control Number: 2022947575

ISBN: PB: 978-1-50996-674-5
ePDF: 978-1-50994-108-7
ePub: 978-1-50994-109-4

Typeset by Compuscript Ltd, Shannon

PREFACE

Judges and legislators are increasingly being called upon to address biomedical developments that were once merely science fiction. This book considers future developments in the technologies enabling the creation, enhancement and extension of human life. All have their basis in some feature of existing biomedical science and range from likely incremental developments to less likely leaps: from refinements to the ability to edit the genes of embryos (heritable genome editing) to bringing frozen bodies back to life (cryonic reanimation). Consideration of these future technologies culminates in hypothetical legal responses: two UK Parliamentary Bills and two appeal court judgments.

These hypothetical legal responses apply the theory articulated and defended in the first two chapters. There is a sense in which chapter 2 may seem to be trying to sell vegetarianism to those who seek crispy bacon and medium-rare sirloin. It goes against the contemporary grain by both rejecting the 'toothbrush theory of philosophy' and adhering to an 'Archimedean point'. The former treats philosophical tools like toothbrushes and insists that everyone should seek their own and refuse to share another's. The latter refers to the principle of levers attributed to Archimedes: 'Give me something to stand on and I can move the world.'[1] Yet, this book explicitly supports the Archimedean claim made by Alan Gewirth that there is a supreme principle of morality.[2]

This book has two purposes. One purpose is to present and apply a theory of adjudication and legislation.[3] Another is to address ethical and legal issues raised by the future developments mentioned above. My central question is thus: how should judges and legislators understand and address the substantive, structural and conceptual challenges arising at the frontiers of biomedicine? In the process of answering this question I hope to provide something of interest even for committed carnivores.[4]

The law and URLs cited in this book were last checked on 1 August 2022.

[1] Archimedes, as quoted in Ripstein 2007, 5.

[2] See principally Gewirth 1978.

[3] In a sense, this book is a sequel to Pattinson 2018.

[4] The metaphors in this Preface do not describe my actual eating or toothbrush preferences – I am a meat eater (albeit with a dislike for bacon) and would like you to keep away from my toothbrush.

ACKNOWLEDGEMENTS

The writing of this book was greatly assisted by the award of a Major Research Fellowship by the Leverhulme Trust.

LEVERHULME
TRUST

I am grateful to those who commented on papers in which I have presented ideas during the process of writing this book, including at the Society of Legal Scholars Annual Conference, Preston in September 2019, a DeepMind webinar in March 2021, the 14th World Conference on Bioethics, Medical Ethics and Health Law, Porto, Portugal in March 2022 and at the Society of Socio-Legal Studies Association Annual Conference, York in April 2022. I would also like to thank those who provided comments on early drafts of one or more chapters: Dave Archard, Deryck Beyleveld, Emma Cave, Zoe Gounari, Andy Greenfield, Gleider Hernández, Marianna Iliadou and Zoe Tongue. Their comments have saved me from many errors, though I remain fully responsible for all those that remain. I owe special thanks to Kaylin Raine, who did a literature search for me on issues related to cryonic reanimation during the term in which the pandemic had delayed her plans to study in Italy.

I dedicate this book to my dearest Zoe and our beautiful boy, Orion.

SDP

CONTENTS

PART II
CASE STUDIES

PART III
CONCLUSION

PART I

Moral and Legal Theory

1

Moral and Legal Values

1.1. Introduction

> I was sure there was a white light. As my eyes focused it morphed into a white sleeve, into which a robotic arm retracted. 'Welcome to New Life', declared the woman to whom the arm was attached. Only moments before, or what had felt like only moments before, I had been sedated into unconsciousness on the understanding that I would soon die and be cryonically frozen.
>
> This was my reanimation; my second life. I had begun my first life genetically enhanced and gestated in an artificial womb. That had been a long life. Every time a body part had failed it had been replaced with a synthetic part, until my cybernetic body had required treatment beyond what was available to medical science. I had then been informed that the best my billions could buy was the chance to be reanimated, when science could either cure my ailment or transfer my consciousness.

This scenario captures a possible future for the technologies explored in this book. You are probably thinking that it is no more than science fiction. One response would be to point out that there have been many steps towards delivery of my imagined billionaire's life, with its super enhancement and super longevity. As will be explained later in this book, humans have been genetically modified, embryos are living longer outside the womb, premature babies are surviving earlier in gestation, pacemakers and artificial limbs are treatment options, and there are cryonically frozen corpses. But many assumptions have to be made to view these as steps on a trajectory towards this imagined future, and numerous additional assumptions are, if I may change my metaphor, hiding below the surface.

My narrator is a billionaire, because it is generally assumed that delivering such dreams will be so expensive that it will be within the purview of only the very rich, thereby magnifying existing socio-economic inequities. Yet, technologies that cost a great deal of money at the outset usually end up becoming much cheaper. It cost around $2.7 billion to sequence the human genome in 2003.[1] By late 2015, the cost had dropped to below $1,500. It is now available to consumers for two or three hundred dollars; as one journalist put it, 'for less than the price of the latest Apple Watch'.[2] This is an example of what seems to be a predictable trend.

[1] See NHGR 2019.
[2] Mullin 2020.

We are, however, generally bad at predicting the future of science and innovation. Dolly the sheep was created using a technique dismissed just over a decade before as 'biologically impossible' by two well respected developmental biologists.[3] My bet is that no interviewee, when asked in 2015 where they would be in five years' time, predicted being furloughed or homeworking due to a global pandemic. 2020 vision was apparently rare! There is an asymmetry between what is obvious before and after an event, scientific discovery or technological innovation. Search engines and social media now seem an obvious way to make money from the internet, but things were not nearly so obvious during the early days of the internet.[4] After something occurs or has been explained we can easily move, like Dr Watson in *The Adventure of the Dancing Men*, from considering it to be 'utterly inexplicable' to 'absurdly simple'.[5] There is no way around this, so the technologies selected for consideration in this book range from those that currently seem to be likely incremental developments to some apparently distant and less likely leaps.[6]

One objection to thought experiments is that they often simplify dilemmas. How realistic is it to imagine a binary choice between pulling or not pulling a lever to substitute one death for five (as per Philippa Foot's trolley problem), or between remaining connected to or disconnecting yourself from an unconscious world-famous violinist (as per Judith Jarvis Thomson's thought experiment on abortion)?[7] How many plausible moral reasons for distinguishing between killing and letting die does James Rachels exclude when he asks you to imagine being in the same room as a starving child with a sandwich you do not need?[8] This book will separate out the technologies alluded to in my opening scenario with an eye on the limitations and assumptions easily cloaked by imaginary futures and thought experiments. Some of the most demanding ethical and legal challenges are presented by the very complexity and uncertainty that it is so tempting to ignore.

One of this book's aims, as I have hinted, is to examine the ethical and legal issues raised by plausible biomedical innovations in the creation, enhancement and extension of human life. The other aim is to present a theory for judicial and legislative development of the law. These two aims cohere because the application of this book's legal theory is best explained by considering how it would deal with developments that are likely to find existing legal rules to be unclear or otherwise wanting. The biomedical innovations examined in this book represent developments of just this type. They would evoke considerable moral concern and this chapter unpacks different types of moral perspectives capable of underpinning such concerns.

[3] See Wilmut et al 1997 and McGrath & Solter 1984, 1319, respectively.
[4] See Ridley 2020, 204–210.
[5] Doyle 1905, ch 3.
[6] Cf the discussion of heritable genome editing in ch 3 and cryonic reanimation in ch 6.
[7] See Foot 1967 and Thomson 1971.
[8] See Rachels 1979, 160. Rachels neutralises, for example, the cost to the actor and the probability that death will result.

This book has three parts. Part 1 (this and the next chapter) contextualises, articulates and defends the framework that is to be applied to four biomedical case studies. This chapter sets out the context for the theory presented in chapter 2. Part 2 addresses four case studies involving the creation, enhancement or extension of human life: heritable genome editing, ectogestation, cybernetic biohacking and cryonic reanimation. Part 3 is the conclusion.

This chapter maps the territory of morality and the trajectory of appeals to moral criteria in the law of England and Wales, enabling subsequent chapters to take a particular path forward. The focus here on the law of a single jurisdiction is necessitated by the later presentation of hypothetical judgments and draft legislation for the biomedical case studies.

1.2. Types of Moralities

The terms 'morality' and 'ethics' are used by different people to capture divergent concepts. They are used as synonyms in this book. For current purposes, *morality* (or *ethics*) is to be understood as referring to action-guiding requirements that are *other-regarding* in the sense that they require an individual to act in the interests of others. For some moral theories (including the theory defended in chapter 2), morality can be defined more narrowly as other-regarding obligations that are *categorical* in the sense of overriding all other interests or obligations. There are various potential sources for other-regarding obligations, giving rise to three types of moralities: cultural morality, refined cultural morality and acultural morality.

Cultural morality refers to the moral convictions of a particular community. As the label suggests, a refined cultural morality cleaves or shapes cultural moral convictions to derive a coherent principle or set of principles. An acultural morality is yet more ambitious in its rejection of reliance on any cultural moral convictions. This section unpacks all three types of moralities.

1.2.1. Cultural Morality and Refined Cultural Morality

According to a BBC nationwide survey of those aged 16+, 83% feel a significant responsibility to be faithful to their partner, 59% consider capital punishment justifiable and 73% believe abortion justifiable.[9] While 78% believe assisted dying in the face of terminal illness justifiable, 49% believe that suicide is never justifiable in any circumstance. Opinion polls of this type are one way of discerning the dominant moral convictions of a particular community, but such a cultural morality is indistinguishable from a set of shared prejudices. Dworkin distinguishes this

[9] See BBC 2019.

type of morality (which he refers to as morality in the 'anthropological sense') from morality in the 'discriminatory sense'.[10]

Discriminatory morality refers to a morality free from 'prejudices, rationalizations, matters of personal aversion or taste, arbitrary stands, and the like'.[11] Dworkin tells us that reasons are to be given for a discriminatory morality and these are to exclude: prejudice (taking account of considerations excluded by the community's conventions), mere emotional reaction (personal feeling without reason or justification), rationalisation (appeal to false or irrational beliefs, or relying on evidence known to be irrelevant or insufficient) and parroting (mere citation of the beliefs of others).[12] A discriminatory moral position must also be held sincerely, be consistent with that person's other moral beliefs and not be presented as self-evident when it is controversial.[13]

Dworkin's discriminatory morality will not appeal to anyone who rejects the normative force of cultural morality, for it offers refinements rather than replacement or justification. This is exemplified by Dworkin's rejection of prejudice, defined as 'postures of judgment that take into account considerations our conventions exclude'.[14] Dworkin is invoking cultural morality ('our conventions') to provide content for discriminatory morality. Discriminatory morality therefore cannot, nor is it meant to, provide reasons for its acceptance to those who refuse to identify as part of the relevant group, accept the group's moral precepts or indeed accept any moral precepts at all. It is, in my terminology, a refined cultural morality.

There are degrees of refinement. Cultural moral convictions shaved of prejudices, matters of personal aversion or taste and the like amount to a minimally refined cultural morality; whereas the derivation of moral criteria from a single shared moral conviction would amount to a maximally refined cultural morality.

Most ethicists and bioethicists work within refined cultural morality. Consider the popularity among Anglo-American scholars of the method often referred to as 'reflective equilibrium', which seeks balance between shared moral convictions and theoretical insights.[15] Beauchamp and Childress state that their four principles of biomedical ethics (respect for autonomy, nonmaleficence, beneficence and justice) 'are derived from common morality', and they identify their approach as 'an appropriately adjusted version of reflective equilibrium'.[16] Nussbaum similarly insists that her 'capabilities approach', which focuses on 'what people are actually able to do and to be', follows the method of seeking reflective equilibrium.[17]

[10] Dworkin 1977, 248–253.
[11] Dworkin 1977, 248.
[12] See Dworkin 1977, 249–251.
[13] See Dworkin 1977, 251–252.
[14] Dworkin 1977, 249.
[15] This terminology has its origins in the work of Rawls (see the most recent edition of *A Theory of Justice*: Rawls 1999, esp 42–45), but is frequently used by others for purposes beyond those conceived by Rawls.
[16] Beauchamp & Childress 2019, 13 and 443.
[17] See Nussbaum 2000, 6 and Nussbaum 2006, 352.

Accordingly, she asks us to use '*our* moral judgments and intuitions' to compare the capabilities approach with contractarianism, utilitarianism and other approaches.[18] In her words, 'intuitions both test and are tested by the conceptions we examine, hoping, over time, to achieve consistency and fit in our judgments taken as a whole'.[19] These approaches utilise the shared (or at least widespread) moral convictions of a particular group, but seek more than the exclusions and weak internal coherence of Dworkin's discriminatory morality. Also consider Harris' strategy in *The Value of Life*, which is to 'test' moral principles by reference to 'hypothetical counter examples' to determine whether they 'hold good … in any imaginable or possible world' and then ask whether the underlying values 'taken as a whole are well calculated to make the world a better place'.[20] Harris analogises moral theorising with a houseboat at sail, whereby every plank is kept under examination for maintenance, repair or replacement 'without sinking the whole enterprise'.[21] This approach and analogy encapsulate the enterprise of seeking a type of reflective equilibrium, according to which cultural morality is part of a process of dynamically reviewing and rendering moral principles into a coherent whole. In contrast to Nussbaum's use of reflective equilibrium, Harris' candidate for the resulting morality is utilitarianism.[22] In common with all attempts to place considered moral convictions into reflective equilibrium, these theorists cannot answer critics who reject the normative force of the relevant moral intuitions. That would require a morality that was in no way dependent upon cultural morality; it would require an *acultural morality*.

1.2.2. Acultural Morality

An acultural morality is one derived from premises that are not tied to acceptance of the contingent moral convictions of a particular group, whether unrefined or refined. There are two types of acultural moralities, distinguished by the nature of their justificatory claims. The first seeks to derive criteria for determining what is morally permissible from the assumption that members of all cultures must accept other-regarding oughts: weak moral rationalism. The second seeks to derive moral criteria from non-moral premises: strong moral rationalism.

Examples of weak moral rationalism pepper the philosophical literature. Hare, in his *Moral Thinking*, seeks to show that anyone who accepts moral oughts (understood as 'universalisable', 'prescriptive' and 'overriding' precepts) is logically committed to accepting preference utilitarianism.[23] A similar project is often attributed to Kant, whereby he is understood in the *Groundwork of the Metaphysic*

[18] See Nussbaum 2006, 352 (emphasis added).
[19] Nussbaum 2000, 151.
[20] See Harris 1985, 235–236.
[21] Harris 1985, 236.
[22] See Harris 1985, 105 and Harris 1998, 257–258 and the discussion in Häyry 2001, ch 5 and Pattinson 2020, 573–574.
[23] See Hare 1981, ch 10 and 219. Hare refers to his method as 'rational universal prescriptivism'.

of Morals as seeking to show that anyone who accepts morality is logically required to accept the Categorical Imperative.[24] Accordingly, Kant and Hare can be understood as seeking to derive their very different moral principles from acceptance of the moral point of view. Yet, they also seek to avoid reliance on the cultural morality of a particular group. While weak rationalism assumes that we owe duties to take account of the interests of others, it otherwise eschews reliance on moral intuitions – in contrast to the method of seeking reflective equilibrium.

Some theorists have gone further by seeking to derive criteria for moral permissibility without assuming that we owe duties – let alone categorical duties – to take account of the interests of others. These are theories within strong moral rationalism. Kant's project in the *Groundwork* is to show that any rational being with a will is rationally required to accept the Categorical Imperative.[25] Accordingly, Kant declares, this moral principle is to be understood as 'a necessary law for all rational beings' on the basis that it is 'connected (entirely *a priori*) with the concept of the will of a rational being as such'.[26] Gewirth, in his *Reason and Morality*, seeks to show that the Principle of Generic Consistency (PGC) is 'dialectically necessary'.[27] This method involves arguing from the internal viewpoint of an agent ('dialectically') from premises that cannot be coherently denied within that perspective ('necessary' premises).[28] Thus, Gewirth seeks to show that for an agent to understand what it is for her to be an agent is for her to accept the Principle of Generic Consistency; according to which all agents have a set of specific rights (see chapter 2). In other words, Kant and Gewirth share a justificatory strategy in relation to their moral philosophy. Both analyse the internal perspective of a being that is able to act for its freely chosen purposes (a rational being with a will/an agent) and thereby seek to derive an acultural morality from agential self-understanding. Their derived deontological principles differ in important ways. For a start, the duties imposed by the Categorical Imperative are not automatically subject to the will of the beneficiary,[29] whereas the duties imposed by the PGC are subject to the will of the rights-holder to whom they are owed.

1.2.3. Moral Relativism versus Moral Universalism

Moral beliefs could be considered universal or relative. *Moral universalists* claim that basic moral beliefs can be true or rational.[30] *Moral relativists* claim that basic moral

[24] See Kant 1785. Examples of those who interpret Kant in this way: Hare 1981, 162; Gauthier 1986, 6–7; Gewirth 1991, viii.

[25] See Kant 1785 [4: 448]: 'we must prove that it belongs universally to the activity of rational beings endowed with a will'.

[26] Kant 1785 [4: 426].

[27] See Gewirth 1978 and the defence in Beyleveld 1991.

[28] See Gewirth 1978, 42–47.

[29] See O'Neill 1998.

[30] There are three variants of moral universalism: basic moral beliefs are capable of being *true* (moral intuitionism/arational cognitivism), *rational* (moral rationalism/rational noncognitivism) or *both* true and rational (moral naturalism/moral realism/rational cognitivism).

beliefs are on a par with regard to their truth and rationality; they are relative to a particular person or group of those who happen to share those beliefs or feelings.

Acultural morality is explicitly universalist. Cultural and refined cultural moralities are more complex. Both are reliant upon the cultural moral convictions of a particular group: the refined version relies on a subset of one or more shared moral intuitions. But those convictions could claim to express universal or relative norms. A refined cultural morality may, for example, rely on the conviction that all humans have equal rights and dignity, as proclaimed by various international human rights instruments.

An objection might be made to the way my framework identifies positions that rely on substantive moral intuitions as cultural moralities even if it is claimed that those intuitions capture universal or objective values. This categorisation is not arbitrary. To validate the content of a moral duty by reference to a moral intuition is to make it contingent upon acceptance of that intuition. But, since any substantive moral intuition can be meaningfully opposed by a counter intuition, all such intuitions must be regarded as either relative to a particular individual or group (as per cultural or refined cultural morality) or capable of being supported by a justificatory process that does not rely upon them (as per acultural morality). A moral intuition does not transcend its cultural basis merely because it is widely shared, fits with other moral intuitions or is expressed in universalist terms.

Some theories are capable of being placed into more than one group, depending on whether their declared features are dispensable. Consider John Rawls', much admired and much maligned, justificatory framework in his *A Theory of Justice*.[31] His theory of justice was published over 50 years ago and its influence continues to this day. It has two key declared components: a moral contractarian framework and the notion of reflective equilibrium. His contractarian exposition involves one of the greatest thought experiments in the history of moral and political philosophy. Rawls asks us to imagine ourselves as about to enter society from the 'original position' in which knowledge of our particular situation (such as the generation to which we belong, and our social status, assets, abilities and overall conception of the good) is hidden from us by a 'veil of ignorance'.[32] Rawls argues that individuals who seek to maximise their individual self-interest in this hypothetical situation would agree to two principles of justice: a principle of liberty and a principle of equality.[33] Rawls further requires the solutions derived from this hypothetical social contract to be placed in 'reflective equilibrium' with our most firmly held convictions.[34] We thereby seek to go back and forth between the conditions in the original position and our shared moral convictions until the result 'both expresses reasonable conditions and yields principles which match our considered judgments duly pruned and adjusted'.[35]

[31] See Rawls 1999 (the first edition of which was published in 1971).
[32] Rawls 1999, ch 3.
[33] See Rawls 1999, esp 107.
[34] See Rawls 1999, 18 and 42–45.
[35] Rawls 1999, 18.

The veil of ignorance is an impartiality condition, requiring us to reason from a moral point of view. Thus, if Rawls' contractarian reasoning were to operate without reliance on specific substantive moral intuitions, the resultant political theory would adopt a weak moral rationalism.[36] But his method of reflective equilibrium permits adjustment to the conditions of the original position, and the derived principles, to take account of our considered moral convictions. By way of example, Rawls includes potential agents within the scope of the principle of equality on the basis that 'this interpretation of the requisite conditions seems necessary to match our considered judgments'.[37] Any conclusions resulting from adjustments made to accommodate moral intuitions will have justificatory force only for those who accept those moral intuitions, so the result is that Rawls' method operates within refined cultural morality.

Chapter 2 will defend the derivation of a particular moral principle (Gewirth's PGC) both within maximal acultural morality and, less ambitiously, within maximal refined cultural morality. There is, however, much more that can be said about the nature of morality and law without at this point committing to any particular criteria for moral permissibility.

1.2.4. Criteria for Moral Permissibility

The three types of moralities outlined above are compatible with vastly divergent criteria for moral permissibility. Cultural morality is the least theoretically demanding and is likely to support a set of obligations and prohibitions of the type favoured by tabloid journalists and populist politicians. Normative theories, setting out specific criteria for determining how we ought to act or weigh other-regarding principles, can be grouped in many ways. Elsewhere I have divided criteria for moral permissibility into five camps: utilitarian, rights-based, duty-based, virtue ethics and mixed theories.[38] Each is a group of normative theories with common central tenets, rather than a specific theory. This five-fold grouping will be used in this book, because it has explanatory value and the existence of a miscellaneous category (mixed theories) ensures that it is exhaustive.

Utilitarians hold that we ought to achieve the best balance of utility over disutility, which typically requires the maximisation of pleasure over pain (classical utilitarianism) or the maximisation of preference satisfaction (preference utilitarianism). Crucially, individual interests are to be added together (for aggregation or averaging) and compared. Jeremy Bentham's classical utilitarianism was aggregative: 'it is the greatest happiness of the greatest number that is the measure of right and wrong'.[39]

[36] cf Gauthier 1986, who uses a contractarian method to argue for moral constraints without assuming impartiality: a form of strong moral rationalism.

[37] Rawls 1999, 446.

[38] See Pattinson 2006 and 2020, ch 1.

[39] Bentham 1775, 393. On Bentham's use of the greatest happiness principle, see Burns 2005.

Rights-based and duty-based theories hold that the duties owed to individuals may be outweighed by more important duties owed to other individuals but cannot be outweighed by adding together the interests of different individuals. These two deontological approaches diverge on whether the moral duties owed to an individual may be waived by that individual. This difference can be expressed in terms of adherence to rival conceptions of rights. These are two conceptions of what Hohfeld termed a 'claim-right': a justifiable claim or entitlement imposing duties on others.[40] The *will-conception* regards the duty imposed on others by my right as subject to my will, in the sense of being waivable by me.[41] I will refer to these as *will-rights*. The *interest-conception* regards the duty imposed on others by my right as tracking my important interests and, crucially, these interests are not intrinsically connected to my will.[42] Since my autonomy interests may be overridden by my other interests, my possession of a right does not imply that I may release you from the correlative duty. I will refer to these as *interest-rights*. Accordingly, rights-based theory holds that individuals have will-rights, whereas duty-based theory holds that individuals have interest-rights. It follows that rights-based theories permit suicide, because a will-right to life permits suicide, subject only to the rights of others. In contrast, the interest-rights recognised by duty-based theories are not automatically subject to the right-holder's will and the interest in life is often regarded as the most important interest, which rules out suicide.[43]

A common objection to rights-based theories is that will-rights can only be possessed by agents and, so the objection goes, this excludes very young children, severely cognitively impaired adults and other proper subjects of moral concern from moral protection. A partial response is to point out that while non-agents would not be the subjects of direct duties, they could still be the subjects of vicarious duties. Inflicting harm on a non-agent would still be impermissible where it happens to violate the will-rights of an agent. And we typically love our children, pets and others deemed to be non-agents so profoundly that harming them is likely to harm us in ways that could amount to an infringement of our rights. But that will not suffice as a defence of a rights-based theory within a cultural or refined cultural morality with a core moral conviction that non-agents are owed direct duties. A more sophisticated response, which will be advanced in the next chapter, is available if will-rights are considered to be *categorical*. That response, which draws out the moral implications of the inescapable fallibility of our judgments

[40] See Hohfeld 1923.

[41] eg Hart 1955. There is a crucial difference between *waiving the benefit of a right* (ie releasing another from the correlative duty) and *waiving the right itself* (ie giving up the right). This is important if the rights-based camp is to capture theories holding that rights are *inalienable*, so that an individual cannot possess the properties of a rights-holder without possessing the associated rights (see eg Gewirth 1978).

[42] eg MacCormick 1977.

[43] eg according to Keown, the right to life is 'a right not to be intentionally killed' and the correlative duty not to kill commands respect over 'a choice to kill, whether another or oneself' (Keown 2018, 38 and 53, respectively).

about others' minds, shows that protecting categorical will-rights requires interest-rights to be granted to those who seem to be only partial agents.

This chapter has so far summarised examples of theorists' work within all but one of the five camps: utilitarian (eg Harris and Hare), rights-based (eg Gewirth), duty-based (eg Kant) and mixed theories (eg Beauchamp and Childress). No examples have yet been cited of virtue ethics, which has its origins in the work of Aristotle and is undergoing a revival, particularly within feminist theory.[44] Theories of virtue ethics focus on virtues and vices, character and motive. If they are to be understood as *moral* theories, then they need to be interpreted as giving rise to other-regarding obligations *to act* either in accordance with a set of virtues or as a virtuous person would act.

More generally, the conception of the good life attributed to a virtuous person need not impose duties to act in the interests of others. Part of the appeal of an ethic extending beyond other-regarding duties is that it enables various feelings and relationships to be regarded as good or bad without those evaluations implying a duty to bring them about or prevent them. There cannot, for example, be a meaningful duty to love someone, because you cannot have a duty to bring about a set of feelings over which you do not have voluntary control. You could meaningfully have a duty to *try* to love someone or even to *act as if* you love someone, but love as a subjective feeling is not the meaningful object of your will. It needs to be emphasised, however, that the language of morality in no way prevents recognising love, friendship, benevolence or other such feelings and relationships as morally good; as long as this is not taken to suggest that the *achievement* of these things could be a moral requirement.

Virtue ethics is to be distinguished from accounts of virtue within other types of normative theory.[45] From the perspective of other theories, a virtue is to be understood as a character trait disposing towards compliance with the tenets of that theory, such as the maximisation of utility or compliance with rights.[46] Since virtues may refer to intrinsic or instrumental goods in this way, particular care needs to be taken when identifying a virtue ethics theory from use of the language of virtues.

1.3. Refined Cultural Morality and the Law

Legal instruments and judicial decisions frequently directly appeal to a refined cultural morality. Consider judicial references to 'right-thinking members of

[44] See Aristotle BCE and Anscombe 1958 (often identified as the inspiration for the revival of virtue ethics). More recent examples include Hursthouse 1991; MacIntyre 2007; Besser-Jones & Slote 2015; Berges 2015.

[45] See Hursthouse 2016, who refers to the latter as 'virtue theory'.

[46] See eg Gewirth 1978, 332–333 and Pattinson 2002, 30–31.

society',[47] the 'reasonable man'[48] and the 'man on the Clapham omnibus'.[49] These are examples of appeals to the discriminatory morality of the United Kingdom. Beyond this jurisdiction, the European Convention on Human Rights could be regarded as encapsulating a European refined cultural morality.[50] Since the underlying cultural morality is not immutable, this helps to explain the European Court of Human Right's willingness to refer to the Convention as a 'living instrument'.[51] Similarly, international human rights instruments could plausibly be regarded as expressing the refined cultural morality of their signatory states: paradigmatically a morality of rights possessed on the basis of human dignity, as per the Universal Declaration on Human Rights 1948 (to which we will return below).

The formal rules and rulings of organised societies are posited as laws and are referred to as laws in this book. That might seem to be an odd statement. It alludes to the conceptual debate over whether a rule is *legally valid* because it is formally posited by an organised system (as per legal positivism) or whether it must also accord with moral criteria (as per legal idealism) – chapter 2 will defend the latter position. It is a debate over whether a rule must be (procedurally or substantively) morally valid to be a *valid* law. Neither position denies that rules formally posited as laws (positive laws) can express cultural moral values or be moral/immoral when assessed against moral criteria.

Those who enact legislation often do seek to systemise and give effect to the community's moral standards. In a representative democracy, those elected have publicly declared adherence to a set of policies and political convictions, and face being judged at the ballot box by reference to whether they have given effect to those declarations and other norms of cultural morality. But can a specific refined cultural morality be discerned from the laws of England and Wales?

This section has three subsections. The first explores judicial use of the five positions (types of normative criteria) outlined in 1.2.4. It is suggested that the law of this jurisdiction exemplifies a shift from the religious to the secular, and towards a more consistently rights-based ethic. The second subsection extends the claim made in the first to the effect that principles can be discerned from the law of England and Wales that plausibly encapsulate a refined cultural morality, carrying the imprimatur of the state's political and legal structures. The third subsection considers whether such principles could assist with debate over ethical matters at the frontiers of biomedicine.

[47] See eg *Sim v Stretch* [1936] 2 All ER 1237, 1240 (Lord Atkin). Cf 'right-thinking bystanders': *R (Burke) v GMC* [2004] EWHC 1879, [149] (Munby J).

[48] See eg *Davis Contractors Ltd v Fareham Urban District Council* [1956] AC 696, 728 (Lord Radcliffe).

[49] See eg *Healthcare at Home Limited v The Common Services Agency (Scotland)* [2014] UKSC 49, [1]–[4] (Lord Reed).

[50] See Beyleveld & Brownsword 1993, 57–58 ('European critical cultural morality').

[51] See eg *Tyrer v UK* (1979–80) 2 EHRR 1, [31]. Cf the 'living tree doctrine' in *Edwards v Canada (Attorney General)* [1930] AC 124 and subsequently developed by the Canadian Supreme Court.

1.3.1. The Moral Trajectory of the Law

References to the values of 'right-thinking members of society' and the 'man on the Clapham omnibus', as cited above, facilitate appeal to a mixed theory. Similarly, the standard of a 'reasonable man' or 'reasonable person' in tort law enables reasoning in accordance with virtue ethics, because that standard (in contrast to a 'reasonable action' or 'reasonable consequences' standard) is well-suited for the purpose of assessing individuals by reference to a virtuous comparator. As is easily anticipated, there are judicial phrases and emphases that align with all five groups of moral criteria.

Let us consider two medical law cases in which the first instance judge used language aligned to one type of moral theory, only to be shot down by the Court of Appeal using language aligned to a rival theory.

In the first, *ex parte B*, the approach of Laws J in the Divisional Court contrasts with that adopted in the Court of Appeal by Sir Thomas Bingham MR.[52] The two courts reached opposed conclusions on whether to quash a health authority's refusal to fund further experimental treatment for a 10-year-old girl suffering from acute myeloid leukaemia. Laws J declared that the girl's 'right to life' was 'vindicated' by the English common law and had been compromised by the health authority's failure to reveal the details of their resource allocation policy. Sir Thomas Bingham rejected the justiciability of this issue, citing the complex policy nature of allocating a limited budget 'to the maximum advantage of the maximum number of patients'.[53] This is, at least in part, a conflict between rights-based and utilitarian positions.[54]

In the second, *Burke*, the approach of Munby J contrasts with that of the Court of Appeal.[55] Leslie Burke's degenerative brain condition would eventually remove his ability to swallow. He sought to challenge the legality of professional guidance, which he read as permitting doctors to withdraw clinically assisted nutrition and hydration (CANH) against his will.[56] Munby J derived 'key ethical (and legal) principles' by examination of the common law and the Convention rights given domestic effect by the Human Rights Act 1998 (HRA 1998).[57] His Lordship reasoned that Burke's 'fundamental rights', including his rights to self-determination and dignity, implied a right to insist on receiving life-prolonging CANH for at least those stages of his illness in which he remained aware of his surroundings.[58] In contrast, the Court of Appeal restricted the right to self-determination to the right to refuse treatment, rather than to insist on receiving a

[52] *R v Cambridge HA Ex p B* [1995] 1 FLR 1055 (QBD); [1995] 2 All ER 129 (CA).
[53] [1995] 2 All ER 129, 137.
[54] A view also expressed by Mullender 1996.
[55] *R (Burke) v GMC* [2004] EWHC 1879; [2005] EWCA 1003. See Pattinson 2015, esp 261.
[56] The case itself used the older language of artificial nutrition and hydration (ANH).
[57] [2004] EWHC 1879, esp [73].
[58] [2004] EWHC 1879, [213]–[214].

particular treatment.[59] For the period Burke had capacity, the hospital treating him would be under a common law duty to provide CANH. This duty was said not to override the wishes of a patient with capacity who refuses CANH, but the patient's wishes to receive CANH 'will not be the source of the duty to provide it'.[60] Thus, while Munby J held that Burke had the *right* to insist on receiving life-prolonging CANH, the Court of Appeal held that he would merely be the *beneficiary of a duty* to provide it, and his only right was to refuse it. Lord Phillips MR, giving the judgment of the Court of Appeal, was not inclined to adopt Munby J's rights-based position with its positive rights. Indeed, his Lordship's downplaying of autonomy[61] suggests reliance on a duty-based or a similarly focused mixed position.

Both first instance decisions, expressed in the language of rights, were overturned using the language of different moral theories. These cases indicate that judges, when they do draw on moral criteria, do not uniformly draw from one type of moral theory. Nonetheless, some appeal cases on medical treatment were expressed in the language of rights.[62] And since the HRA 1998 came into effect in 2000, there has been a noticeable judicial coalescence around the language of rights and individual self-determination, even when developing the common law. Consider the Supreme Court's decision in *Montgomery v Lanarkshire Health Board*.[63] This case, decided in 2015, considered when healthcare professionals would be negligent for failing to disclose the risks of treatment to their patients. The standard of care, at common law, was revised from what a reasonable doctor would disclose to what a reasonable patient or (on the basis of what the doctor ought to have realised) the particular patient would want disclosed.[64] The principle explaining and justifying the court's conclusion was identified by Lord Kerr and Lord Reed, with whom the other Justices agreed. They argued that the law had developed to recognise 'patients as persons holding rights, rather than as the passive recipients of the care of the medical profession',[65] and that 'respect for the dignity of patients requires no less'.[66] The notion that rights are grounded in dignity and intrinsically connected to the exercise of the rights-holder's will is the essence of a rights-based position. The move from *Sidaway* (the standard of a reasonable doctor) to *Montgomery* (the standard of a reasonable and particular patient) thereby represents a move from a duty-based to a rights-based ethic.

[59] [2005] EWCA Civ 1003, [31].

[60] [2005] EWCA Civ 1003, [32].

[61] Once Burke lost capacity, his best interests were not to track his previous wishes because 'it is best to confine the use of the phrase "best interests" to an objective test'. [2005] EWCA Civ 1003, [29]. Cf *Aintree University Hospitals NHS Foundation Trust v James* [2013] UKSC 67, [45]: 'The purpose of the best interests test is to consider matters from the patient's point of view'.

[62] See eg *Gillick v West Norfolk and Wisbech AHA* [1986] AC 112, 186 (Lord Scarman) and *Re MB* [1997] 2 FLR 426.

[63] [2015] UKSC 11.

[64] [2015] UKSC 11, [87]. Overruling *Sidaway v Board of Governors of the Bethlem Royal Hospital* [1985] AC 871.

[65] [2015] UKSC 11, [75].

[66] [2015] UKSC 11, [93].

We have seen that judicial reliance on rights-based reasoning was bolstered by the HRA 1998 and has become embedded in the common law. That Act gives domestic effect to the rights of the European Convention of Human Rights. The Act's long title declares that its purpose is to 'give further effect' to those rights. The preamble to the Convention states that it aims to secure 'the universal and effective recognition and observance of the Rights' in the Universal Declaration of Human Rights 1948. Articles 1 and 2 of the Declaration claim the rights to which it gives recognition are possessed equally by all humans by virtue of their dignity.[67] Thus, the rights to which the HRA 1998 gives effect in national law have their origin in instruments proclaiming their special status as rights whose force does not rest on their recognition by positive law.

There has been a corresponding transition from judicial references to principles derived from Christianity to secular expressions of cultural moral values. In the famous case of *Donoghue v Stevenson*, decided in 1932, Lord Atkin relied on a principle expressed in biblical language: 'The rule that you are to love your neighbour becomes in law, you must not injure your neighbour'.[68] In 1958, Devlin J gave a direction to a jury that is widely regarded as importing the principle (or doctrine) of double effect into English law.[69] This principle has its origins in Catholic theology, and Patrick Devlin had been brought up a Roman Catholic and educated at a Catholic boarding school.[70] By way of contrast, appeals to moral values in later cases (including *ex parte B, Burke* and *Montgomery*) have been expressed in purely secular language. Judges are now unlikely to identify a principle using faith-based language and concepts, which is a tendency lamented by some commentators.[71]

In sum, the law of this jurisdiction displays a trajectory towards a particular type of refined cultural morality: rights-based and secular. In the context of the international human rights instruments of the twentieth century, the notion of universal human rights could be considered a central tenet of the transnational moral zeitgeist. However, refined cultural morality derives from cultural morality and cultures evolve over time. In the United Kingdom, politicians have made repeatedly calls for repeal or amendment of the HRA 1998, to give greater weight to 'British rights' or, as Douglas has noted, 'to give a greater place to duties and responsibilities'.[72] In December 2021, the UK Government published a consultation document in which they proposed to reform the HRA 1998 to focus on 'quintessentially UK rights, such as freedom of speech and the right to trial by jury' and to 'restore the common sense application of human rights in the UK'.[73]

[67] Art 1: 'All human beings are born free and equal in dignity and rights'. Art 2: 'Everyone is entitled to all the rights and freedoms … without distinction of any kind'.

[68] [1932] AC 562, 580.

[69] *R v Adams* [1957] Crim LR 365, 375 and see the discussion in Pattinson 2018, ch 2.

[70] See Morton 1992.

[71] See eg criticism of the understanding of the 'sanctity of life' principle in *Airedale NHS Trust v Bland* [1993] AC 789 from Finnis 1993, esp 336–337 and Keown 1997.

[72] Douglas 2018, 360.

[73] Ministry of Justice 2021, 3 and 5.

The Government reiterated the United Kingdom's continuing commitment to rights, including all the substantive rights protected by the European Convention. Nonetheless, opposition was expressed to judicial development of those rights, particularly under the 'living instrument' doctrine, whereby the Convention rights are interpreted in line with changes in society and the cultural norms of member states.[74]

1.3.2. Discerning Additional Moral Principles from the Law

We have seen that the notion of rights derived from dignity explains and justifies the common law decision in *Montgomery* and can be inferred from the Human Rights Act 1998 and any replacement legislation that gives effect to the rights in the European Convention on Human Rights. This subsection will argue that analysis of English law may similarly discern the principle that the developing human has proportional status.

From a moral point of view, a developing human could be said to have intrinsic value as a recipient of direct duties (moral status) and/or value to someone or some group with moral status (vicarious value). There is a well-known divergence of views over whether the developing human is owed direct moral duties with the same weight as those owed to you or me (full status), duties of less weight (limited status) or no direct duties at all (no status). The most popular limited status position holds that the value of the embryo or fetus[75] is gradualist or proportional to gestational development until it obtains full moral status at birth or beyond.

In theory, the developing human could be granted three types of legal protection: (a) direct protection, (b) retrospective protection when born alive or (c) vicarious protection as a result of protection of the pregnant legal person. Domestic law grants all three forms of protection.[76] While the fetus is not a legal person, it is not treated as a valueless thing.[77] The law therefore cannot be aligned to either the full status position, which would imply legal personhood, or the no status position, which would imply no direct legal protection. Instead, the law aligns with a limited status position. That is to say that *the principle that best explains and justifies the approach in legislation is the proportional status position*, because such a principle translates, from the point of view of enforcement, into a threshold approach of increased protection.

An embryo created outside the body falls within the Human Fertilisation and Embryology Act 1990. In England and Wales, the fetus inside the pregnant

[74] See Ministry of Justice 2021, 17–22, citing *Tyrer v UK* (1979–80) 2 EHRR 1 as 'an early example' of this doctrine.
[75] The word 'fetus' is often spelt 'foetus', but I prefer the etymologically correct spelling for its simplicity: see also Williams 1994, 71 (n 1).
[76] See Pattinson 2020 chs 7–9.
[77] See Pattinson 2002, ch 4; Scott 2004; Cornock & Montgomery 2011.

individual's body is covered by two Acts of Parliament,[78] subject to s 1(1) of the Abortion Act 1967, as amended by the 1990 Act.[79] Before implantation, any clinical or research use of the embryo must be licensed but it may be lawfully destroyed without relying on any of the grounds in the Abortion Act. In fact, it must be destroyed if either gamete provider withdraws consent to its storage or use.[80] The fetus has greater protection within the womb. The most permissive ground for abortion under the Abortion Act only applies up to 24 weeks (s 1(1)(a)), but the more restrictive grounds for abortion apply up to birth (ss 1(1)(b)–(d)). Legal personality is only acquired at birth.[81] Thus, the law grants increasing protection to the developing human according to four legally relevant thresholds: (i) preimplantation (up to 14 days);[82] (ii) implantation to 24 weeks; (iii) post-24 weeks; and (iv) birth.

A principle of proportional status is also capable of explaining and justifying the decision in *St George's Healthcare NHS Trust v S* to the effect that 'a 36-week foetus is not nothing: if viable it is not lifeless and it is certainly human', yet those who are pregnant and satisfy the legal capacity test have the right to refuse medical treatment even if acting on the refusal will result in the death of a fetus.[83]

One of two interpretative approaches is, however, required to render this principle compatible with the principle that humans have rights derived from dignity. *Approach A* excludes embryos/fetuses from the principle that humans have rights derived from dignity and considers them to be owed direct, proportional duties for some other reason. *Approach B* considers possession of rights and dignity to vary in degree among those who are biologically human.

Approach A is compatible with rights given effect under the auspices of the HRA 1998 and the international instruments to which the HRA itself (directly or indirectly) gives effect. The Strasbourg Court has, for example, repeatedly refused to require states to extend the article 2 right to life to the fetus.[84] The Convention itself purports to give effect to the Universal Declaration of Human Rights (UDHR), article 1 of which proclaims: 'All human beings are *born* free and equal in dignity and rights' (emphasis added). This could be explained as a limit on the coverage of the relevant international instrument (and jurisdiction of the Strasbourg Court), or as a principled distinction. The latter raises the question as to what is the overarching principle for possession of moral status, given that birth is largely a matter of the fetus' location and disconnection from the uterine

[78] The Offences against the Person Act 1861, ss 58 and 59 and Infant Life (Preservation) Act 1929, s 1.

[79] The 1967 Act applies to England, Wales and Scotland.

[80] Subject to a cooling-off period: 1990 Act, Sch 3, para 4A.

[81] eg *Paton v BPAS* [1979] QB 276; *In Re F (In Utero)* [1988] Fam 122; *C v S* [1988] QB 135; *Burton v Islington Health Authority* [1993] QB 204.

[82] Strictly, up to the development of the primitive streak or 14 days, whichever is earlier: 1990 Act, s 3(3)(a).

[83] [2002] EWHC 2871, 45. See further Pattinson 2018, ch 5.

[84] See eg *Paton v UK* (1981) 3 EHRR 408; *H v Norway* (1992) 73 DR155; *Open Door Counselling and Dublin Well Woman v Ireland* (1993) 15 EHRR 244; *Boso v Italy* (No 50490/99); *Vo v France* (No 53924/00).

environment.[85] The relevance of birth in English law will be considered further in chapter 4, which envisions gestation taking place completely outside the womb (see 4.3.5).

Approach B requires some or all of the relevant rights to be interest-rights: while some humans can meaningfully be granted will-rights, the embryo/fetus cannot. It also requires an understanding of dignity that is capable of both justifying those rights and increasing their weight according to the level of gestation. A possible candidate for this is suggested in chapter 2.[86]

1.3.3. Use and Limits of Principles Derived from the Law

We have seen that the law of England and Wales encapsulates a particular type of refined cultural morality. This subsection further explores such discerned principles by reference to the Nuffield Council on Bioethics (NCOB) and its 2017 report on non-invasive prenatal testing.[87] One concern (and there are many) is that principles discernible from the law are simply too abstract to assist in public debates on issues at the frontiers of biomedicine.

The NCOB is the United Kingdom's leading bioethics committee. It aims to inform policy and public debate so that the benefits of 'recent developments in biological and medical research' may be 'realised in a way that is consistent with public values'.[88] However, matters at the forefront of bioethics are likely to split refined cultural morality into sub-cultures, so giving effect to this aim raises what may be called the *moral acceptance dilemma*, whereby the more specific the moral principles identified, the less likely that those principles will be uncontroversial in the community as a whole. Consider, for example, the contrasting approaches to the 'principle of moral status' adopted in the NCOB's 2005 report on *The Ethics of Research Involving Animals* and its 2006 report on *Critical Care Decisions in Fetal and Neonatal Medicine*.[89] The animal research report advances the view that 'consideration of the relative moral status does not settle the question of the permissibility of animal research, or of any other use of animals, in a helpful manner'.[90] This view will be rejected by moral approaches (within refined cultural or acultural morality) holding that full moral status vests according to possession of particular characteristics that can meaningfully distinguish particular animals from humans

[85] Arts 1 and 2 of the UDHR raise additional interpretative questions with regard to the UDHR's approach to all post-birth humans: see Beyleveld 2012, 11–12.

[86] See 2.3.1, where it is argued that protecting categorical will-rights (granted on the basis of agency-as-dignity) requires (in response to the philosophical problem of other minds) recognition of proportional rights of this type. This approach, however, would also have implications for post-birth humans beyond those currently accepted by English law.

[87] See NCOB 2017. *Declaration of interest:* I was one of the seven members of this working group. I was also a member of the NCOB from 2015–2021 and its Deputy Chair from 2019–2021.

[88] www.nuffieldbioethics.org/about-us/aims-and-values.

[89] See NCOB 2005 and 2006 and the discussion in Chan & Harris 2006, 46.

[90] NCOB 2005, para 3.24.

and other types of animals. The fetal and neonatal medicine report rejects the view that 'full moral status is reached only at some point after birth' on the basis that identifying some point in postnatal development has 'serious dangers' and would require subjective decisions.[91] They conclude that 'the moment of birth, which is straightforward to identify, and usually represents a significant threshold in potential viability, as the significant point of transition not just for legal judgments about preserving life but also for moral ones'.[92] This view will be rejected by approaches holding that full moral status must vest in humans earlier or later than the moment of birth.

As the examples above suggest, the NCOB's response to the acceptance moral a dilemma is to expressly permit differently constituted working groups to identify and apply divergent moral frameworks and accept that others may simply disagree with the approach taken. Indeed, the NCOB's website expressly states that it does not 'have a standard ethical approach' and its reports 'have adopted different ethical principles and frameworks'.[93] The NCOB's reports have accordingly adopted normative criteria ranging from the 'broadly utilitarian' (questionably asserted to be 'a starting point which is shared by most people in the UK') to the 'virtue-guided'.[94] More often, they appeal to a mixed position without reference to philosophical ethics.[95]

A 2017 report examines 'non-invasive prenatal testing' (NIPT), which involves using a blood test to analyse free-floating DNA fragments in a pregnant woman's bloodstream that come from both her cells and cells from the placenta.[96] NIPT can be undertaken from around nine weeks of pregnancy. It is 'non-invasive' in the sense that a needle is not inserted into the abdomen or cervix and so it does not present the risk of miscarriage associated with invasive procedures, such as chorionic villus sampling and amniocentesis. It can be used to ascertain, with a high degree of accuracy, the sex of the fetus[97] or whether the fetus has some single gene disorders inherited from the father or arising at conception, such as achondroplasia and Apert syndrome.[98] NIPT can also be used as a 'screening' test to estimate the chance that a fetus has other conditions (such as Down's syndrome), with an invasive test then being needed to provide a diagnosis. The evidence suggests that NIPT is more accurate at identifying conditions associated with an extra (whole or part) chromosome (particularly Down's syndrome), than alternative non-invasive screening tests.[99] Further, NIPT could be used to sequence the whole genome or

[91] NCOB 2006, para 2.19.
[92] NCOB 2006, para 2.19.
[93] www.nuffieldbioethics.org/about-us/how-we-work.
[94] NCOB 1999, 3 and NCOB 2013, 84–86, respectively. See also the reliance on three 'professional virtues' in NCOB 2015, xvii–xviiii.
[95] See further Schmidt & Schwartz 2016, 436.
[96] See NIPT 2017.
[97] I am using the term 'fetus' to cover the developing human at all stages of development and 'sex' to refer to the X and Y chromosomes.
[98] See NCOB 2017, 3.
[99] See Taylor-Phillips et al 2016.

exome, which has the potential to identify a vast array of genetic variations, with varying degrees of accuracy.[100]

The 2017 report's 'ethical starting points' are stated to be '[Value 1:] choice, autonomy and consent; [Value 2:] avoidance of harm; and [Value 3:] equality, inclusion and fairness'.[101] These values and a set of associated principles are utilised by the report to support four sets of policy recommendations.[102] My concern here is with two of these policy recommendations: (1) where certain preconditions are satisfied, women and couples should be able to access NIPT to test for 'significant medical conditions or impairments'[103] and (2) NIPT should 'not generally' be used to test whether the fetus has a less significant medical condition, has an adult onset condition or is a carrier of a medical condition, or to reveal the sex of the fetus.

The chair of the working party and his co-author have noted that the report 'did not give a closely argued justification of the position adopted'.[104] Brownsword and Wale have argued that the NIPT report insufficiently defends its 'relatively conservative position'.[105] However, while this is not considered in the report itself, the report's three values can be discerned from examination of domestic law. Above I argued that principles discernible from English law include the principles that patients possess rights grounded in human dignity and developing humans have proportional status. Protecting choice, autonomy and consent (Value 1) is a direct implication of what it means for patients to possess rights,[106] protecting rights can be understood as seeking avoidance of harm (Value 2) and these rights are based in, and protect, the dignity of the human person and thus the recognition of equality, inclusion and fairness (Value 3). Nonetheless, as Brownsword and Wale point out, there is an explanatory gap between the 2017 report's values and its conclusions.

The 2017 report concludes that NIPT should generally be available to test for 'significant medical conditions or impairments'. Brownsword and Wale argue that while the general availability of NIPT can be supported by Value 1, it is not clear how that or the other two values support the report's restrictions on the exercise of parental autonomy and choice. They express particular concern with regard to the recommendation that NIPT should 'not generally' be used to test for fetal sex when not connected to a significant medical condition.

NIPT to determine fetal sex is widely available in the United Kingdom through private companies. This aligns with the view of many academics that parental autonomy supports access to both information about the sex of their embryo/fetus and

[100] See further Shakespeare & Hull 2018, 37–38.
[101] NCOB 2008, para 1.55. See further xvii and paras 1.56–1.83.
[102] See NCOB 2017, esp ch 6.
[103] The stated preconditions concern matters such as the predictive accuracy of the test and the provision of high-quality information and support to the pregnant person and their partner.
[104] Shakespeare & Hull 2018, 41.
[105] Brownsword & Wale 2018, 647.
[106] Brownsword & Wale (2018, 650) note that 'after *Montgomery*, it is easy to argue that, in reproductive contexts, women should be aware of the clinical options that are available to them and be free to make their own choices'.

sex selective practices.[107] Yet, the 2017 report recommends that NIPT providers should not continue to generate and report information about the sex of the fetus, unless 'there is concern that the fetus may be showing signs of a significant sex chromosome aneuploidy or is at risk of a sex-linked disorder'.[108] This practice is said to display intrinsically sexist values and could lead to undesirable social consequences:

> The ability of NIPT to reveal the sex of the fetus at a much earlier stage does … increase the risk of terminations on the basis of sex alone. The Working Group believes that sex selective terminations will almost always be based solely on sexist and discriminatory attitudes.[109]

Further, it is argued that the United Kingdom should not undermine international efforts to counter the use of prenatal tests to favour male over female birth in countries such as China, India and some Middle Eastern countries.[110]

Brownsword and Wale object that this reasoning views NIPT 'as a precursor to a termination (rather than information pure and simple about the sex of the child)' and they ask for 'a narrative that both explains and justifies' the regulatory conditions imposed on testing from preimplantation genetic diagnosis (PGD) to NIPT.[111] This criticism calls for a response.

The two principles derived earlier offer potential to explain and justify why NIPT is not solely a matter of the pregnant individual's rights. But the earlier analysis does not tell us when the pregnant woman's rights will prevail over those of the fetus or others outside those instances where the legislature or court has already made that determination. Additional principles, however, drop out of further analysis of the 1967 and 1990 Acts.[112]

The 1967 Act permits abortion on four grounds, only one of which makes any reference to the traits or condition of the fetus, as opposed to the likely consequences of continuing the pregnancy. Abortion is permitted up to birth where two doctors certify that there is a 'substantial risk' that the child would be born 'seriously handicapped' (s 1(1)(d)). The arcane language of this provision is to be understood as referring to a high likelihood that the fetus will have a significant medical condition, which does not include fetal sex alone. The 1990 Act addresses the testing and selection of embryos for implantation and prohibits 'any practice designed to secure that any resulting child will be one sex rather than the other', save to avoid sex-related serious disability, illness or other sex-related 'serious medical condition'.[113] Thus, diagnosis of a serious medical condition provides

[107] See eg Savulescu 1999 and McCarthy 2001.
[108] NCOB 2017, para 6.16.
[109] NCOB 2017, para 6.15.
[110] NCOB 2017, para 6.15.
[111] Brownsword & Wale 2018, 658 and 659, respectively.
[112] Wale 2015 points to some features of the law on abortion (which I examine below) to argue that publicly funded provision of NIPT should be compatible with the framework for lawful abortion. In my view, the key legal principles have wider implications.
[113] Sch 2, 1ZA(1)(c) and 1ZB.

grounds for the termination of a fetus and non-selection of an embryo, whereas the identification of its sex (when not associated with a serious medical condition) does not.

The 1967 Act also permits abortion up to 24 weeks on the so-called social ground: where two doctors certify that the continuance of the pregnancy involves risk, greater than termination, of physical or mental injury to the pregnant woman or any existing children of her family (s 1(1)(a)). In practice, this is interpreted to support early abortion on the grounds that the pregnancy is undesired, irrespective of the pregnant individual's associated views or motivation.[114] This does not, however, imply that the social ground is incompatible with a principle opposed to reproductive decisions being based solely on the sex of the fetus. Giving effect to such a principle by narrowing the social ground or requiring intrusive questions of the woman's motivations would have repercussions far beyond preventing or reducing terminations motivated by fetal sex. In contrast, the 2017 report's recommendation that NIPT providers be prevented from generating and reporting information about the sex of the fetus does not alter otherwise permitted access to abortion or PGD.

Brownsword and Wale aver that NIPT need not be a precursor to a termination and a woman may seek information about the sex of the child for other reasons. But those other reasons reduce to either parental curiosity or gender-role expectations. If we are to respond using principles discerned from the law, these other reasons also need to be considered in light of (a) the principles derived from the 1967 and 1990 Acts and (b) the principle that persons of different sexes/genders have equal status and should not be subject to unjustifiable differences in treatment, which underpins the rights protected by the HRA 1998 and the Equality Act 2010. Curiosity readily masks gender-role expectations and is only a sufficient reason for access to information about another where there are no countervailing considerations connected with others' rights. Parental desires for information about fetal sex to enable preparations to be made for the child's future environment are characterised by or give expression to gender-role expectations.[115] Gender-role expectations and associated gender-stereotypes have purpose-restrictive implications for both the future child and others in society. While some mechanisms for challenging the display and perpetuation of gender-stereotypes are likely to have wide and potentially serious negative consequences for individual rights, this does not seem to be the case with regard to hindering access to early information on fetal sex. Thus, it is a *plausible* claim that principles discernible from the law can be utilised to support the 2017 report's recommendation on fetal sex.

This analysis goes some way towards addressing concerns that a morality discerned from the law will lack sufficient specificity to address developments at

[114] For a defence of this interpretation see Morgan 1988 and Laurie et al 2016, 9.65. See also the decision not to prosecute in CPS 2013 and the discussion in Pattinson 2020, 247–248.

[115] See further Berkowitz & Snyder 1998; Pattinson 2002, ch 6; Pattinson 2020, 299–300; Hendl 2017.

the frontiers of biomedicine. But does a set of refined cultural moral values of this type have sufficient authority or justification to answer the moral acceptance dilemma? No, it does not, for at least three reasons. The first concerns the role of the NCOB. While some public bodies (and some national ethics committees) are set up by legislation to act on behalf of the state, the NCOB was established by a charity and is independent of the United Kingdom's political system.[116] It is therefore free to depart, in its moral reasoning, from the refined cultural morality encapsulated by the law without tensions arising from its status as a body set up to give effect to the will of the legislature. Secondly, some legal rules and rulings could potentially be explained and justified by more than one principle, or simply be inconsistent with other legal rules or rulings.[117] When this occurs, a decision has to be made on what to give priority and that takes us straight back to the moral acceptance dilemma. Thirdly, the moral status of positive law is highly contestable, even as the source of a refined cultural morality within a democratic state. Procedural legitimacy is typically conceded to legislative expressions of the will of a democratically elected parliament. But few would be willing to concede that elections of any type bestow representatives with decisive authority over moral matters, or that the United Kingdom's political system gives sufficient expression to the views and values of the population. These are issues to which we will return in chapter 2, which will address the problem of justifying, ranking, interpreting and delimiting moral and legal principles.

1.4. Conclusion

This chapter has prepared the ground for the next chapter, which will present a theory for judicial and legislative development of the law. That theory will then be applied to biomedical case studies, thereby addressing the past, present and future of the law addressing biomedicine.

[116] The NCOB was set up by the Nuffield Foundation and is now also funded by Wellcome and the Medical Research Council. Its chair is appointed by those funders and it appoints its own members.

[117] These rules and rulings are products of particular processes, to which we will return in ch 2.

2

Contextual Legal Idealism

2.1. Introduction

This chapter presents the framework that is applied in the rest of the book. It defends a particular moral principle and the view that the legal enterprise inescapably involves moral reasoning (legal idealism), as opposed to being conceptually separable from morality (legal positivism). The specific form of legal idealism used in this book is applied without assuming the social context to be different from what it is: contextual legal idealism.

2.2. Justifying the Principle of Generic Consistency

In *Reason and Morality*, Gewirth makes the controversial claim that the Principle of Generic Consistency (PGC) is the supreme principle of morality.[1] The PGC grants negative and positive will-rights to agents (ie those who capable of acting for their own freely chosen purposes). In the terminology of chapter 1, Gewirth argues for a right-based acultural morality.

This section will present a revised form of Gewirth's argument for the PGC as the supreme principle of acultural morality, briefly address some objections to Gewirth's method and then very briefly present Beyleveld's argument for the PGC as a maximal refined cultural morality.

2.2.1. The Dialectically Necessary Argument

Gewirth argues that the PGC is 'dialectically necessary': the argument is conducted from the internal perspective of an agent ('dialectically') by drawing out the implications of premises that cannot be coherently denied within that perspective ('necessary' premises and implications).[2] The PGC is thereby presented as a strict implication of agential self-understanding.

[1] See Gewirth 1978.
[2] See Gewirth 1978, 42–47.

My summary follows Beyleveld's refinements and division of the argument into three stages.[3] *Stage I* establishes that I (any agent) ought to defend and pursue my possession of what I always need to act at all or with general chances of success: the 'generic needs of agency'. *Stage II* establishes that this commits me to claiming rights to the generic needs: the 'generic rights'. *Stage III* establishes that I must accept that all agents have the generic rights: the PGC.

Stage I

In claiming to be an agent, I must (by definition) accept that:

(1) 'I act (or intend to act) for a purpose that I have freely chosen',

which entails

(2) 'My purpose is good (worth pursuing).'

Since

(3) 'If there are necessary needs (things I must do or have) for me to pursue or achieve my purpose, then I ought to pursue or satisfy those needs or give up pursuit of my purpose' (which is the Principle of Hypothetical Imperatives)

and

(4) 'There are things that are necessary for me to pursue or achieve any purpose', which is to say: 'There are generic needs of agency',

it follows that

(5) 'My having the generic needs is (categorically instrumentally) good', which is to say: 'I (categorically instrumentally) ought to pursue and defend my having the generic needs.'

To put this a little less abstractly, let me express the argument from the viewpoint of a named agent. I will call that agent Orion, which is also the name of my son. In Stage I, Orion considers what it means for him to voluntarily choose to pursue (or intend to pursue) a purpose. He must attach a positive value to his purpose sufficient to motivate him to pursue it, even if he happens to think that his purpose has a negative value on some other ground. Imagine, for example, that Orion is a fan of the *Star Wars* movies and has heard of the spin-off television series called *The Mandalorian*. If he freely chooses to watch the first episode of *The Mandalorian*, he attaches motivational value to watching it, even if he considers it to have negative value on some other criterion (because, say, he considers television series to be poor substitutes for movies) or later regrets the decision (because he now wants a Baby Yoda toy, which his father is unwilling to buy).

[3] See Beyleveld 1991, 13–46. My expression of the argument also draws on Beyleveld 2015 and my previous summaries in Capps & Pattinson 2017 and Pattinson 2018.

Since he must proactively value his purpose, Orion must attach instrumental proactive value to anything that is necessary for him to achieve that purpose. That is to say, Orion ought to pursue whatever is necessary to achieve his purpose or abandon that purpose. This follows from the Principle of Hypothetical Imperatives (PHI), which he must accept in order to understand what it is for him to be an agent:

> if I wish to pursue a chosen purpose and having X, or doing Y, is necessary to achieve that purpose, then I ought to pursue/defend having X, or doing Y, or give up pursuing that purpose.[4]

There are some things that Orion needs to achieve his particular purpose (eg he needs access to equipment on which to watch the first episode of *The Mandalorian* and access to a copy of that episode) and some things that are so important that he needs them for *any* purpose (eg continued life while he pursues that purpose). Those things that he needs to act at all or with general chances of success, whatever his particular purpose, will be referred to as the *generic needs* of purposive action.[5] Since Orion requires the generic needs to achieve any purpose, he must accept that he categorically ought to pursue and defend his possession of the generic needs, unless he is willing to accept generic damage to his capacity to act.

Stage I thus combines the dialectically necessary concepts of a chosen purpose, the PHI and the generic needs of agency to conclude: (5) 'I (categorically instrumentally) ought to pursue and defend my having the generic needs.'

Stage II

From (5) it follows:

(6) 'Other agents categorically ought not to interfere with my having the generic needs against my will, and ought to aid me to secure them when I cannot do so by my own unaided efforts, if I so wish',

which is to say,

(7) 'I have both negative and positive rights to have the generic needs.' In short, 'I have the generic rights.'

In Stage II, Orion recognises that he requires the generic needs of agency in order to pursue and defend his possession of them. Now consider Artemis (representing any other agent), who could affect Orion's possession of the generic needs. Orion must be against Artemis interfering with his possession of the generic needs

[4] Beyleveld 2012, 4 and Beyleveld & Bos 2009, esp 16–18.

[5] Gewirth preferred the label the 'generic features of action' (see eg Gewirth 1978, 21), whereas Beyleveld (1997, 12 and subsequent works) uses the label 'generic conditions of agency'. These terms are synonyms. My preference is to refer to these as the generic needs (of action/agency) for ease of expression when later applying this concept.

against his will and in favour of her helping him to secure possession of the generic needs, when he wishes to have her help and is unable to secure them without help. Thus, Orion must claim that Artemis categorically ought not to interfere with him having the generic needs *against his will*, and categorically ought to aid him to secure them when he cannot do so by his own unaided efforts, *if he so wishes*. It is therefore dialectically necessary for Orion to claim that he has negative and positive will-rights to have the generic needs of agency. That is to say, it is dialectically necessary for Orion to claim: (7) 'I have the generic rights.'[6]

Stage III

From (7) it follows (as shown by the Argument for the Sufficiency of Agency):

(8) 'I have the generic rights because I am an agent'

which, by the logical principle of universalisability, entails

(9) 'Every agent has the generic rights because it is an agent.'

Thus,

(10) 'All agents have the generic rights.'

Thus, by the logical principle of universalisability,

(11) It is dialectically necessary for every agent to accept that all agents have the generic rights: the PGC.

Stage III involves the move from Orion's dialectically necessary claim that he has the generic rights to the dialectically necessary claim that Artemis has the generic rights. This move relies on the *logical principle of universalisability*:

> if some predicate P belongs to some subject S because S has the property Q (where the 'because' is that of sufficient reason or condition), then P must also belong to all other subjects S_1, S_2, …, S_n that have Q.[7]

Applied to Orion: *if* Orion's possession of Q provides him with a sufficient reason to hold that he possesses P, *then* Artemis' possession of Q provides Orion with a sufficient reason to hold that Artemis also possesses P. Use of this logical principle in the argument requires it to be dialectically necessary for Orion to accept: (8) 'I have the generic rights *because* I am an agent.'

Orion must accept this by virtue of the Argument for the Sufficiency of Agency (ASA), which is an argument presented by Gewirth on a single page of *Reason and Morality*.[8] If Orion were to deny (8), then he would imply that he has the generic

[6] Gewirth (1978, ch 2) identified these as both procedural and substantive rights: 'freedom and well-being.'

[7] Gewirth 1978, 105.

[8] See Gewirth 1978, 110. Gewirth refers to it as the Argument *from* the Sufficiency of Agency.

rights *because* he has a property that is not necessarily possessed by agents (such as being called Orion, being human, being male, having a wonderful father, etc). This implies that if he lacked that property he would not have the generic rights, but that contradicts (7), which was derived without reliance upon that property. It follows that it is dialectically necessary for Orion to claim that he has the generic rights *because* he is an agent.

The logical principle of universalisability is applied twice. First, it follows that Orion must accept that Artemis also has the generic rights.[9] Secondly, since Artemis must reason in the same way from her own perspective, it follows that she denies that she is an agent if she does not accept that Orion has the generic rights.[10] Thus, it is dialectically necessary for every agent to accept that all agents have the generic rights: the PGC.

2.2.2. Objections

If you have objections to the dialectically necessary argument, you will not find yourself in want of company. Minds much greater than mine have objected to every link in Gewirth's chain of reasoning and the PGC is only as secure as the weakest of those links. Defending the argument requires a book in itself; indeed more than one book, for Gewirth's *Reason and Morality* did not anticipate all plausible criticisms. Beyleveld's *The Dialectical Necessity of Morality* recast the argument (in a form to which my summary owes considerable debt) and brought Gewirth's later responses together with his own. Here I propose to address some of the most pressed or challenging objections to the whole enterprise, rather than to particular steps in the argument.[11]

Let me, here, try to convey these objections in a single paragraph of my own. Humans are emotional beings; furless bipedal primates or even creations of God, capable of feeling love and hate, hope and despair, elation and misery. Appeals to intuited impartiality, self-interest or pure sentiment can resonate in non-rational ways; whereas appeals to severed reason are hollow and disconnected from our cultural and psychological identities as embodied and socially embedded beings. The idea of a justificatory reason detached from a motivational reason must, so the thought goes, be left to the realm of the non-moral; for the realm of moral has an intrinsic allegiance to feeling. A perfectly rational being could be a sociopath, but a sociopath could never truly be a moral being.

I have deliberately elided many thoughts, not to suggest that they must co-exist but to convey my sense of their cumulative psychological and social force.

[9] Gewirth (1988, 253) calls this 'possessive universalization'; Beyleveld (1991, 59) 'internal application of the LPU'.

[10] Gewirth (1988, 253) calls this 'judgmental universalization'; Beyleveld (1991, 59) 'external application of the LPU'.

[11] Readers with other objections should consult Beyleveld 1991; Beyleveld 2017a, 241–244; Beyleveld 2017c (which responds to Enoch 2006).

Three objections fall out of these thoughts. The first is the idea that the locus of the dialectically necessary argument is an artificial construct, unlike any real human being. I will call this the *atomised agent objection.* The second condemns the dialectically necessary method for ignoring the importance of emotion to morality. I will call this the *emotion objection.* The third objection is to the distinction between a justificatory and motivating reason. This may be expressed as a rhetorical question: why should I care about the PGC being dialectically necessary? I will call this the *Humean internalist objection.*

Before addressing these objections, I wish to draw attention to the distinction between the justification of the PGC and its application. My current focus is on the dialectically necessary argument for the PGC. This chapter will go on to consider how the PGC is to be applied to us as human beings – a species of furless bipedal primate whose frontal lobes can easily be overshadowed by their adrenal glands – who live and identify with particular contexts and social relationships. If the PGC is indeed dialectically necessary, then it has implications for how agents (including human agents) may or ought to facilitate, encourage or respond to emotions and associated behaviours. Objections are not always sensitive to the distinction between the justification and application of the PGC. This is part of the response to Brooks and Sankey, who combine the atomised agent and emotion objections when they question how well ethical rationalism 'accounts for agents in their concrete, everyday lives'; agents as 'human beings with emotions'.[12] A similar criticism is found in the work of Mullally, who argues that Gewirth's argument 'defines the self simply by reference to its capacity for agency'.[13] She adds that 'if the self is stripped of its concrete, affective and emotional aspects, then what we are left with is an empty mask'.

According to the atomised agent objection, dialectically necessary reasoning requires agents to be conceptualised as individuals abstracted from their physical and social selves. This misunderstands the function of dialectical necessity and the attributes of agency. Agents are the locus of the argument because they are the only beings for whom the question as to whether there are any moral duties is intelligible. Only agents are intelligible addressors or addressees of practical precepts (norms specifying what may or ought to be done). Such beings need not be human, be gendered, exist in a community or interact with others; but a *particular agent* could be all of these things (as is the case for you and me). That is because no particular agent is *merely* an agent.[14] I cannot be an agent without being the particular agent that I am, just as I cannot be the particular (human and socially embedded) agent that I am without being an agent.[15] Contrary to the claims of this objection, a dialectically necessary argument does not ignore the status of an agent as a particular agent; it merely seeks to show what it means for a particular agent to understand itself as *both* a particular agent *and* an agent as such.

[12] Brooks & Sankey 2017, 135 and 137. See the response in Beyleveld 2017a, 248–250.
[13] Mullally 2006, 33.
[14] See Brown 2016, esp 82–84.
[15] See Beyleveld 2017a, 243–244; Beyleveld 2017b, 7.

According to the emotion objection, the dialectically necessary method overlooks the importance of emotion to morality. Emotions are, however, a crucial component of agency (and the application of the PGC). To be an agent is to have the capacities required for internal reflection and voluntary purposivity, which include the capacities required to possess feelings, desires and motivations. That is not to deny that there can be vast differences between particular agents in terms of the levels of emotional feelings or sensitivities. But dialectically necessary reasoning neither assumes nor requires us to be Star Trek's Vulcans. It does not require us to be any less human or emotional than we actually are. It merely requires possession of the attributes of agency, because only those who possess such attributes can act on practical precepts; and a human agent is still an agent.

The Humean internalist objection alludes to David Hume's view that morality depends on passions.[16] It goes beyond Hume's published views by claiming that a reason for acting morally must serve a desire. This idea that moral values can only be based on sentiment or self-interest has wide appeal among contemporary philosophers.

One way of evading this objection is by treating dialectical necessity as a form of prudential reasoning, so that the agent's self-interest provides the agent with a reason for acting morally.[17] But that would be to misunderstand dialectical necessity, which is about agential self-understanding.[18] Dialectical necessity cannot, nor is it meant to, show that it is in an agent's prudential self-interest to act in the interests of others.

A categorical moral principle is not something that makes you do or desire something. It is a principle stating that you ought to do something in the interests of others where you are able to both do it and not do it, and might have no desire to do it. A categorical principle therefore cannot be justified in terms of what you desire. Further, contrary to appearances, prudential reasoning does not offer an alternative to dialectical necessity; it presupposes it.[19] Prudential reasoning relies on the Principle of Hypothetical Imperatives (PHI).[20] But that principle is not itself a hypothetical imperative: the PHI is not a desired end or a necessary means to achieve a desired end, it is a principle presupposed by any intelligible attempt to reason in terms of means and ends. It is dialectically necessary: necessary for an agent to understand what it means to be an agent. Thus, paradoxically, the PHI is itself a categorical imperative (and the PGC is a categorical imperative

[16] See Hume 1739–1740, 3.1.2.1: 'morality … is more properly felt than judg'd of'. This view is shared by many contemporary theorists: see eg Rorty 1993.

[17] Cf Chitty 2008.

[18] See Beyleveld & Bos 2009, esp 13 (which responds to Chitty 2008).

[19] And not just because a self-interested agent is still an agent. The argument in this paragraph draws on Beyleveld & Bos 2009, esp 16–18 and Beyleveld 2017b, esp 242.

[20] eg when Gauthier (1986) argues that a rational self-interested person (a 'utility maximiser') must accept other-regarding obligations (be a 'constrained maximiser'), he is arguing (in accordance with the PHI) that a straightforward utility maximiser either chooses to become a constrained maximiser or gives up her goal of maximising her utility overall.

because it accords with the PHI). Since dialectically necessary reasoning draws out the necessary implications of an agent understanding what it is to be an agent, to ask why dialectical necessity gives you a reason to act is to ask for a reason to follow reason. That makes no sense. The Humean internalist objection is therefore incoherent.

2.2.3. Dialectically Contingent Arguments

Gewirth contrasted his dialectically necessary method with the dialectically contingent method. This less ambitious method also examines the logical implications of claims made by protagonists or interlocutors (hence it is dialectical), but it 'begins with … statements or judgments that reflect the variable beliefs, interests, or ideals of some person or group' (hence it is contingent).[21] Beyleveld has devised several arguments of this type for the PGC.[22]

One of Beyleveld's arguments combines the least controversial stage of the dialectically necessary argument (Stage I) with the belief that all human beings are equal in dignity and rights.[23] It was argued in 1.3.1 that this belief explains and justifies particular common law decisions and can be inferred from the European Convention on Human Rights and therefore any national implementation of the Convention rights. Indeed, as the declared ground for the rights in the Universal Declaration of Human Rights (UDHR), it is implied by any instrument that purports to give effect to the UDHR.

Stage I of the dialectically necessary argument requires Orion (any agent) to accept (as dialectically necessary) that he categorically instrumentally ought to defend and pursue his possession of the generic needs of agency. The UDHR's impartiality assumption takes as given the other-regarding and universalisability steps in Stages II and III of the dialectically necessary argument. If Orion is to avoid either denying the UDHR's impartiality assumption or that he is an agent, then he must accept that he categorically ought to pursue or defend Artemis' possession of the generic needs (if she so wills) and that Artemis has (indeed all agents have) the generic rights. In short, combining Stage I and the UDHR's impartiality assumption implies the PGC.

The PGC can thus be defended as an acultural or refined cultural morality. The dialectically necessary method, if sound, would establish the PGC as the supreme principle of acultural morality. The dialectically contingent argument just outlined relies on a single cultural moral belief, so presents the PGC as a maximal refined cultural morality.

[21] Gewirth 1978, 43–44.
[22] See Beyleveld 1996 and 2012.
[23] See Beyleveld 2012.

2.3. Applying the PGC

Gewirth distinguishes direct from indirect applications of the PGC.[24] Direct applications involve judging whether actions are compatible with the generic rights of an agent: the imposition of the PGC on the 'interpersonal actions of individual persons'.[25] These judgments can be complex or controversial, or require authoritative selection between otherwise optional possibilities (such as whether vehicles should drive on the left- or right-hand side of the road).[26] Procedures must therefore be applied and obeyed as, indirect applications of the PGC, to 'govern multiperson activities and institutions'.[27]

2.3.1. Direct Application

When Orion claims the generic rights, he is claiming will-rights to whatever he needs to act or act successfully, regardless of his specific purpose. These *generic needs* vary in degree.[28] They divide into those required for him to act at all (*basic needs*), maintain his ability to act (*nonsubtractive needs*) and improve his ability to act (*additive needs*). Since his basic needs are preconditions of his nonsubtractive needs and these are preconditions of his additive needs, his generic needs can be ordered according to the 'criterion of degrees of needfulness for action'.[29] This criterion therefore provides a hierarchical ranking for the generic rights: basic, nonsubtractive, then additive generic rights. Applying this criterion, Orion would infringe a more important right if he were to inflict non-consensual physical injury upon Artemis (depriving her of a basic need), than if he were to break a promise to her (depriving her of a nonsubtractive need) or impede an opportunity for her to learn a new skill (depriving her of an additive need).

Determinations of generic needs require empirical judgments to identify the agent's nature and context. As a human agent, Orion's basic needs will include his biological life and sufficient mental equilibrium to pursue his chosen purposes, and the means to these, such as food, drink, shelter, clothing and health.[30] A glass of orange juice could, depending on the context, satisfy varying levels of generic need or a mere desire, or even deprive him of a generic need. If he is severely dehydrated or hypoglycaemic and orange juice is the only available source of hydration and sugar, then he has a basic need for that orange juice. If he has no urgent biological need for hydration or sugar, then to deprive him of a glass of orange juice

[24] See Gewirth 1978, chs 4 and 5, respectively.
[25] Gewirth 1978, 200.
[26] See Beyleveld & Brownsword 2006.
[27] Gewirth 1978, 200.
[28] See Gewirth 1978, 53–63.
[29] See Gewirth 1978, 53–58 (which uses the previous label of 'criterion of degrees of *necessity* for action') and Gewirth 1996, 45–46. This criterion follows from the PHI.
[30] See Gewirth 1978, 54.

that he already possesses could still inflict a nonsubtractive harm or, if he has yet to possess it, an additive harm. If he asks for orange juice from a vendor only to discover that the last has just been sold, he might suffer only an unfulfilled fleeting desire, rather than generic harm. If he is allergic to orange juice, then mixing his drink with it could cause anaphylactic shock and death, thereby depriving him of basic needs. It follows that while there is not a generic right to orange juice (because it is not needed by agents to pursue purposes as such), giving effect to Orion's generic rights will sometimes require that he have a right to orange juice.

The rights claimed and recognised by Orion are both negative and positive. The positive generic rights are limited by two provisos.[31] According to what I will call the *own unaided effort proviso*, Orion only has a duty to aid Artemis to secure her generic needs where she is unable to do so by her own unaided effort. This is because her dialectically necessary claim to rights derives from her categorical instrumental needs, and the assistance of another agent is not so needed where she can achieve her purposes without assistance. According to what I will call the *comparable cost proviso*, Orion only has a duty to aid Artemis to secure her generic needs where such action does not deprive him of the same or more important generic needs, as measured by the degree of needfulness for action. This is because Orion must first recognise the dialectical necessity of his own claim to the generic rights before recognising the dialectical necessity of Artemis' equal generic rights.

If Artemis steps into the path of a car while distracted by her phone, Orion must not remain wilfully silent, but he is not required to put himself between her and the car. Since the generic rights are will-rights, Artemis may release Orion from the corresponding duties to assist her. But he must not be too eager to infer such release (by, for example, her failure to ask others to shout out warnings) or too willing to assume that she needs or desires his assistance (by, for example, imputing her need to be escorted home on the basis of her gender). Since assisting those in need often requires coordinated collective action, in a complex society the discharge of many positive duties will fall primarily on the state and its institutions.[32]

Before applying the PGC at all, Orion first needs to identify those who are agents. Since he has direct access to his own mind, he can be certain of his own possession of the reflective purposivity constitutive of agency. But he does not have such direct access to the mind of any other. Even if it were possible to connect another's brain to his own *and* this meant that he had experiences that appeared to him to be internal access to that other's thoughts, he would still lack the purposive control over the direction of those thoughts required to confirm agency. If he had such purposive control, then he would have to regard those thoughts as his own, rather than those of another. There is, in other words, an epistemic gap between his knowledge of his own mind and his knowledge of another's mind.[33]

[31] See Gewirth 1978, 217–230.

[32] See Gewirth 1996, 59; Beyleveld 2012, 14; Bauhn 2016, 222–225.

[33] Coggon 2012, 190 (fn 159) argues that the response to this problem presented below (and first presented in Beyleveld & Pattinson 2000) fails 'to account for the sceptic's objections that form the basis

To explicate the implications of the PGC, let us imagine that Orion interacts with Dawn (who behaves as if she is an agent) and Sirius (who is a newborn baby and so does not behave as if he is an agent). Orion does not directly experience their thoughts (or their pains, pleasures or feelings) in the way that he does his own. He might happen to be willing (as most of us are) to infer agency from Dawn's behaviour and similarly infer that Sirius is capable of feeling pleasure and pain but not capable of reflective purposivity, so is only partially or potentially an agent. Gewirth's own application of the PGC involves him making these very inferences. He simply assumes that (anyone represented by) Dawn is an agent and (anyone represented by) Sirius is a partial or potential agent ('marginal agent'). Gewirth would grant generic rights to Dawn directly and invoke the Principle of Proportionality to grant partial generic rights to Sirius.[34] But such inferences of agency and partial agency depend on unverifiable metaphysical assumptions. Orion's willingness to draw them is no guarantee of their soundness, for he has no way of eliminating the possibility that Dawn is merely a sophisticated automaton without a mind, or that Sirius is a locked-in agent somehow currently prevented from fully displaying his abilities to others. Further, Gewirth's invocation of the Principle of Proportionality to extend the population to which the PGC applies in the abstract is inconsistent with the dialectically necessary argument for the PGC, because the (dialectically necessary) sufficient ground for possession of any generic rights is agency (see the ASA, above) and the generic rights are will-rights (thereby only capable of being possessed by agents).[35]

Even though Orion cannot strictly know whether Dawn is an agent, he can treat her as an agent because she behaves like one. Treating Dawn as an agent and acting accordingly would involve him restricting some of his freedom of action. But treating Dawn as a non-agent, despite being able to do otherwise, would violate her generic rights. Thus, since the PGC is categorically binding, Orion is required to treat Dawn as an agent and act in accordance with her presumed generic rights. If the dialectically necessary argument for the PGC is valid, it follows that it is dialectically necessary for Orion (who represents any agent) to treat Dawn (who represents anyone who displays sufficient agency-like behaviour to make it possible to treat them as agents) as an agent with generic rights. In this book, I will refer to those others who behave like agents in this sense as *agent-behavers*.[36]

of their theory's extension'. But the problem of other minds is not a fictional construct: it is the logical implication of the distinction between 'I' and 'not I'.

[34] See eg Gewirth 1978, 120–124.

[35] Gewirth's reasoning on 'marginal agents' has also been criticised by Hill 1984 and Pluhar 1995, ch 5. The substance of the following argument, for the dialectical necessity of moral precaution, was first presented in Beyleveld & Pattinson 2000 (which was itself based on an unpublished paper from 1998). This argument has been criticised by Holm & Coggon 2008, to which see our response in Beyleveld & Pattinson 2010.

[36] The label 'ostensible agent' is used in Beyleveld & Pattinson 2000 and Pattinson 2018, but this could be misinterpreted as suggesting that the relevant other is seemingly *but not actually* an agent (as opposed to seemingly but not necessarily an agent). The label 'apparent agent', used in Beyleveld & Pattinson 2010, could equally be misinterpreted as suggesting that the relevant other is *clearly* an agent or is *seemingly but not actually* an agent. The PGC must be applied under precaution precisely because it is impossible to know whether or not another is an agent.

A neologism is required due to the absence of a commonly used word or expression, rather like the absence of a word for the stringy white fibre that clings to bananas.[37]

Orion can also not strictly know that Sirius is not an agent. But, crucially, he cannot treat him as an agent or intelligibly grant him generic rights (or any will-rights). Nonetheless, it is both possible and intelligible for Orion to guard against mistakenly treating Sirius as a non-agent by acting towards him in ways that would respect his generic rights should he (unknowably) happen to be an agent. Moral precaution here therefore requires Orion to grant Sirius interest-rights tracking his presumed generic interests. These interest-rights are correlative to duties not to kill, inflict pain or otherwise harm Sirius in ways that would infringe his generic interests if he were an agent, and duties to provide appropriate assistance for him to gain what would be his generic interests if he were an agent. I will refer to those others (like Sirius) who display only some of the characteristics and behaviours displayed by those who behave like agents as *partial agent-behavers.*

A single-variable conflict between respecting a will-right of an agent-behaver (Dawn) and respecting the equivalent interest-right of a partial agent-behaver (such as Sirius) is to be dealt with in the way most likely to comply with the PGC, given the epistemic gap. This is an instance of the 'criterion of avoidance of more probable harm'.[38] As outlined above, the PGC requires that the agency-like characteristics and behaviours displayed by others be treated as if they are evidence of agency. Greater behavioural display of this type is, by definition, displayed by agent-behavers than by partial agent-behavers. It follows that, in a single-variable conflict of the type under consideration, a will-right of an agent-behaver is to take precedence over the equivalent interest-right of a partial agent-behaver. To put it in more general terms, partial agent-behavers are owed duties in proportion to the degree to which they approach being agent-behavers. Thus, all other variables being equal and standard species expectations applying: the life of an embryo counts for less than the life of a fetus, the life of a fetus counts for less than that of a newborn at full-term and a newborn's life counts for less than the life of a child who has reached the stage of being capable of being treated like an agent. In multi-variable conflicts, where other relevant factors arise, matters are not so simple and it is then necessary to apply the PGC indirectly.

2.3.2. Indirect Application

The PGC provides dialectically necessary justification and content for many popular slogans of moral and political philosophy. These includes Mill's harm principle and Marx's socialist slogan. Mill declared: 'The only purpose for which power can be rightfully exercised over any member of a civilized community, against his will,

[37] See Regan 2003, 80, citing Bill Lawson.
[38] Beyleveld & Pattinson 2000, 44.

is to prevent harm to others.'[39] The PGC permits agents to do anything they wish, provided only that what they do does not violate other agents' possession of their generic rights. It therefore provides a dialectically necessary justification for Mill's harm principle, where its content is provided by the generic needs. Marx declared: 'From each according to his ability, to each according to his needs.'[40] The PGC imposes extensive positive duties to assist others (which must be primarily operationalised through the state) according to the duty-bearer's ability to do so (the comparable cost proviso) and the right-holder's needs (the comparable cost and own unaided effort provisos). It therefore provides a dialectically necessary justification for Marx's slogan, where its content is provided by the positive generic rights.

The PGC is, however, incompatible with many details of the theories of Mill and Marx and many other political slogans, beliefs or theories. It is, for example, incompatible with the liberal idea that the state should be neutral upon the particular conceptions of morality held by individuals. The PGC will only permit state neutrality where its direct or indirect application does not require intervention. Many features of the political and legal system in this (or any other existing) jurisdiction are liable to give rise to infringements of the PGC.

In a 2006 article, Beyleveld and Brownsword present a thought experiment in which we are asked to imagine that we live in 'Gewirthia'.[41] This imaginary country is assumed to have a developed scientific and technological sector and to operate in the globalised world of the twenty-first century. Where it differs from any existing country is that all its citizens accept the PGC as both the supreme principle of morality and the constitution's first principle of dispute resolution. Crucially, and this is the point of the thought experiment, even in such an imaginary country, political and regulatory structures would be required to settle disputes over the direct application of the PGC. Beyleveld and Brownsword argue that structures would be required to authoritatively select between optional possibilities that cannot co-exist (such as whether vehicles should drive on the left- or right-hand side of the road) and authoritatively respond to both value complexity or controversy where allowing individuals to act on divergent judgments would cause or threaten generic harm to others. Two types of value complexity need to be distinguished. I will refer to the first as the problem of value calculation and the second as the problem of variable identification.

The problem of value calculation arises when multi-variables affecting different individuals need to be assessed and weighed together. Assessing options according to the requirements of the PGC requires such multi-variable judgments concerning the probability (under precaution) that potentially affected individuals are agents, the importance of the (presumed) generic need affected and the probabilities of

[39] Mill 1859, ch 1.
[40] Marx 1891, 11.
[41] Beyleveld & Brownsword 2006, esp 143.

actions having effects on those (presumed) generic needs.[42] Consider, for example, weighing the probable loss of a cat's hind limbs against a small chance that Dawn will suffer a small diminution in her ability to learn a new skill. As is common to all complex interpersonal cost-benefit calculations, it is not clear how such apparently different scales of probability/importance are to be objectively weighed.[43]

The problem of variable identification arises where there is 'a dialectically necessary answer to an application of the PGC', but the application is so complex that rational and reasonable doubt arises about the correct answer.[44] Imagine, for example, that there is a dispute between equally informed scientists over the probabilities and outcomes to the population of a particular set of options, and a decision is required before it is possible for them to obtain further data.

Ideally, any dispute resolution procedure would operate with the consent of all those affected, but even in Gewirthia unanimous agreement will often be unobtainable. The justification for proceduralism also requires that Gewirthia avoid 'an infinite regress of one layer of proceduralism on another'.[45] Beyleveld and Brownsword argue that a citizen must recognise that the fallibility of their own judgments and a free, fair and transparent democratic process is the 'optimal compromise' by which committed Gewirthians can mutually co-exist in a complex society governed by the PGC.[46] Because individual rights of sufficient weight trump decisions yielded by majoritarian politics or processes, independent judicial oversight is also required.[47]

Consideration of Gewirthia raises issues often associated with the work of Rawls. Chapter 1 briefly considered Rawls' defence of his two principles of justice, which he argued must be met before a society may be regarded as fully just. His self-declared purpose in *A Theory of Justice* was to identify 'what a perfectly just society would be like' on the ground that we need to begin with 'ideal theory' to enable 'the systematic grasp' of the more pressing problems of everyday life.[48] This led Rawls to presuppose ideal conditions, such as a general willingness to comply with the chosen principles (general compliance) and generally favourable social conditions (such as satisfaction of essential human needs). Gewirthia is a tool of ideal theory, for Beyleveld and Brownsword are asking us to imagine a country that does not and has never existed in which something like Rawls' two ideal conditions apply. Many contemporary political theorists push back against counterfactual assumptions about the world in which we live, insisting that we either reject ideal theory and start with the 'real world' or now move to non-ideal

[42] The latter requires consideration of the likelihood of generic effects, as well as its predicted duration and reversibility.

[43] See further Beyleveld & Pattinson 2010.

[44] Beyleveld & Brownsword 2006, 148.

[45] Beyleveld & Brownsword 2006, 150.

[46] Beyleveld & Brownsword 2006, 152. See also Gewirth's 'method of consent': see Gewirth 1978, 304–312.

[47] See Beyleveld & Brownsword 2006, 153–154.

[48] Rawls 1999, 8.

theory as the next step.[49] As is easily anticipated, non-ideal theorists differ with regard to their target, in terms of what they identify as the ideal assumptions they want to replace or from which they want to move on.[50] Much depends on the question being asked. The work of Rawls (and Beyleveld and Brownsword) expressly recognises that we also need non-ideal theory to understand how we ought to regulate human conduct.

Gewirthians cannot treat their perceptions of the empirical and social world, or their intuitions about those perceptions, as conclusive. That is, in part, because the PGC delimits both how we may respond to inferences drawn from our observations and other sense-data (see, for example, the precautionary thesis above) and when we may regard a social enterprise or practice as giving rise to action-guiding norms (see the case for legal idealism below). As the Gewirthia thought experiment demonstrates, expressly excluding variables (as per ideal theory) can provide insight into the indirect application of the PGC. The next step is to reintroduce those variables. Additional work is required to enable us to make comparisons between existing or otherwise deliverable options and consider how we may move from where we are towards a global community of recognised and enforced generic rights.[51]

My task in this book is to start with the United Kingdom as it is, with its existing institutions, historical compromises, inequalities, discriminatory practices, moral pluralism and the like. There are two imaginary features to my thought experiment. First, as declared from the outset, I will imagine the manifestation of some specific biomedical developments to which a regulatory response is required. Secondly, I will consider how a committed Gewirthian would act if exercising one of two central roles: a judge when deciding a hypothetical case or a Member of Parliament when proposing legislation. For ease of expression, I will provide names to my imagined judge and politician; both of whom will be women. Both will be envisioned as having sufficient de facto judicial/political authority to ensure that the resulting decision/legislation reflects her competent and good faith judgment on the requirements of the PGC in the context in which she operates. The nature of any indirect application of the PGC is that there can be a range of legitimate outcomes, so the resulting hypothetical judgments and legislation should not be considered the only defensible outcomes in all their details. Unlike a citizen of Gewirthia, my imagined official will not publicly reason *qua* official from her commitment to the PGC as the supreme principle of acultural morality, for it is difficult to plausibly postulate retention of her imagined de facto authority if she were to do so. But she would not deny or otherwise hide this commitment – many politicians and judges are known to have a strong personal morality. Her ability

[49] Cohen is often cited as an exception, because he adopts a 'radically fact-insensitive kind of "pure" ideal theory' (see Robeyns 2008, 343). But he accepted that, when regulating our affairs, 'facts constrain possibilities of implementation *and* determine defensible trade-offs (at the level of implementation) among competing principles': see Cohen 2003, 244 (original emphasis).

[50] See the overviews presented in Robeyns 2008 and Valentini 2012.

[51] See eg Gewirth 1996, the sequel to *Reason and Morality*, entitled *The Community of Rights*.

to reason from the PGC in this non-explicit way is facilitated by the convergence of the PGC with many of the cultural moral assumptions implicit in the United Kingdom's claim to be a liberal democracy.

2.3.3. Legal Idealism

Hart is to legal theory what Rawls is to political theory: a twentieth-century juggernaut to which most subsequent Anglo-American work in the field has been a response. Hart, in *The Concept of Law*, argued that law is to be conceptualised as separable from morality.[52] I shall refer to the thesis that law is not necessarily conceptually connected to morality as the 'separability thesis'.[53] Despite defending the separability thesis, Hart argued that law is normative in the sense that a valid law gives rise to a legal obligation to obey it.[54] I do not propose to address the details of Hart's argument, because it follows from the dialectical necessity of the PGC that an agent cannot regard any purposive enterprise as valid or as giving rise to obligations, unless doing so is consistent with the PGC.

Beyleveld and Brownsword point out that if the debate over whether the concept of law is not merely a linguistic quibble, then the starting point for this debate must be neutral on the separability thesis.[55] Arguments starting from a loaded premise beg the question by assuming what they are attempting to prove. A sound argument for the separability thesis therefore cannot start from the claim that the concept of law must capture the empirical features of existing formal regulatory systems, because those empirical features are likely to be inconsistent with the requirements of morality (so this starting point rejects legal idealism). Conversely, a sound argument against the separability thesis cannot start from the claim that the concept of law must exclude wicked rules or regulatory systems (as this starting point rejects legal positivism). Beyleveld and Brownsword advance 'the enterprise of subjecting human conduct to the governance of rules' as such a neutral referent.[56] As they point out, the dialectically necessary argument requires attempts to regulate human conduct by rules to be conceived in terms of the PGC. It follows that, under the PGC, legal validity is a subcategory of moral validity. Law may, for example, be conceived as morality from the point of view of enforcement.

Theories rejecting the separability thesis are typically referred to as 'natural law' or 'legal idealist' theories. Some prefer to use the former label for theories within moral universalism or even for theories making particular types of theological claims. The dialectically necessary argument for the PGC as a moral universalist

[52] See Hart 2012 (first edition published in 1961).
[53] This label was probably first used in this way in Coleman 1982, 140–141.
[54] See Hart 2012, 82–92.
[55] See Beyleveld & Brownsword 1986, esp 79–82.
[56] See eg Beyleveld & Brownsword 1986, esp 2 and 120, citing Fuller 1969, 96.

principle is neutral upon whether God exists.[57] I will describe a PGC-compatible legal theory as *legal idealist* to avoid associations with traditional natural law theory, such as Aquinas' claims for divine providence.

If the debate over the separability thesis is merely about language usage or dominant cultural beliefs, then legal positivism prevails in the Anglo-American world. Unless discussing the conceptual debate, this book uses the word 'law' and related terms in just that sense. When the word is used in this way to refer to the formal rules and rulings of a polity or group of polities, the PGC provides criteria for critique, rather than identification. Positive law need not, as a matter of empirical fact, comply with the PGC even if it is regarded as valid and action-guiding by the citizens of the relevant polity. The conceptual debate is evoked if it is asked whether those beliefs are coherent or justified.

Human conduct can also be regulated, in the sense of directed or channelled, by means other than rules and rulings. Brownsword has contrasted regulation by rules with 'technological management'.[58] Technological management seeks to design or automate products, places or processes to preclude certain conduct or behaviour. It has a long history: walls have been used to keep out unwanted visitors for thousands of years and income tax has been deducted from employees' wages for more than two centuries.[59] But technological management is now ubiquitous: hotel lights frequently operate using the door keycard to prevent lights being left on, banks dispense cash by ATM to ensure fast and accurate counting, and restrictions are now routinely embedded in digital products to control use. These examples could date quickly. The future is likely to render 'self-driving' cars commonplace and could even bring implanted devices or deliberate genetic modifications that restrict an individual's ability to act in certain ways. Once implemented, technological management can limit human agency and therefore limit the subjection of human conduct to rules. Moral and legal rules are only relevant to those who are able to choose whether to follow those rules at the relevant time. Thus, technological management can operate as a limit on law.

2.4. Contextual Legal Idealism

My purpose in this chapter is to outline a legal theory for application in the current and anticipated globalised world: contextual legal idealism. In both Gewirthia and many existing countries, judicial decisions and legislation are regarded as acts of provisional closure in the sense of being enforced until overruled or repealed.

[57] There could be implications of the argument from the PGC: Beyleveld & Brownsword 2001, ch 6 argue that a categorical moral principle requires radical agnosticism.

[58] See Brownsword 2004; 2017; 2021; 2022. Other theorists have also considered these issues, see eg Lucy 2022.

[59] Income tax was first introduced in Britain in 1793 and later reintroduced by the Income Tax Acts of 1803 and 1842.

Given the need for cooperative action to give effect to the PGC in a complex society and the de facto existence of a plurality of moral views inconsistent with the PGC, Gewirthians will need to seek moral second- (or third-) bests if they are to avoid ending up with even worse outcomes (as measured by the PGC). This is common to any morality not adopted by consensus among the majority or the most powerful in a pluralist society.

2.4.1. Modified Law as Integrity

I have elsewhere utilised a modified version of Dworkin's 'law as integrity' to support a robust approach to judicial interpretation of the (positive) law.[60] Dworkin argued that the role of a judge when deciding a 'hard case', where the legal rules are not settled, is to interpret the law as supported by an integral web of principle.[61] Accordingly, the judge is to 'find, in some coherent set of principles about people's rights and duties, the best constructive interpretation of the political structure and legal doctrine of the community'.[62] This involves the judge seeking out a principle that 'both *fits* and *justifies* some complex part of legal practice' and provides 'the consistency of principle' required for the law to be an integral whole.[63] Dworkin illustrates this process using the metaphor of a chain novel.[64] If a novelist writes the first chapter of a book, then another novelist writes the second and yet another writes the third chapter, and so on, the resulting manuscript will only form a coherent novel if each writer seeks to place his or her chapter within the framework set by the previous writers. Hercules, Dworkin's ideal judge, treats precedents like a chain-writer would treat chapters written by other novelists. Hercules will frequently find more than one interpretation capable of fitting the 'bulk' of the previous materials and will then move to the justifiability stage.[65] This will involve examining the interpretative options by reference to a 'coherent theory justifying the network [of structures and decisions] as a whole'.[66] In other words, by reference to what in Dworkin refers to in his earlier work as a morality 'in the discriminatory sense' and I refer to as a refined cultural morality.[67] His aim is to put together a coherent set of rights and responsibilities that provide the best overall interpretation of the legal materials of the community.

Something akin to Dworkin's method was adopted in chapter 1 to discern refined cultural morality from (positive) law, in terms of principles that both explain and justify existing legislative rules and judicial decisions. As pointed out

[60] See Dworkin 1986 and Pattinson 2018.
[61] See Dworkin 1986.
[62] Dworkin 1986, 255.
[63] Dworkin 1986, 228 (emphasis added).
[64] See Dworkin 1986, ch 6, esp 228ff.
[65] See Dworkin 1986, esp 245.
[66] Dworkin 1986, 245.
[67] See eg Dworkin 1977, 248 and the discussion in 1.2.1.

there, and as Dworkin recognises, incompatible principles can be discerned from examination of existing rules and rulings. Dworkin's view that Hercules would deal with conflicting principles that 'fit' with existing laws by 'justification', using a theory of the background morality of his community, runs into the problem that the content and justification of that morality is often the very thing in dispute.[68] It also runs into the problem that requiring judicial reasoning to have a necessary moral component assumes legal idealism over legal positivism in a way that begs the question against the latter. The dialectical necessity of the PGC answers both problems, because it implies that the PGC governs any valid attempt to identify legal rules and principles. It follows that both limbs of Dworkin's method, 'fit' and 'justification', must be interpreted by reference to the PGC. Law as integrity, modified accordingly, can then be understood as an indirect application of the PGC through judicial reasoning.

I need to say something more about the 'fit' limb, because existing (positive) legal rules might themselves be incompatible with the PGC. Since none of us live in Gewirthia, the previous rules and rulings of the state were not even presented as attempts to apply the PGC. Nonetheless, many of the rules and rulings of the polity in which the judge operates might happen to be amenable to being interpreted in ways that treat them as if they are indirect applications of the PGC. Where this is the case, a Gewirthian judge must interpret the laws in just that way.[69] To do otherwise would prevent the judge from being able to adjudicate or would involve usurpation of a legislative role. Such usurpation occurs where judges substitute an existing democratically enacted rule that is plausibly consistent with the requirements of the PGC with their own choice of rule that has no greater claim to consistency with the PGC. Substitutions of that type are properly left to official bodies with a greater democratic mandate than possessed by judges. (I will come back to legislative law-making and the democratic mandate possessed by a legislative body in 2.4.2.)

There are societies in which a judge could not plausibly view many existing (positive) laws in a way that is consistent with the PGC. Dworkin envisages Judge Siegfried who acts within a Nazi-like 'legal' system.[70] A Gewirthian Siegfried does not act in a valid legal system, so would be faced with a terrible choice: (1) resign, (2) undermine the state's laws from within or (3) act outside a legitimate judicial role by giving effect to those immoral rules to protect his own skin. The second of these is more likely to protect the generic rights of others. But the extent to which this is feasible without comparable harm to the judge's own generic needs will determine the extent to which the judge has a duty to do so.

Explicitly articulating the premises of judicial reasoning in a written judgment provides transparency and enables properly reasoned critique. In Gewirthia, judges

[68] See discussion of 'the moral acceptance dilemma' in 1.3.3.

[69] Where the relevant rule or ruling is simply inconsistent with any good faith attempt to apply the PGC, then the judge must do her best to evade or undermine it. See the next paragraph for consideration of a society where this is the case for many laws.

[70] See Dworkin 1986, 105.

would (*ex hypothesi*) have the resources and practical authority to reason in this way from explicit recognition of the PGC. However, in no existing society would a judge be able to do this without losing the respect and support of fellow judges and society at large. And, in practice, that respect and support is needed to persuade other judges to affirm and follow her judgments. Fortunately, the judgments of a Gewirthian judge who does not directly refer to the PGC can be indistinguishable in their expression from the judgments of a Dworkinian Hercules or, in many cases, those of judges who are not cognisant of their theoretical assumptions. The PGC therefore supports judicial reasoning in accordance with fit and justification without explicit reference to the PGC as the best of the available options outside Gewirthia. This amounts to judicial reasoning within contextual legal idealism.

In the UK constitutional context, judges declare adherence to the doctrine of precedent. If *stare decisis* operated strictly, so that precedents were regarded as strictly binding, this would pose problems for a Gewirthian judge. However, in practice, precedents are treated as carrying no more than significant presumptive authority, which is consistent with the notion of fit and justification just outlined.[71]

2.4.2. Legislative Law-making

A legislative chamber is likely to be better placed to make some types of indirect applications of the PGC than a judicial panel. Paradigmatically, this is the case for what Fuller called 'polycentric' disputes: complex disputes whose resolution is likely to have repercussions on wider policy concerns or persons who are not party to the proceedings.[72] Such disputes often require inputs and regulatory responses beyond those available to a court. The extent to which a legislative chamber is able to competently and legitimately address polycentric disputes, however, depends on its membership, function and practices. In Gewirthia, a legislative chamber would be explicitly empowered to give effect to the PGC, so would be constitutionally bound (as a matter of positive law) by the direct applications of the PGC and would be populated and structured to facilitate competent and good faith indirect applications of the PGC. The UK legislative system is very different and has many features that are inconsistent with the direct application of the PGC. Let me briefly examine two of these.

Parliamentary sovereignty, the sovereignty of the Crown in Parliament, is considered to be 'a fundamental principle of the UK constitution'.[73] Formally, this principle means that Parliament may enact any laws it wishes and 'no person or body is recognised by the law of England as having a right to override or set aside the legislation of Parliament'.[74] Stephen famously declared that this held

[71] See Duxbury 2008 and Pattinson 2018, 148–151.
[72] See Fuller 1978.
[73] *R (Miller) v Secretary of State for Exiting the EU* [2017] UKSC 5, [43].
[74] Dicey 1915, 3–4, quoted with unstated ellipses in *Miller* [2017] UKSC 5, [43].

even if Parliament enacted a law requiring 'all blue-eyed babies' to be killed.[75] Stephen recognised that it was implausible that such a law would be enacted, to which it may be added that it is even more implausible that the current judiciary would uphold such a thing to be a valid law. In one case, Lord Hope declared: 'Parliamentary sovereignty is an empty principle if legislation is passed which is so absurd or so unacceptable that the populace at large refuses to recognise it as law'.[76] Nonetheless, there remains a moral problem with this constitutional principle: if the PGC is the supreme principle of morality, then only it is sovereign. The United Kingdom has not adopted the first-best primary constitutional principle (the PGC as per Gewirthia), the second-best (a principle of human rights grounded in dignity) or even the third-best (a principle recognising the primacy of a more limited set of relevant rights). What it has is repeated judicial proclamation of the principle of parliamentary sovereignty, formally repealable rights-based legislation (the Human Rights Act 1998) and formally non-sacrosanct common law principles that assert the constitutional importance of human rights.[77]

The second feature, or rather set of features, I want to consider concern the process for electing Members of Parliament. The vast majority of MPs are elected as representatives of political parties with policy manifestos that most candidates had no hand in devising and few voters actually read. Political parties are not publicly funded, so derive the income needed to operate from private donations and subscriptions. All MPs are elected on the basis of a first-past-the-post system, whereby the candidate in a particular constituency with the highest number of votes is elected. The highest number of votes could represent a minority of those who do vote, and those who vote could represent a minority of those eligible to vote. Consequently, the election process enables some individuals and groups to have greater influence than others, and the resulting parliamentary chamber does not fully represent the general will.

To make matters worse, MPs populate only the lower house of Parliament (the House of Commons) with the upper house (the House of Lords) being unelected. The House of Lords comprises appointees, plus 90 hereditary peers elected for life from among themselves and two *ex officio* members.[78] As I write, the House of Lords has 761 members, compared to the 650 MPs eligible to sit in the House of Commons.[79] As a legislative chamber, the House of Lords 'is surpassed in size only by China's National People's Congress'.[80] What is more, legislation is enacted by the Crown in Parliament, meaning that an unelected Head of State has a formal role in this process.

The United Kingdom's constitutional structure clearly fails to provide anything approaching a first-best option for populating a competent and representative

[75] Stephen 1882, 143.
[76] *R (Jackson) v AG* [2005] UKHL 56, [120].
[77] See eg *Thoburn v Sunderland City Council* [2002] EWHC 195 (Admin), [64] (Laws LJ).
[78] House of Lords Act 1999, s 2.
[79] members.parliament.uk/parties/Lords.
[80] Wilks-Heeg et al 2013.

legislative body. Extensive constitutional reform is required to align the UK constitution – indeed, any existing constitution – with the PGC. The means by which such reform is brought about must itself comply with the requirements of the PGC and, in a constitutional structure in which basic needs are capable of being met, that reform will need to be incremental, rather than by overthrow of the entire existing system of power. My task in this book is not to focus on constitutional change as such, but to consider the operation of contextual legal idealism at the lower level of enacting legislation addressing non-constitutional matters. More specifically, I seek to consider what an elected representative could achieve within the United Kingdom's current constitutional framework when introducing a Bill addressing developments at the frontiers of biomedicine.

2.4.3. Imagined Judgments and Legislation

In *Revisiting Landmark Cases in Medical Law*, I used an imaginary judge for the purpose of rewriting the lead judgments of nine cases. In contrast to Dworkin's Hercules, who was said to possess 'superhuman talents and endless time',[81] my imagined judge was not given any superpowers and, 'to reject the mistaken suggestion that an ideal judge is a male judge', was a woman.[82] Athena seemed to me to be a more fitting name for the person carrying the burden placed by Dworkin on to the shoulders of Hercules, given that Athena was the name of the Greek goddess of wisdom and the embodiment of reason and justice. For this book, I need two imagined people: a judge and a politician.

My judge will be *Lady Athena* and positioned as the Masters of the Rolls in the Court of Appeal (chapter 4) or President of the UK Supreme Court (chapter 6). She will give the lead judgment in two cases arising from hypothetical biomedical developments (see chapters 4 and 6).

My politician will be called *Themis Walpole* and placed in the role of UK prime minister. Themis is a Greek goddess of justice.[83] Walpole was the surname of Britain's first prime minister, Sir Robert Walpole, which I use in the absence of a suitable Greek god or goddess.[84] Themis Walpole will lead the government putting forward two Bills addressing hypothetical scientific developments (see chapters 3 and 5). The imagined outcomes are Bills, rather than Acts, to highlight a key difference between the judicial and legislative process. In contrast to draft judgments, Bills are public documents and therefore receive public input and are usually amended before enactment. Thus, while I imagine Themis Walpole

[81] Dworkin 1986, 245.

[82] Pattinson 2018, viii.

[83] Themis and her daughter Dike were goddesses of justice; the equivalent Roman goddess was Justitia.

[84] Themis had another daughter, Eunomia, who was a minor goddess of good order and law, but to my eyes Themis Eunomia looks a bit like a medical term.

having the practical authority to ensure that her Bills are enacted without losing their central features, I do not imagine that she can ignore legitimate concerns that would be overlooked in the absence of the open discussion intrinsic to the democratic process. Further, a Bill can use tens of thousands of words and be full of details that are unnecessary for my purposes; so rather than present complete drafts of hypothetical legislation, I will adopt brief Explanatory Notes explaining the purpose of the draft legislation and summarising its provisions. In practice, detailed Explanatory Notes accompany all Government Bills and some Private Members' Bills.

2.5. Conclusion

The rest of this book will develop and apply the framework that has been articulated in the first two chapters. It will address four case studies on biomedical developments that create, enhance or extend human life. Each of these focuses upon anticipated advances in biomedical research and clinical practice that present challenges to the coherence of extant legal doctrine and categories. Each will culminate in either hypothetical legislation enacted by the United Kingdom Parliament or a hypothetical decision of an appeal court. The next two chapters present case studies on human reproduction: heritable genome editing (chapter 3) and ectogestation (chapter 4). Chapter 5 is a case study on the self-shaping of human beings: cybernetic biohacking. Chapter 6 is a case study on a response to the end of life: cryonic reanimation. I thereby intend to articulate the application of contextual legal idealism to the challenges presented by existing legal tensions and future socio-scientific developments.

PART II

Case Studies

3

Heritable Genome Editing

3.1. Introduction

In November 2018, Jiankui He posted a video on YouTube.[1] It was no ordinary video. It announced, in English, the birth of twin girls in China from embryos genome-edited for HIV resistance. Grace had given birth to Lulu and Nana. Even these pseudonyms were suggestive: Grace, whose name alludes to divine favour, had given birth to girls with the names of fictional women whose sexual charms had caused controversy in early twentieth-century movies. Lulu is the name of the lead character in the 1929 German movie *Pandora's Box*: 'a seductive, thoughtless young woman whose raw sexuality and uninhibited nature bring ruin to herself and those who love her'.[2] Nana is the eponymous protagonist of a nineteenth-century French novel and subsequent French movie of 1926: a seductress who 'destroys every man who pursues her'.[3] A third genome-edited child, born slightly later, was given the pseudonym Amy.[4] Amy is the name of the lead character in a 1927 German novel, made into the 1930 American movie *Morocco*. In the movie, Amy dances and kisses in ways 'considered scandalous for the period'.[5] There are many interpretative possibilities here: intentional allusions to God, opening Pandora's box and sexual transmission of HIV; blatant misogyny or female empowerment; or no more than coincidence.[6]

Just over a year after making this announcement, He was sentenced to three years in prison for conducting 'illegal medical practices'.[7] Shorter sentences were given to two colleagues who assisted him. This chapter considers a future in which the technology enabling the alteration of selected DNA (genome editing) has advanced considerably. The focus is on targeted genomic modifications that could be passed on to subsequent generations: *heritable genome editing*.

This chapter will first explain the basics of genetic science and current genome editing technology, so the next section (3.2) can be skipped by those already

[1] youtu.be/th0vnOmFltc. His name is typically written in accordance with Chinese practice with his surname first: He Jiankui.

[2] en.wikipedia.org/wiki/Pandora%27s_Box_(1929_film).

[3] en.wikipedia.org/wiki/Nana_(novel).

[4] See Gutierrez 2022.

[5] en.wikipedia.org/wiki/Morocco_(film).

[6] You might think I've spent too long looking up other uses of these names on Wikipedia.

[7] See Normile 2019 and Cyranoski 2020. He was released in April 2022: see Regalado 2022.

familiar with this material. Four norms will then be discerned from international instruments and domestic legislation and a key associated ethical issue discussed (3.3). This chapter will then present an imagined scenario for the future of genome editing technology (3.4) and apply the PGC (3.5), before outlining draft legislation to amend the existing legislation in light of the imagined scenario (3.6).

3.2. Genetic Science and Genome Editing

This section will explicate the basics of genetic science (including DNA, genes and genetic disorders) and genetic modification (ranging from recombinant DNA to CRISPR).

3.2.1. Genetic Science

Many of us are told that we resemble our biological parents. Some of us are lucky enough to inherit our parent's endearing features; others inherit less valued traits. Many generations of the Habsburg dynasty passed down a distinctively long jaw and droopy lower lip, which became known as the 'Habsburg lip'. Charles II of Spain, the last of the Habsburg monarchs, had a lip so pronounced that he could not even chew his own food.[8] This genetic trait was, at least, not life-threatening. Huntington's disease is. Those with this condition usually display no symptoms until they reach middle age or beyond. It then causes progressive neurodegeneration, leading to involuntary movements, loss of motor control and dementia, with death occurring 10 to 20 years later. There is currently no cure.

No special tests were needed to diagnose the Habsburg lip. It was evident to any observer from the moment of birth. In contrast, Huntington's disease can remain undiscovered until the onset of symptoms. Both the Habsburg lip and Huntington's disease run in families. Not all genetic disorders are similarly associated with a family history. Down's syndrome, which is the result of an extra part or copy of chromosome 21, is usually the result of a spontaneous mutation, so children with the condition are frequently born to those without any family history of it.

The units of heredity, enabling traits to be passed from parent to child, are known as *genes* and are composed of DNA.[9] The sum total of our DNA is known as the human *genome*. Our DNA is found wound up in tiny cell structures – most of it on chromosomes in the cell nucleus (nuclear DNA) and a much smaller amount in little subcellular bodies called mitochondria (mitochondrial DNA). Each of our

[8] See Watson et al 2017, 4, who use the alternative spelling of the family name: 'Hapsburg'.

[9] DNA is the acronym of deoxyribonucleic acid. DNA molecules consist of two sugar-phosphate backbones that wind round each other to form a double helix, from which nucleotide bases jut inwards like the steps of a ladder: see Watson and Crick 1953.

cells has the 46 chromosomes that we inherited from our parents: 23 from each.[10] Our cells therefore contain a combination of our biological parents' genes. The genes themselves are found at distinct locations (called *loci*) along the chromosomes. At each locus there are a number of different variants that the gene can take (called *alleles*).

We evidently do not see the genes of those around us. What we see is the product of the interaction between their genes and many non-genetic factors, which is known as the *phenotype*. Very few traits are the product of variation at a single gene. For those traits that are directly correlated to one gene, it can make a difference whether the allele at one particular locus on each of the paired chromosomes is the same. A dominant allele will be expressed irrespective of whether it is matched on the other chromosome. A recessive allele will only be expressed if its effects are not counterbalanced by a different allele on the other chromosome.

Huntington's disease is an example of a dominant disorder. Inheriting one copy of the defective gene from either of your parents will mean that you will get Huntington's disease. It also follows that, even without a genetic test, we know that the biological child of someone with Huntington's disease has at least a 50 per cent chance of developing the condition. In contrast, phenylketonuria (PKU) is a recessive disorder. Only those born with two copies of the relevant allele (gene variant) will be unable to produce the enzyme needed to metabolise the protein phenylalanine. Without this enzyme the normal cellular process that converts this protein into another does not occur. Such individuals will, if brought up on a normal diet, accumulate an abnormal imbalance between these two proteins, which can severely disrupt cognitive development and cause retarded growth, epilepsy and hyperactivity.

Most single gene (*monogenic*) disorders are very rare.[11] And the majority of traits, including most genetic disorders, are associated with many genes (*polygenic*). Conversely, a single gene can affect multiple traits, which is known as *pleiotropy*.[12] The interaction between genetic and non-genetic factors can be extremely complicated. The reason for this is that genes act indirectly. Genes are expressed when they direct the production of a protein, or part of a protein, in a cell and they can sometimes regulate the expression of other genes. Genes cannot perform either function without an appropriate cellular environment, and the consequences of producing a protein will depend on the protein in question, the other proteins in the cell, where in the body it is produced and an individual's external environment.

Where a gene contributes to the expression of a particular trait, it can act as a necessary, sufficient or contributing condition. Few genes are *sufficient* conditions

[10] There are exceptions: sperm carry only 23 chromosomes, red blood cells do not contain DNA and the cells of those with one of the few chromosomal abnormalities compatible with life can have an extra chromosome or part chromosome (eg Down's syndrome). Eggs are more complex, because fertilisation reduces their two copies of 23 chromosomes (on the maternal spindle) down to 23 (and generates the second polar body) – I am grateful to Andy Greenfield for drawing this to my attention.

[11] There are roughly 3,600 monogenic disorders (see Lander 2015, 6), but individually most have 'frequencies typically in the range of one in 10,000 to one in 1 million births' (NAM et al 2020, 40).

[12] See Lobo 2008.

for a trait (in the sense that possession of a specific allele will lead to the expression of the trait in any human who survives until the time of onset). Similarly, few are *necessary* conditions for a trait (in the sense that only individuals with that allele can express that trait). The vast majority of alleles associated with complex traits are merely *contributing* conditions. That is to say that the variations of a particular gene can contribute to a trait without being either a necessary or sufficient condition for that trait. For example, a mutation in the *BRCA1* gene can increase susceptibility to breast cancer, but those with this mutation might not get breast cancer and those without it can still get breast cancer. In addition, the same genotype can result in different levels of expression of a disease (expressivity) in different people.

You are 99.9 per cent genetically identical to any randomly selected human.[13] Only a few traits have been mapped to specific genes that are identifiable at the molecular level – as specific sequences of DNA. Not all correlations between genes and traits reveal a causal connection. A statistical correlation between having Huntington's disease and watching football would not, for example, be sufficient evidence to conclude that watching football causes Huntington's or that Huntington's causes the development of an interest in watching football. Particular issues are raised by the claim that there are genes for various behavioural traits. Claims that there is a gene for intelligence, homosexuality and criminality, for example, have notoriously relied on statistically unpersuasive evidence or problematic specification of the relevant trait.[14]

3.2.2. Genome Editing

Techniques for modifying DNA in living cells have been around for over 40 years. Discoveries in the late 1960s and early 1970s gave us 'recombinant DNA technology'.[15] This technology made it possible to transfer long strands of DNA or whole genes into living cells using modified viruses (viral vectors). Even by the 1990s, however, use of this technique effectively involved throwing genes into the genome 'in the hope that in some cases they would land somewhere useful'.[16] To get a rough picture of why the place where a gene lands matters, imagine it as a paragraph and the genome as a stack of books.[17]

By the early 2000s scientists had a draft sequence of the entire human genome and so could read the three billion letters of our genetic code.[18] These 'letters' are

[13] See Watson et al 2017, 259.
[14] See further Pattinson 2002a, ch 3.
[15] See Watson et al 2017, 84.
[16] See Ridley 2020, 145.
[17] See Carey 2019, ch 1.
[18] See IHGSC 2004. In 2000, many complex regions of the draft human genome were unfinished or contained mistakes, but the complete human genome sequence (save for the Y chromosome) has now been published: see Nurk et al 2022.

A, C, G and T, which stand for the chemicals that make up the nucleotide bases of DNA: adenine (A), cytosine (C), guanine (G) and thymine (T). These four chemicals combine to spell out three-letter 'words', which specify the amino acid to be used as a step in making a protein. It is a precise language and a change in even a single letter can sometimes have significant effects. A brutal example is Lesch-Nyhan syndrome, which can be caused by the mutation of a single letter in a specific gene.[19] Boys with this genetic condition are often mentally disabled, suffer extreme pain similar to gout and compulsively self-mutilate; often chewing off their lips, biting off their fingertips or gouging out their eyes. They usually die in their teens.

The current genome editing toolbox includes a range of techniques that are cheaper, easier and more precise than anything before.[20] The most promising of these is CRISPR-Cas9 technology, which is commonly referred to as CRISPR (pronounced 'crisper').[21] CRISPR emerged as a major genome editing tool with the publication of two pivotal papers in 2012.[22] It adapts a bacterial immune mechanism that uses a particular enzyme (Cas9) as genetic 'scissors' to disarm viral DNA. The breakthrough came when it was shown that this bacterial defence system could be reprogrammed to cut any DNA sequence at a predetermined locus. This enables genome editing down to a single letter (nucleotide base).[23] Emmanuelle Charpentier and Jennifer Doudna won the Nobel Prize in Chemistry in October 2020 for their contributions to this development.[24]

Jiankui He, with whom this chapter started, used CRISPR to edit embryos.[25] The embryos that were to become the babies Lula and Nana had been edited with the aim of making them less susceptible to HIV.[26] He (pronounced 'Huh') had apparently selected opposite-sex couples in which the man was HIV-positive and the woman HIV-negative and had then edited their embryos with the intention of disrupting a gene that codes for a protein that enables HIV to enter white blood cells. He was reportedly not trying to prevent transmission of HIV from the father's sperm (the likelihood of transmission in that way is very low and can be lowered further by washing the sperm) but was seeking 'to protect the babies from infection in later life'.[27] Genome editing was therefore used as an experimental form of genomic immunisation for a virus that they were extremely unlikely to

[19] See Davison et al 1989.

[20] The first technologies in this toolbox were meganucleases, zinc-finger nucleases (ZFNs) and transcription activator-like effector nucleases (TALENs): see Khan 2019 and EGE 2021, 9 (n 1) and 13.

[21] CRISPRs (clustered regularly interspaced short palindromic repeats) are repeated nucleotide bases with spaces and Cas9 is short for CRISPR-associated protein 9.

[22] See Jinek et al 2012 and Gasiunas et al 2012.

[23] See NAM et al 2020, 59–60.

[24] www.nobelprize.org/prizes/chemistry/2020/press-release.

[25] CRISPR had been used on early human embryos before but they were not implanted: see eg Liang et al 2015 and Fogarty et al 2017.

[26] See Cyranoski 2020.

[27] Normile 2018.

get. What is more, with current antiretroviral medications most people who get the virus now live long and healthy lives.[28]

Three likely complications of genome editing are mosaicism (different cells displaying different edits), off-target DNA edits (changes to DNA in the wrong place) and off-target effects (the desired edit affecting non-target traits). Musunuru, a scientist who has seen a copy of He's unpublished manuscript, describes evidence of 'rampant' mosaicism 'in both Lulu's and Nana's embryos, as well as in Lulu's placenta, making it likely the twins themselves are mosaic'.[29] This makes it likely that the twins remain 'fully vulnerable to HIV'. Further, 'off-target edits could cause problems such as cancer and heart disease, and could be passed on to Lulu's and Nana's future children'.

Since a single gene can sometimes affect multiple traits (which is known as pleiotropy), even simple genetic modifications can have unpredicted consequences.[30] Lander cites the 'cautionary tale' of genetic modification of the *TP53* gene to protect mice against cancer, which unexpectedly caused premature ageing.[31] Jiankui He sought to inactivate the *CCR5* gene, which encodes a receptor used by HIV to enter cells, but its inactivation seems to increase complications from other infections.[32] Such consequences will remain unpredictable until the genome is much more thoroughly understood. Thus, the potential benefits of He's experimental genome editing were negligible and the likelihood of serious complications high. Indeed, Baylis has argued that He's manuscript should remain unpublished because the experiments were so poorly designed and executed that they 'lacked scientific merit'.[33]

Discussions of genome editing typically distinguish two types. *Somatic* genome editing involves altering the DNA of somatic (body) cells. *Germline* genome editing involves altering the DNA of the specialised cells that can transmit genetic information from generation to generation: gametes, their precursors and the cells of early embryos. Not all germline edits are intended to be heritable, because they could be made for research, rather than clinical purposes.[34] That is to say, that genome-edited germ cells or embryos could be destroyed before implantation. *Heritable genome editing*, as undertaken by He, is the most controversial. This term is used here to refer to the deliberate alteration of selected DNA with the aim of establishing a pregnancy with the edited embryo to yield an individual with an edited genome.[35]

While this chapter is focused on heritable editing of the *genome* (the complete set of DNA possessed by an organism), heritable modifications could also be made

[28] www.nhs.uk/conditions/hiv-and-aids/treatment.
[29] Musunuru 2019.
[30] See Lobo 2008 on pleiotropy.
[31] See Lander 2015, 7, citing Tyner et al 2002.
[32] See Lander et al 2019, 166.
[33] Baylis 2020.
[34] A point made by others: see NAM et al 2020, 18.
[35] My definition owes much to discussion with Andy Greenfield.

to the *epigenome* (a multitude of genome-wide chemical modifications that affect whether and how genes are expressed).[36] Variants of targeted editing tools such as CRISPR could be used to alter the expression of specific genes without changing the underlying DNA sequences.[37] This chapter does not directly address what others have called 'non-genetic inheritance mechanisms'.[38]

3.3. The Boundaries of Current Law and Policy

Until relatively recently, two restrictive norms attracted widespread support: (1) rejection of all clinical use of germline modification and (2) rejection of genomic modification for the purposes of enhancement. I will refer to these as *norm one* and *norm two*, respectively. This section will show how they have been given expression by various documents and instruments, but support for such broad prohibitions is waning.

Norm one rejects the clinical application of *all* deliberate modification of the human germline. Support for this norm has been challenged by a technology that will be addressed in the next paragraph. *Norm two* permits human genomic modification for the purposes of treatment or prevention of a disease or illness (genetic treatment), but not enhancement (genetic enhancement). This distinction between treatment and enhancement has application outside the context of genome editing.

Mitochondrial replacement technology (MRT) is a disruptive technology with regard to support for *norm one*. This technology can be used to prevent the transmission of mitochondrial disorders from mother to child by replacing the mitochondrial DNA in the mother's egg, or an embryo created from it, with that from a donated egg or embryo. Mitochondrial DNA codes for 37 genes (compared to more than 22,000 in the nuclear DNA).[39] All of these genes are crucial and more than 50 inherited metabolic diseases are thought to be caused by mutations in mitochondrial DNA. An embryo's mitochondria come from the egg and can pass on a genetic disorder even if the mother displays only mild or no symptoms. MRT is sometimes said to produce 'three-parent babies'[40] because it uses DNA from three gametes: from the egg of a woman who carries a mitochondrial disorder, from an egg donated by a woman who does not carry a mitochondrial disorder and from a sperm. Since these cells pass genetic information from one generation to another, this technology involves alteration of the germline. It follows that the clinical application of MRT is opposed by *norm one*. And it is consistent with *norm two*

[36] These definitions derive from NAM et al 2020, 202.
[37] See Pei et al 2019.
[38] See eg Lewens 2018.
[39] See IBC 2015, [98].
[40] See eg Hamzelou 2016 (which reported the birth of the world's first baby from 'new "3 parent" technique') and Reardon 2017.

only if it is properly regarded as therapeutic or preventative, rather than an enhancement technology. The technology is now generally referred to as therapy or treatment, but this raises questions as to for whom or what it is treatment.[41] As we shall see, however, these norms do not exhaust those recognised by legal instruments and policy documents. There is, in particular, support for narrowing *norm one's* prohibition to distinguish MRT from heritable genome editing (presented below as *norm four*).

3.3.1. The International Position

Many international instruments take a restrictive approach towards germline genomic modification. Two instruments from 1997 are worthy of particular consideration.

The first of these is the Council of Europe's Convention on Human Rights and Biomedicine. This is often referred to as the Oviedo Convention, from the city in which it opened for signature in April 1997. Article 13 states that an intervention 'seeking to modify the human genome may only be undertaken for preventive, diagnostic or therapeutic purposes and only if its aim is not to introduce any modification in the genome of any descendants'. The Convention thus prohibits the clinical application of both genetic enhancement (as per *norm two*) and germline modification (as per *norm one*). The Convention does not directly deal with germline modification for research purposes, but article 18(2) prohibits the creation of embryos for research. As we shall see below (in 3.3.2), UK law departs from both articles.[42] The United Kingdom could therefore make reservations to these articles under article 36, which permits opt-outs 'to the extent that any law then in force in its territory is not in conformity with the provision'; though no UK government has been willing to become a signatory to the Convention. Further, the existence of UK legislation that adopts an approach inconsistent with the Oviedo Convention makes it unlikely that the Strasbourg Court will use articles 13 and 18(2) as interpretative references for the Convention on Human Rights and Fundamental Freedoms, as it has done for other articles.[43]

The Universal Declaration on the Human Genome and Human Rights (UDHGHR) was adopted by the United Nations Educational, Scientific and Cultural Organization (UNESCO) in November 1997. It is not a legally binding instrument. Article 5 declares that 'research, treatment or diagnosis affecting an individual's genome' shall be undertaken only with that individual's informed

[41] See eg HFEA 2019, para 3.3 ('mitochondrial donation treatment'). Cf Scott & Wilkinson 2017, 892–893 (who argue that MRT is only treatment if it occurs after the development of the embryonic pronuclei and 'thus is something that happens to a determinate individual', which they argue is only the case for one of the two major MRT techniques).

[42] But only in part with regard to art 13.

[43] See *Glass v UK* (2004) 39 EHRR 15, [58]; *MAK v UK* (2010) 51 EHRR 14, [77]; *Lambert v France* (2016) 62 EHRR 2, [59].

consent or (where consent cannot be given) in that individual's best interests. Article 11 prohibits 'Practices which are contrary to human dignity, such as reproductive cloning'. To this Article 24 adds that UNESCO's International Bioethics Committee (IBC) should make recommendations 'in particular regarding the identification of practices that *could* be contrary to human dignity, such as germline interventions'.[44] Thus, the clinical application of germline genome editing is presumed to be contrary to human dignity and, in any event, genome editing is only permissible if it is in the best interests of the individual affected.

In 2015, the IBC called for 'a moratorium on genome editing of the human germline'.[45] In contrast to its position on creating cloned embryos for reproductive purposes, it did not recommend a permanent ban of heritable genome editing on the basis that the 'debate remains open on the *ethical* acceptability' of mitochondrial replacement techniques.[46] Thus, for the time being at least, the IBC supports *norm one*.

Article 12 states that the benefits of biomedical developments, 'concerning the human genome, shall be made available to all, with due regard for the dignity and human rights of each individual'. It goes on to declare that 'applications' of such biomedical research 'shall seek to offer relief from suffering and improve the health of individuals and humankind as a whole'. Thus, clinical applications of genomic editing must accord with *norm two* and those that are preventative or therapeutic (in the sense of seeking to relieve suffering and improve human health) may only be permitted if they are made available to all. This second feature encapsulates another norm, which I will refer to as *norm three*. Its expression in article 12 admits some interpretative flexibility over what it means for something to be 'made available to all' with due regard to individual dignity and rights. In theory, *norm three* could be interpreted purely negatively (eligibility should not unjustifiably discriminate between individuals) or positively (financial support should be provided to enable all eligible individuals to gain access).

The Oviedo Convention and UDHGHR enshrine refined cultural moral values (on which see chapter 1) determined by negotiation between the contributing states. Cultural moral values evolve with socio-scientific developments and, in the quarter of a century since these instruments were adopted, these developments have included the sequencing of the human genome, mitochondrial replacement therapy and CRISPR. An indication of contemporary values in professional circles can be found by consideration of the more recent report of the International Commission on the Clinical Use of Human Germline Genome Editing.[47] This commission was convened by the US National Academy of Medicine (NAM), US National Academy of Sciences (NAS) and the United Kingdom's Royal Society following the birth of the world's first genome-edited babies. It reported in 2020.

[44] Emphasis added.
[45] ICB 2015, para 118.
[46] Original emphasis.
[47] See NAM et al 2020. An earlier report recommended that scientists be allowed to genome edit human embryos for research: NASEM 2017.

The International Commission, like the report of the Nuffield Council on Bioethics issued two years before,[48] does not assert a categorical objection to germline genetic modifications. Instead of adopting *norm one*, it draws on 'the pathway leading to clinical use of mitochondrial replacement techniques in the UK'[49] – on which see 3.3.2. Its first recommendation concerns the necessary ethical conditions for any clinical application of genome editing, requiring that 'it has been clearly established that it is possible to efficiently and reliably make precise genomic changes without undesired changes in human embryos'.[50] But, this recommendation goes on to state, these criteria are not yet satisfied.[51] When they are, the report outlines criteria in which a state may (if it so decides after extensive social dialogue) permit germline genome editing.[52]

The report presents a six-level hierarchy of potential uses of heritable genome editing.[53] These categories (with the exception of Category F) are presented as progressively more problematic at the current time:

A (serious monogenic diseases in which all children would inherit the disease genotype);
B (serious monogenic diseases in which only some of the couple's children would inherent the disease-causing genotype);
C (monogenic diseases with less serious impacts);
D (polygenic diseases);
E (other applications); and
F (monogenic conditions that cause infertility).

Up to Category E these are interventions aimed at addressing 'disease-causing genotypes' and are therefore potentially compatible with *norm two*.

According to the report, only Category A and a 'very small subset of couples in Category B' are part of 'a responsible translational path for initial uses' of heritable genome editing.[54] Initial clinical use should be limited to the avoidance of a monogenetic (single gene) disease that causes 'severe morbidity or premature death', where the prospective parents have either 'no option' or 'extremely poor options' for having a genetically related child without that disease. The report argues that most prospective parents who wish to avoid having a child with a serious monogenetic disease have other options, such as using IVF and preimplantation genetic diagnosis (PGD).[55] These criteria for initial clinical use are intentionally restrictive.

[48] See NCOB 2018.
[49] NAM et al 2020, 26. See also the discussion of mitochondrial replacement therapy at 23–26.
[50] NAM et al 2020, 7.
[51] See also ISSCR 2021, 6 and 14, which declares heritable genome editing to be 'currently unsafe' and 'should not be permitted at this time'.
[52] See, in particular, NAM et al 2020–8-12 and recommendations 2, 4 and 6.
[53] See NAM et al 2020, 100–111.
[54] NAM et al 2020, 111.
[55] This view was previously expressed in Lander 2015 and Lander et al 2019, 166–167. Lander was a member of the International Commission.

They would not apply, for example, where one prospective parent has the Huntington's disease gene until they have attempted at least one cycle of PGD without success. That's because recommendation four defines 'extremely poor options' as those where the likelihood of the embryos being unaffected is '25 percent or less' or PGD has been unsuccessfully attempted.[56]

For Category C the report states that caution 'argues against undertaking first-in-human uses'.[57] For Categories D and E the report declares that they are not currently suitable on the basis that contemporary scientific understanding and technology is insufficient to produce predictable results and these categories raise 'additional societal and ethical concerns'. I will return to the report's categories below with particular focus on Category E.

3.3.2. Domestic Law

The Human Fertilisation and Embryology Act 1990 (the 1990 Act) established a regulatory scheme to license and prohibit activities connected with the creation and use of embryos outside the body. This Act set up the Human Fertilisation and Embryology Authority (the HFEA) as the relevant regulatory and licensing body. It expressly declared that a treatment licence could not 'authorise altering the genetic structure of any cell while it forms part of an embryo', but the HFEA was empowered to grant associated research licences.[58] Thus, the 1990 Act as originally enacted sought to uphold *norm one* but assumed that all germline modification would involve interventions on embryos.

The 1990 Act was amended by the Human Fertilisation and Embryology Act 2008. The amended Act allows only 'permitted gametes' and 'permitted embryos' to be placed in a 'woman'.[59] Permitted gametes are defined as obtained from the testes or ovaries and whose nuclear or mitochondrial DNA has not been altered. Permitted embryos are defined as created by the fertilisation of a permitted egg by a permitted sperm, where no nuclear or mitochondrial DNA has been altered and no cell has been added other than by cell division. These definitions expressly encompass the modification of both gametes and embryos. Crucially, the amended Act goes on to state that regulations may alter these definitions to permit 'a prescribed process designed to prevent the transmission of serious mitochondrial disease'.[60] The relevant regulations came into force in October 2015 and permit the clinical use of MRT.[61]

[56] The report also points out that technical problems are raised by attempts to edit out Huntington's disease, because it is a genetic disorder caused by expansion of a repeated DNA sequence: see NAM et al 2020, 66.

[57] NAM et al 2020, 111.

[58] 1990 Act, Sch 2, paras 1(4) and 3(4), respectively.

[59] 1990 Act, as amended, s 3(2). These terms are defined in s 3ZA.

[60] 1990 Act, as amended, s 3ZA(5).

[61] See Human Fertilisation and Embryology (Mitochondrial Donation) Regulations 2015/572.

The UK government was keen to deny that these regulations reject *norm one*. It accepted that MRT does 'result in germ-line modification', but 'rejected claims that the techniques constitute genetic modification'.[62] The basis of this denial was that MRT replaces subcellular structures, rather than deliberately alters the sequences of bases of any DNA molecule.[63] The Nuffield Council on Bioethics points out that this rests on an 'odd and potentially unstable' distinction between germline modification at the 'cellular level' (as per MRT) and at the 'molecular level' (genome editing using CRISPR and related technologies).[64] It seeks to recast *norm one* as rejecting only the latter. Since this is narrower than *norm one* as I have expressed it, I will refer to it as *norm four*.

There are other potential cellular germline modifications to which the government's distinction could apply, such as some instances of creating functional gametes outside the body from pluripotent stem cells (*in vitro*-derived gametes).[65] This could not be permitted in the United Kingdom without further amendment of the 1990 Act – the existing power to amend the definition of permitted gametes by regulations is restricted to preventing the transmission of serious mitochondrial disease. Omissions of this type are not a problem for the application of *norm four*, because that norm (like the other three norms) is intended as a necessary but not a sufficient condition for permissible clinical application. A much greater problem arises from the Nuffield Council report's claim that it is possible to envisage genome editing techniques that are contrary to *norm four*, yet not prohibited by the amended 1990 Act.[66] The report cites a technique in which a sperm precursor is CRISPR-edited and returned to the testes (where the recipient has been sterilised in the meantime to remove other sperm) so that the conception occurs with a partner through unassisted reproduction. It points out that these activities do not require a licence under the amended 1990 Act. The courts have interpreted other provisions in the 1990 Act purposively to evade legislative gaps created by narrow literal interpretations.[67] But this particular gap could not be evaded by a plausible purposive interpretation.[68] While giving effect to *norm four* is a plausible purpose of the prohibition of placing modified gametes/embryos into a woman, the term 'place in a woman' is used by various provisions to exclude standard sexual reproduction.[69] To interpret that phrase otherwise would enable

[62] DH 2014, 15.

[63] See the discussion in NCOB 2018, 4.7.

[64] NCOB 2018, 4.7 and 4.8.

[65] See further NAM et al 2020, 12–13.

[66] See NCOB 2018, 4.9.

[67] See, in particular, *R (Bruno Quintavalle) v Secretary of State for Health* [2003] UKHL 13 and *R (Josephine Quintavalle) v HFEA* [2005] UKHL 28. It is now a 'well-settled view that the courts should adopt a purposive approach to statutory interpretation where possible': *Rittson-Thom v Oxfordshire CC* [2021] UKSC 13, [33].

[68] A purposive interpretation could plausibly be used to answer another question posed in NCOB 2018, 4.9 (fn 359).

[69] The phrase is used in ss 3(2), 4(3), 4(4), 4A(1), 13(6D)(b) and 13(8)(c) to specify activities in connection with embryos and gametes that require a licence or are prohibited.

effect to be given to *norm four* but would undermine another purpose of the Act – the purpose of regulating only assisted reproduction and not sexual activities undertaken in the bedroom. Thus, further amendment of the 1990 Act would be required to regulate or prohibit this technique and to capture the possibility of other anticipatable methods of undertaking heritable genome editing (see 3.6.2). Imagine, for example, that it were possible to use a pessary to successfully deliver genome editing reagents (to the uterus or fallopian tubes) shortly before or after sexual intercourse.[70]

3.3.3. Opposition to Genetic Enhancement (Norm Two)

Norm two seeks to distinguish attempts to maintain or restore an individual to some baseline of health (prevention and treatment) from attempts to elevate an individual above that level (enhancement). Notice that what is advanced as permissible includes prevention of disease or impairment: article 13 of the Oviedo Convention permits genetic modification for 'preventive, diagnostic or therapeutic purposes' and article 5 of the UDHGHR permits 'research, treatment or diagnosis'. This is particularly important if *norm two* is considered independently of *norm one's* rejection of germline modification. Editing the genome of the early embryo, gamete or gamete precursor is unlikely to be directed at treating a disease suffered by the subject at that time, as opposed to preventing its later occurrence. As pointed out in a recent report, the early embryo 'can be a carrier of a gene that will lead to a disease in the course of further development, but cannot suffer from a disease in the way a born human being can, with physical symptoms and the personal and social experience of illness'.[71]

Norm two requires a baseline of health against which enhancements are to be identified. That baseline is usually articulated as a level of health or ability typically possessed by members of the species.[72] Enhancement is thereby understood as 'the improvement of a statistically and medically "normal" feature or function'.[73] Alternatively, the bar could be set higher, so as to reject only attempts to enable the subject to develop traits not currently possessed by any human, such as echolocation, electric or magnetic sense, or telepathy. The key question is whether any such line carries normative weight.

It is difficult to see how any such line could be regarded as capturing an intrinsic value unless we assume some form of species essentialism or the perfection of the status quo. But could drawing the line at what is species-typical or species-extant be understood as expressing concern about granting some individuals

[70] I am grateful to Andy Greenfield for suggesting this possibility.
[71] EGE 2021, 29.
[72] See eg the discussion in Buchanan et al 2000, 72; President Council on Bioethics 2003, 13; EGE 2021, 29.
[73] EGE 2021, 29.

unfair advantages over others? A distinction between treatment/prevention and enhancement has been invoked in other contexts for which this would appear to be a plausible feature of the underlying intuition. Consider, for example, opposition to the use of steroids to enhance sports performance, while supporting their use for treatment of clinically recognised disorders. Similarly, it might be thought, genetic intervention to prevent an individual being born with a debilitating disease does not unfairly benefit the manipulated subject over others, whereas genetic intervention to provide a superhuman trait would. But blanket opposition to enhancement is too blunt an instrument to address concerns about inequity. Any genomic modification has the potential to perpetuate or exacerbate inequity and this could be addressed more directly. A plausible retort (to which I will return in 3.5.4) would be that enhancement inequity arises only where the individual is improved beyond the level available to all or is unfairly selected for improvement. *Norm three*, which seeks to restrict beneficial clinical uses of deliberate heritable genomic modification to those that can be made available to all, could therefore be understood as a response to the potential for inequity that is more direct than the blanket rejection of genetic enhancement.

Holding a line against genetic enhancement also presents practical problems. Juengst and co-authors point out that technologies developed for the purpose of prevention or treatment could give rise to 'incidental enhancements'.[74] They cite as a candidate example the ongoing research into modifying a particular human gene to prevent Alzheimer's disease, noting that research on mice shows that upregulating that gene enhances cognition and lifespan in mice by up to 30 per cent.[75] Modifying the relevant gene in humans might therefore not only prevent neurological decline but also enable incidental enhancement by improving cognitive capacities and extending lifespans. Incidental enhancements of this type would also increase pressure to genome edit for direct enhancement, just as drugs licensed for one condition are used for other conditions – so-called 'off-label' use.[76] The appropriate response to such concerns must turn on the defensibility and ambit of the reason for seeking to prohibit enhancement in the first place.

3.4. A Future Scenario

One purpose of this book is to apply contextual legal idealism to future developments in biomedicine. This chapter will present a hypothetical Bill to address a scenario in which genome editing technology has advanced considerably from the current state of the art. My future scenario is not intended to be the most desirable or even the most plausible. Few ethical and regulatory problems would arise if, for example, somatic genome editing became an effective treatment option for a

[74] See Juengst et al 2018.
[75] They cite Chen et al 2018; Kurosu et al 2005; Dubal et al 2014.
[76] See Green 2007, 60.

currently untreatable fatal disease. Nonetheless, my scenario is limited to specific, plausible biomedical developments. A much wider array of socio-political and ethical issues would arise if, in contrast, we were to imagine the dystopian worlds of Aldous Huxley's *Brave New World* or Andrew Niccol's 1997 film *Gattaca*.[77] Descension into something akin to the dystopias of science fiction would require systematic socio-political failures because these are worlds of both advanced science and tyrannous governments.

My scenario will involve development of the ability to genome edit embryos, gametes or gamete precursor cells to express three traits after birth to such a level of precision that mosaic and off-target edits/effects are negligible: (1) immunity to coronaviruses; (2) superhuman vision and (3) selected eye colour. In such a scenario it is inevitable that other traits would also have become editable, but my focus will be on these three. My focus is thus on germline modifications at a molecular level (rejected by *norms one* and *four*) and two of these involve enhancements (rejected by *norm two*).

Jiankui He genome-edited embryos for immunity to HIV, which has a low transmission rate in countries such as China and the United Kingdom and symptoms which are treatable. During the recent global pandemic, COVID-19 proved to be particularly infectious and fatal even to some of those provided with the best available clinical care. The longevity of protection offered by a standard vaccine is currently unclear. Imagine that it became possible for *immunity to all coronaviruses* to be provided by genome editing of gametes or embryos. That immunity could protect against future mutations to COVID-19 beyond what is currently possible with standard vaccination.[78] Indeed, one way in which this trait differs from the other two focal traits is that it is focused on a moving target. Pathogens (viruses and disease-causing micro-organisms) are continually evolving, and genetic immunity to one category of virus could require modifications to the immune system or cell structures that have implications for the body's ability to fight other pathogens. This means that the risk of unpredictable biological effects from genome editing for immunity to all coronaviruses is probably much greater than those associated with genome editing for superhuman vision and eye colour. If those other off-target effects cannot be rendered negligible, then this must be factored into any moral assessment. In my scenario, to prevent reliance on safety concerns and focus the debate on more ethically complex matters, the available evidence is envisaged as suggesting that the likelihood of unwanted side-effects is negligible and genetic immunisation has greater efficacy than standard vaccination.

Superhuman vision is to be understood as enhanced vision beyond that previously possessed by any human. There are significant variations in typical unaided human eyesight but even those with top-level eyesight suffer from age-related deterioration in vision. Typical human vision has three colour channels, derived from three types of cone cells. This is known as trichromacy. Those who are colour

[77] See Huxley 1932 and *Gattaca*, distributed by Columbia Pictures in 1997, respectively.
[78] There are, however, planned trials of a universal vaccination for all coronaviruses: see Lawton 2021.

blind usually have a defect in one of these cones. Around 12 per cent of women have four cone cells, which is known as tetrachromacy.[79] Such women might not realise that they can see colours that are invisible to the rest of us. One famous tetrachromat is the artist Concetta Antico, who is reputed to be able to see an exceptionally wide palette of colours and have enhanced vision in low light.[80] The greater incidence of colour blindness in men and the possession of tetrachromacy by some women is because the relevant genes are on the X chromosome. It is plausible that precise genome editing to that chromosome could grant colour vision to a male child beyond that currently found in the human population and match or enhance that currently available to female tetrachromats.

Eye colour is likely to become manipulable by germline genome editing much earlier than the other two focal traits.[81] It has been selected because it is usually a purely cosmetic trait. There are associations between particular eye colours and specific conditions, such as studies indicating that those with lighter iris colours have a higher prevalence of age-related macular degeneration.[82] But here I assume that eye colour is manipulable without any negative biological consequences.

The 2020 report of the International Commission, outlined in 3.3.1, presents a hierarchy of potential uses of heritable genome editing from Category A (serious monogenic diseases in which all children would inherit the disease genotype) to Category E (other applications).[83] Category E encompasses applications that are contrary to *norm two* on the basis that they do not involve heritable diseases.[84] All three of my focal traits fall into this category. The report cites attempts to confer resistance to an infectious disease by editing a gene as an example of this category, which would encompass immunity to all coronaviruses. It also cites as examples both introducing a rare allele associated with a particular phenotype and adding a set of genes in an attempt to confer new abilities that are not currently found in humans, which would encompass superhuman vision. Eye colour does not clearly fall within one of their examples for Category E, but it is evidently in this category and outside the others.

The previous section identified four norms concerned with the regulation of *clinical use of deliberate heritable genomic modification:*

- *Norm one:* blanket rejection.
- *Norm two:* rejection for the purposes of enhancement.
- *Norm three:* only permissible where it can be made available to all, with due regard to individual dignity and rights.
- *Norm four:* rejection at the molecular level (genome editing), but potentially permitted at the cellular level (eg mitochondrial replacement therapy).

[79] See Jordan 2010; Robson 2014; research.ncl.ac.uk/tetrachromacy.
[80] See Robson 2014.
[81] A recent study has, however, identified 50 new genes associated with eye colour: Simcoe et al 2021.
[82] See Frank et al 2000.
[83] Category F (monogenic conditions that cause infertility) is not presented as the bottom of this hierarchy.
[84] See NAM et al 2020, 106–108.

Heritable genome editing for the selected focal traits – coronavirus resistance, superhuman sight and eye colour – would be inconsistent with *norms one* and *four*. Supporters of these two norms divide into those who seek a permanent restriction on the relevant clinical applications and those who seek only a time-limited restriction. Those who support no more than a moratorium on clinical use of heritable genome modification/editing are likely to do so because of current unknowns and likely complications – see the discussion of mosaic and off-target edits/effects above (3.2.2). In 2019, a group of leading specialists from seven countries expressly called for a five-year 'global moratorium' on 'clinical uses of germ-line editing', thereby supporting *norm four* as a time-limited restriction.[85] The 2020 report of the International Commission supported a prohibition for the time being, even with regard to Category A (see 3.3.1).

Superhuman sight and eye colour are on the enhancement side of *norm two's* treatment-enhancement divide, whereas preventing a disease by genomic immunisation is on the other side of that divide. *Norm three* is potentially applicable to any permitted genomic modification. The question to be considered in the next sections is whether (and to what extent) giving effect to these four norms or permitting these three focal traits is compatible with the theory of contextual legal idealism presented in this book.

3.5. Application of the PGC

The PGC requires all agents to be granted will-rights to what they need to act at all or with general chances of success – the generic rights. Four meta-principles for the *direct* application of the PGC were outlined in 2.3.1. First, the generic rights are to be *ranked* according to the criterion of degrees of needfulness for action: basic, nonsubtractive and additive rights. Secondly, *positive rights* are limited by the own unaided effort and comparable cost provisos. Thirdly, *full moral status* is to be granted to those others who display the characteristics and behaviour expected of agents: *agent-behavers*. Fourthly, *proportionally lower moral status* is to be granted to those others who are only partial agent-behavers.

The PGC needs to be applied *indirectly* to authoritatively select between optional possibilities that cannot coexist and to deal with the problems of variable identification and value calculation (see 2.3.2). The procedures required must be contextually responsive, and we now operate in a globalised world in which individuals with appropriate resources can travel to other jurisdictions to circumvent inconvenient national laws. That means that citizens of democratic nations that ban or restrict activities connected to any particular technology can travel to places with more permissive laws.

[85] See Lander et al 2019.

By way of example consider travel for access to abortion. In 2019, 2,135 women travelled to England and Wales for abortion, which was a decrease from 4,687 in 2018.[86] Most of these travelled from Ireland and Northern Ireland, so this significant decrease seems to be largely explainable on the basis of the legalisation of abortion in Ireland on certain grounds on 20 December 2018.[87] Numbers travelling to this jurisdiction for abortion dramatically decreased further in 2020 and 2021: to 943 in 2020 and 206 in 2021.[88] Those low numbers are, however, primarily a consequence of travel restriction relating to the COVID-19 pandemic.

Even if the United Kingdom were to ban or strictly regulate heritable genome editing, it is likely to be only a matter of time before more embryos with modified genomes are implanted elsewhere and are born, raised and later work here.[89] These practical implications could be relevant to regulatory responses advanced on the basis of predictions as to likely consequences, but it also needs to be borne in mind that legislation can have a declaratory purpose – declaring what is impermissible, even if it is possible to evade those prohibitions by travel to a more permissive jurisdiction.

The next section (3.5.1) will provide an initial evaluation of the four prohibitive norms derived from the principal international and national instruments, before addressing the chapter's three focal traits (3.5.2) and then giving particular attention to the case for *norm four* (3.5.3).

3.5.1. The Four Norms

Some potential uses of genome editing would violate the generic rights of individuals, but there is no intrinsic connection between this technology and possession of either agency or generic needs. It follows that blanket rejections of heritable genetic modification (*norm one*), heritable genome editing (*norm four*) or genetic enhancement (*norm two*) are not abstract implications of possession of human dignity or human rights. In fact, the PGC could plausibly permit or even require interventions that contravene these norms. Heritable genome editing is theoretically capable of affecting all levels of generic need and could therefore give effect to generic rights. Additive rights (as rights to pursue improvement in levels of purpose fulfilment) encompass rights to be enhanced, which could sometimes include genetic enhancement.

We have seen that heritable genome editing involves selective manipulation of DNA within gametes, their precursors or the early embryo. The immediate subject of manipulation is granted moral protection by the principle of proportion under

[86] See DHSC 2020,15 and DHSC 2022.
[87] Northern Ireland liberalised its abortion law with effect from 31 March 2020, but abortion practice in that jurisdiction remains restrictive.
[88] See DHSC 2021 and 2022.
[89] See Macintosh 2018, 3.

precaution (see 2.3.1). While a germ cell or early embryo is not an agent-behaver, this principle grants moral protection to partial agent-behavers in proportion to the closeness of their approach to displaying the characteristics and behaviour expected of another agent. Any living cell displays some (albeit minimal) agency-associated behaviour, and the displayed characteristics of a fully functional early embryo are greater than those of a germ cell. Further, as will be explained in the next chapter (see 4.5), the relative moral status of reproductive cells and the embryo is greater than that of cells that lack the potential to develop into future agent-behavers.[90] It should also be borne in mind that moral evaluation must take account of the moral status of all affected beings and entities, which includes those who are intended to come into being in the future. The manipulated entity thus has direct moral status, which increases where the action in question is characterised by particular future intentions so that it must be treated as a future agent-behaver.[91]

The bioethics literature frequently invokes Feinberg's notion of a 'right to an open future'. Feinberg defended a child's right to an open future as a limit on parental control of their child's upbringing through socialisation and education.[92] He intended this as shorthand for all the 'rights-in-trust' that serve to protect the child's future autonomy. Feinberg points out that these rights can be violated now if the ability of the child to exercise them, when it becomes an adult, is removed or impaired now. This idea has been developed by others. Buchanan and co-authors express this right as correlative to duties on parents

> to help their children during their growth to adulthood to develop capacities for practical judgment and autonomous choice, and to develop as well at least a reasonable range of the skills and capacities necessary to provide them the choice of a reasonable array of different life plans available to members of their society.[93]

They argue that it operates as a limit on the 'substantial discretion' granted to parents with regard to both environmental and genetic interventions.[94] If understood as applying to the developing human before birth, the right to an open future operates as a constraint on heritable genome editing.[95] We have seen that under the PGC the subjects of manipulation do indeed have moral status, and this requires protection of their presumed generic rights. Generic rights are rights to what is generically needed to pursue and achieve purposes as such. They are rights to all-purpose needs and abilities, rather than rights to specific purposes. From this it follows that the rights of the genetically manipulated subject (as a partial, potential and sometimes future agent-behaver) support interventions that are likely to improve its ability to conceive and successfully achieve future purposes as

[90] See also Beyleveld & Pattinson 2010 and Pattinson 2018, 133–136.
[91] See further Pluhar 1995, 111; Beyleveld et al 1998; Pattinson 2002, 28–29.
[92] See Feinberg 1980, esp 92.
[93] Buchanan et al 2000, 170.
[94] Buchanan et al 2000, 171.
[95] See eg Davis 1997.

such, and those rights oppose other interventions. The right to an open future is a convenient shorthand label for these considerations. The manipulated subject's rights are not, of course, the only relevant rights. Prospective parents who seek access to genome editing will sometimes do so to satisfy a mere desire and at other times to save themselves from predicted generic harm, which is relevant to their rights. Further, as we shall see in 3.5.3, the rights of others are relevant to the case for *norm four.*

3.5.2. The Three Focal Traits

Since the PGC is not intrinsically opposed to heritable genome editing, regulatory restraints can only be justified if they seek to prevent predicted generic harms caused by application of this technology in the relevant context. My future scenario assumes significant advancement in the precision and predictability of genome editing technology, so that it is able to deliver three focal traits: immunity to coronaviruses, superhuman vision and selected eye colour. These traits are not identity-affecting in the sense that that their introduction could plausibly be regarded as morally equivalent to killing and replacing the subject.[96]

At first sight it appears that effective genetic *immunity to coronaviruses* could only be a good thing, in that COVID-19 and related viruses directly cause generic harm and variations are likely to remain in the global population. But, given that there are efficacious traditional vaccinations for COVID-19, it is likely that population effects from editing a small number of gametes/embryos and benefits to edited individuals would be limited. It would therefore require only a small risk of potentially serious complications from such genetic manipulation of the immune system or cellular structure to tilt the ethical balance against utilising genome editing technology for this purpose. If, however, we assume that the available evidence suggests that the likelihood of other unwanted effects is negligible and genetic immunisation has greater efficacy than standard vaccination, then only two types of potentially legitimate objections to genome editing for this purpose remain. The first is that genome editing for this purpose would be likely to have negative social consequences that undermine generic rights: the *social consequence objection*. The second is that access to genome editing for this purpose would likely be inequitable: the *justice objection*. We will return to these objections in 3.5.3 and 3.5.4, respectively.

What if, contrary to the assumptions made in my future scenario, it transpired that genomic immunity to coronaviruses was needed to protect the basic generic needs of the wider population? Imagine that herd immunity (where vaccination indirectly protects the unvaccinated) to COVID-19 could only be attained if at least

[96] The threshold for loss of personal identity is to be determined by reference to the PGC: see Pattinson 2017. See also Scott & Wilkinson 2017 (esp 907 on nuclear genetic modifications that 'may not be identity-affecting').

some members of the population had genomic immunity to coronaviruses. Such a situation would make genome editing for coronavirus immunity very different from genome editing for the other two focal traits. Since herd immunity protects the generic rights of vulnerable members of the population who are unable to get vaccinated, the rights protected by clinical application would go beyond those of the edited subject and its parents. There would therefore be a very powerful case for active state support for use of the technology in this way and a prima facie obligation to add this edit where an embryo is undergoing genome editing for other traits. Except where I specifically address this alternative scenario, in my future scenario the evidence is assumed to suggest that genome editing is not required for herd immunity to COVD-19.

While genetic immunity to coronaviruses would protect the manipulated subject's future health, the aim of genome editing for *superhuman vision* would be to enhance the subject's future eyesight beyond that of other members of the species. Human eyesight is already improvable by non-genetic means, such as glasses, infrared cameras and surgery. Nonetheless, unless genome editing for superhuman vision presents undesirable side-effects (such as causing colour confusion or hindering communication about colours with those who lack enhanced vision), it would increase the likely success of vision-dependent purposes. It is therefore an enhancement tracking additive needs. Thus, prohibition in my future scenario would require appeal to the social consequence and/or justice objection.

Genome editing for *eye colour* is envisaged as a purely cosmetic change. As such it could already be effected using coloured contact lenses or, in some cases, eye tattooing. Where the eyes are matched and that colour is within the usual range, the colour would be unlikely to have any negative social consequences in the United Kingdom at the current time. In this regard eye colour differs from baldness, height and many other traits that make us physically distinguishable. Unlike immunity to coronaviruses and superhuman vision, genome editing for eye colour would not ordinarily be relevant to the generic needs of the manipulated subject in the future. Its permissibility must therefore depend on the rights of the prospective parents and the impact of the social consequence and justice objections.

3.5.3. The Social Consequence Objection

Fears about the impact of genome editing on society are commonly expressed. Particularly powerful concerns point to the potential of the technology to instantiate, perpetuate or magnify discrimination and marginalisation. The focus could be on access to the technology (to which we will return in the next section) or the predicted consequences of use of the technology. Where predicted negative consequences are gradual, they are often articulated using the language of the slippery slope. An initially acceptable act or purpose is predicted to gradually lead us towards an unacceptable outcome. Slippery slope arguments can support a ban of the relevant activity only if the outcome is morally impermissible, it is a likely consequence, there is no morally preferable way of avoiding its occurrence and the moral desirability of permitting the relevant activity does not outweigh the risk of that outcome.[97]

One compelling concern is that genome editing for certain traits will undermine the perceived value of particular groups of agent-behavers. Considerable academic attention has been devoted to the impact of genetic testing and the potential impact of heritable genome editing technology on those who have (or are perceived to have) disabilities. There are, however, competing accounts of what counts as a disability and what are permissible responses to disabilities and those with disabilities.[98] The abilities, impairments and impediments that are relevant to the generic rights are those that affect an agent's possession of the generic needs. Some traits with a plausible genetic component[99] are likely to affect any human agent's ability to achieve its purposes. Traits such as enhanced memory and intelligence would increase future purposivity, whereas traits such as reduced life expectancy or increased pain would impair future purposivity. Of my three focal traits, coronavirus immunity and superhuman vision are concerned with functional abilities relevant to successfully achieving future purposes, whereas eye colour is not a functional trait in this way. Complications arise because the individual impact of many genetic traits depends on the agent's other abilities and the social and physical context in which they live. Dyslexia would be functionally irrelevant in a hunter-gatherer society and a functional impairment in a modern society. But even in a modern society its functional impact will depend on the individual's environment and the availability of supportive equipment and structures. Indeed, the functional impact of virtually all traits (including severely impaired sight, hearing and motor functions) is a product of the interaction between that trait and the agent's physical and social context. Those who are blind are not disabled in the pitch-dark, and in the light they can be greatly assisted by an environment designed to provide appropriate tactile and auditory signals.

Genome editing for particular traits could trigger or increase negative social perceptions of both those who are modified and those who are unmodified. Those who are modified could be held to higher expectations – perhaps those with superhuman vision would be expected to perform social tasks for which their enhanced sight makes them particularly well equipped. Conversely, those who are unmodified could be regarded as having less social worth – perhaps those without superhuman vision would be considered to be less suitable for some social purposes, or considered disabled relative to their modified peers. As others point out, there is already 'stigma and discrimination against those considered genetically disadvantaged, including disabled people and communities', so heritable

[97] See Pattinson 2000.

[98] Cf eg Savulescu 2001; de Melo-Martin 2004; Stoller 2008.

[99] In the sense that particular genes are necessary, sufficient or contributing conditions for the relevant trait: see 3.2.1.

genome editing can easily further undermine their social status.[100] Moral evaluation of such predictions turns on the criteria outlined above. These criteria point against blanket prohibitions of genome editing directed at removing traits that impose functional restrictions, because successful genetic modification of such traits would be likely to support the subject's possession of the generic needs and the disadvantages experienced by existing disabled people and communities are more directly addressed by providing them with additional support.

Predictions of harmful social consequences have particular weight when directed at genome editing for traits that are irrelevant to the subject's future status as an agent-behaver or future possession of the generic needs. One concern is that permitting genome editing for cosmetic traits would be likely to cause harmful social fashions to develop. Perhaps genome editing for eye colour could cause fashions to develop for particular eye colours or eye colour patterns, so that those with unfashionable eye colours become regarded as flawed and their parents regarded as having failed to act in their child's interests. If a particular eye colour were used to badge those who have been genetically enhanced, then it could plausibly become a status marker for possession of superhuman traits. Fashions and negative social attitudes are already triggered by many cosmetic traits, such as those relating to hair, height and body structure, so it is plausible that the same could occur for eye colour. In the context of preimplantation genetic diagnosis, Beyleveld has provided an instructive analogy:

> the example of the desire for perfectly shaped teeth that has swept the US, resulting in children whose parents are unable to afford the treatment that can correct 'imperfections' that are now perceived as deformities, suffering deep traumas as a result.[101]

This concern has weight when applied to genome editing for a purely cosmetic trait, because it would initially track a mere desire (rather than the generic needs of the future child or the parents), the predicted harmful consequences to agent-behavers are plausible and regulatory prohibition is likely to effectively prevent these consequences. Thus, this social consequence objection has particular force against genome editing for eye colour on the basis that there is no functional benefit to counterbalance the plausible risk of negative social consequences. Prohibition of genome editing for eye colour is therefore a potential outcome of the indirect application of the PGC.

3.5.4. The Justice Objection (Inequitable Access)

We have seen that parental rights and the subject's right to an open future provide prima facie support for deliberate heritable genome editing. The latter right provides support for genome editing for traits that are relevant to the modified

[100] See Andorno 2020, 353.
[101] See Beyleveld 2000, 474.

subject's future possession of the generic needs, such as superhuman vision and immunity to coronaviruses in my future scenario. The PGC therefore does not directly require the genetic intervention to be regarded as treating or preventing a health condition, as per *norm two*.

We do not, however, live in a social context in which access to prenatal genetic and reproductive technologies is available to all those who could benefit. Genome editing is costly and requires other expensive genetic and reproductive services, such as *in vitro* fertilisation and preimplantation genetic diagnosis. What is more, as Andorno and co-authors point out, commercial pressures and incentives in the (largely private sector) fertility industry

> could foster the adoption of heritable human genome editing by those able to afford it. Unequal access to perceived genetic 'upgrades' could then exacerbate the recent dramatic rise in socioeconomic inequality.[102]

In other words, access is likely to be inequitable, reflecting and potentially magnifying underlying socio-economic inequities. Here, following Braveman and Gruskin, I refer to 'equity'/'inequity' rather than the more standard 'equality'/'inequality'.[103] Equity is more explicitly normative. It directly conveys the demands of distributive justice for a fair distribution of resources, opportunities and burdens across a given population. Equality can carry the same meaning but is potentially wider because not all inequalities are unfair. That is to say that disparities within a given population do not necessarily indicate an unjustified prioritisation of the generic needs of one subpopulation over another. Consider, for example, expected inequalities between the health of the young and the old and between the birth-weights of female and male newborns.[104]

It was suggested earlier (in 3.3.3) that the intuitive plausibility of *norm two's* distinction between treatment/prevention and enhancement rests, at least in part, on it seeming to capture objections to providing an individual with an unfair advantage over others. But the potential of genome editing technology to perpetuate or exacerbate inequity could be addressed more directly than the blanket rejection of either genetic enhancement or genome editing as such. *Norm three*, which requires beneficial clinical uses of deliberate genomic modification to be made available to all, could be understood as a norm more tailored to preventing inequitable access.

Norm three could be interpreted minimally or maximally (3.3.1). Interpreted as mere rejection of unjustifiable discrimination between those individuals who seek access, it does no more than articulate a condition for PGC-compliant access to any intervention tracking generic needs. Could the PGC support a maximal interpretation, which is to say a norm requiring state-supported access for all those likely to benefit?

[102] Andorno 2020, 353.
[103] See Braveman & Gruskin 2003.
[104] See Braveman & Gruskin 2003, 255.

We should first consider how a norm requiring state-funded access to genome editing in specific situations would fit with the PGC's limits on positive rights (on which see 2.3.1). The *own unaided effort proviso* would generally mean that financial support would not need to be provided to those who could feasibly access a resource without state support and the *comparable cost proviso* operates where providing support would prevent the state from addressing more pressing generic needs. But, while the own unaided effort proviso limits the positive rights of individual agents, it does not straightforwardly operate as a restriction on identifying the positive rights of a group of agents. For one thing, those governing a state may conclude that the negative consequences (to protection of generic needs) of assessing the financial needs of potential beneficiaries could be worse than providing free access to the group as a whole. The offsetting benefit of efficiency gains from not means testing the rich were, for example, relied on by the 1942 Beveridge report when recommending the setting up of a 'comprehensive medical service for every citizen'[105] – which was to be given effect by the creation of the NHS. The application of the comparable cost proviso is similarly more complex when the fulfilment of a positive duty falls to the state, because the opportunity costs of providing one type of support need to be assessed by reference to the state's other (actual and potential) activities and its (actual and potential) means of obtaining the requisite resources, and there will be a huge array of both in a modern state. It follows that whether the costs of providing state-funded access are comparable is often contextual and open to a range of reasonable conclusions.

Superhuman vision and immunity to coronaviruses are not, on the assumptions and analysis articulated earlier, traits of major functional benefit for prospective parents, the modified subject in the future or other members of society.[106] Since the state may readily invoke the comparable cost proviso as a reason for directing its resources to other societal and public health needs, the case for a maximal norm requiring state-supported access to genome editing for these traits is not particularly compelling. The more pressing question is therefore whether access should merely be non-discriminatory among prospective parents who have the required resources or should be prohibited for everyone to avoid exacerbating existing social inequities. Here, politicians attempting to apply the PGC competently and in good faith in a particular context could reasonably reach different conclusions. On the one hand, the state should not too readily interfere with the actions of prospective parents who are plausibly acting in accordance with the generic needs of their future children. On the other hand, these are not particularly important traits for the modified subject's future generic needs and there are already significant inequities between the rich and the poor. My imaginary UK

[105] See Beveridge 1942, 48.

[106] Remember that it is assumed here that genome editing for coronavirus immunity is not needed for herd immunity to Covid-19. If this assumption did not hold, then the state's response would need to take account of the level of genome editing required for herd immunity. Would it, for example, suffice to add an additional edit to some embryos already approved for genome editing?

prime minister acts in a particular context and will, below, support the former while putting in place a mechanism to keep track of its social consequences.

3.6. Hypothetical Bill

This section applies contextual idealism. As explained in chapter 2, I assume narrowly specified developments in both science (see the future scenario in 3.4) and politics (see the discussion of Themis Walpole as UK prime minister in 2.3.2). To retain the focus on heritable genome editing, other topics are not considered. My hypothetical Bill therefore takes the form of amendment to the Human Fertilisation and Embryology Act 1990, as already amended by the 2008 Act, to address the conditions under which genome editing would be licensable by the Human Fertilisation and Embryology Authority.

A Bill begins in either the House of Commons or the House of Lords. My hypothetical Bill will start in a House of Commons in which a majority government is led by Themis Walpole. It would then need to go through various stages in each House before it could be passed and receive Royal Assent, at which point it would become an Act.[107] An Act comes into force soon after Royal Assent (usually two months later) or at a time set by the government. It is the Second Reading where the House has its first opportunity to debate the main principles of a Bill. That debate is usually opened by a government minister, who sets out the case for the Bill and explains its provisions. No amendment may be made to the Bill at this stage and this stage concludes with a vote on whether the Bill is to proceed. My summary of the case to be put before Parliament by Themis Walpole (which would in practice be put by the relevant minister)[108] is therefore directed to this stage. Subsequent parliamentary stages, which this chapter will not address, involve line-by-line consideration of the detail of a Bill and provide opportunities for the House to make amendments.

3.6.1. The Case to be Put to Parliament

It was argued in chapter 2 that modified law as integrity provides a method for judges to reason in accordance with the PGC.[109] That method requires a judge to discern a set of legal principles that both explain and justify existing legal rules and rulings, with the PGC as the overarching principle. It is applied in chapters 4 and 6 to support Lady Athena's lead judgments in appeal cases. The United Kingdom's legislative chamber is not restricted by the narrow facts and arguments that

[107] See www.gov.uk/guidance/legislative-process-taking-a-bill-through-parliament.

[108] The second reading of the Bill that was to become the Human Fertilisation and Embryology Act 2008 was opened by Alan Johnson, Secretary of State for Health.

[109] See 2.41 and 2.4.2. See also Pattinson 2018.

happen to come before a court, and it has resources, a range of inputs and (in the case of the House of Commons) a democratic status lacked by the courts. A legislative chamber with such features is better placed than the courts to reform and create new legal rules and principles. A legislature seeking a competent and good faith application of the PGC would seek to ensure that the law as a whole forms an integral web of legal principle under the PGC. That means that a new Act of Parliament would need to either fit its principles and rules within the jurisdiction's existing web of legal principles or contribute to reform of those principles with the aim of giving greater effect to the PGC. Themis must therefore seek to ensure that her Bill is not only internally coherent but fits with, or appropriately reforms, the law as a whole.

The application of the PGC in the face of predictive and evaluative uncertainties – referred to as the problems of variable identification and value calculation in 2.3.2 – means that there will often be multiple alternative defensible regulatory outcomes. Since this chapter's focus is on heritable genome editing, I will not here seek to reopen debate on the rules and structures that currently apply to assisted reproduction where they are plausibly consistent with a competent and good faith attempt to apply the PGC or raise issues beyond the scope of this chapter.

Many features of the United Kingdom's regulatory approach are plausibly consistent with the requirements of the PGC. Assisted reproduction provides ways of responding to involuntary childlessness, which the evidence suggests can be as emotionally crippling as grief and therefore relevant to basic generic needs.[110] It was argued in chapter 1 that the principle that best explains and justifies the approach in the 1990 Act and other UK legislation to the developing human is adherence to the proportional status position (1.3.2) and it was argued in chapter 2 that this principle is a direct implication of the PGC (2.3.1). Further, ex ante regulation of assisted reproduction enables more effective protection of the early human, potential parents and other affected groups than ex post litigation. There are, of course, many other features of the 1990 Act and its associated regulatory structures and some of these are more problematic.[111] There have been many biomedical, social and legal developments since the 1990 Act was amended by the 2008 Act, and a chorus of academics have expressed the view that the 2008 Act was itself a missed opportunity to provide greater ethical coherence.[112] The legislation is now ripe for deeper review. However, since the purpose of this chapter is to address heritable genome editing, Themis will not consider the case for deeper reform of the Act or the Human Fertilisation and Embryology Authority, as the statutory licensing authority. Crucially, since this chapter has not considered the case for reforming the 1990 Act's references to sex and gender, the Bill will not amend the Act's use of terms such as 'man', 'woman', 'male', 'female', 'mother' and 'father'.

[110] See eg Menning 1977; Menning 1980; Hull 1992, 2; Fisher & Hammarberg 2012.

[111] For a more detailed overview of the UK's regulation of assisted reproductive and genetic technologies see Pattinson 2020, chs 8 and 10.

[112] See eg Fox 2009; Eijkholt 2011; Alghrani 2018, 31.

Themis, or her appointed minister, will open the Second Reading of the Human Fertilisation and Embryology (Heritable Genome Editing) Bill by articulating its governing principles. One of these is that the purposes for which genome editing may be permitted must not extend beyond the purposes for which preimplantation genetic diagnosis (PGD) is permitted. That is to say that it cannot be permissible to make heritable genome edits where it is not permissible to test embryos to confirm whether those changes are required or have succeeded. The reverse does not hold: it could be permissible to genetically test gametes or embryos where it is not permissible to genome edit in response to what the test reveals. Examples include situations where genome editing in response to what the test reveals would go beyond what is sufficiently safe and reliable, or where the test is for tissue (HLA) compatibility with a sick sibling (as the genome editing would not then be for the benefit of the subject).[113]

In its current form the Human Fertilisation and Embryology Act 1990 (the 1990 Act) prohibits certain uses of PGD. In particular, embryo testing for treatment purposes is only permitted:

(a) to establish if an embryo has an abnormality that might affect its capacity to result in a live birth;
(b) to establish if an embryo has a 'gene, chromosome or mitochondrion abnormality';
(c) to avoid a sex-related serious medical condition;
(d) for histocompatibility (tissue typing); or
(e) to establish the identity of gamete providers.[114]

The Human Fertilisation and Embryology Authority (the HFEA) licenses embryo testing on a condition-by-condition basis and lists those conditions on a central list.[115] There are currently 600 conditions on that list.

The 1990 Act (as amended in 2008) expressly prohibits testing gametes or embryos to ensure that the resulting child 'will be one sex rather than the other', unless the purpose is avoidance of a serious medical condition.[116] This excludes genetic testing to sex select for 'family balancing' or other social reasons. The Act also expressly prohibits preference being given to an embryo that is known to have a gene, chromosome or mitochondrial abnormality involving a significant risk that the person with the abnormality will develop a serious medical condition.[117] This means that it is unlawful to select an embryo for implantation following PGD to provide prospective parents with a deaf child (perhaps, to render it more amenable

[113] On the latter, so-called saviour siblings, see the discussion in Pattinson 2020, 300–304.
[114] 1990 Act (as amended), Sch 2, para 1ZA.
[115] See www.hfea.gov.uk/treatments/embryo-testing-and-treatments-for-disease/approved-pgt-m-and-ptt-conditions.
[116] 1990 Act, Sch 2 paras 1ZA(1)(c)/(3) and 1ZB.
[117] 1990 Act, s 13(9).

to the deaf culture of its deaf parents)[118] or an achondroplasic child (perhaps, to enable it to fit into the spatially restricted living conditions of parents with congenitally restricted growth). These prohibitions are plausible indirect applications of the PGC.[119] Themis will therefore invoke these prohibitions when making the case for prohibiting genome editing for non-functional (cosmetic) traits, such as eye colour. She will also draw on the pre-existing legislative principle that clinics treating prospective parents may only use genetic and reproductive technologies that accord with the best interests of the future child.[120] She will argue for permitting the HFEA to license genome editing for superhuman vision and immunity to coronaviruses, but require periodic review of the social effects of these developments. Given the principle that genome editing may only be available for traits for which it is permissible to test, Themis will widen the grounds on which PGD is licensable to encompass traits with wide or all-purpose functional effects for the future child for which genome editing is a viable option.

The amendment Bill will permit genome editing where specific approval has been given by the HFEA to a licensed clinic. It will adopt a procedure similar to that applied to living organ donation by section 33 of the Human Tissue Act 2004.[121] What this means is that the HFEA will need to approve every clinical application of genome editing and be satisfied that specific conditions have been fulfilled. Following the model provided by section 33 of the 2004 Act, the features of the new approval process are to be specified in regulations to enable periodic adjustment in light of future developments and experience of the procedure in operation. It is envisaged that the regulations will require the HFEA approval panel to comprise at least three members.[122]

The Explanatory Notes in the next subsection use the standard headings and introductory wording used since 2015 for Explanatory Notes to government Bills.[123] To save space I have omitted headings/sections that provide statements or details beyond what is relevant to the focus of this chapter. To ensure stylistic felicity I have also drawn some text from the Explanatory Notes to the Human Fertilisation and Embryology Act 2008.[124]

[118] On 'Deafness' as a culture, see Ivers 1995 and Davis 1997, 567–575. It was widely reported that a deaf lesbian couple had used a sperm donor with congenital deafness to enable them to have a deaf child: see Spriggs 2002.

[119] On the prohibition of sex selective use of prenatal tests see 1.3.3 and Pattinson 2002, esp 151–153. On the prohibition of selecting for a disability see Pattinson 2002, 160–163.

[120] See the discussion of the 1990 Act's s 13(5) 'welfare of the future child' requirement in Pattinson 2020, 281–283. As argued there, a rights-based theory must interpret that provision in a specified way to avoid what Parfit (1984, ch 16) called this the 'non-identity problem'.

[121] s 33 of the 2004 Act states that the removal or use of 'transplantable material' from a living person for the purposes of transplantation is illegal unless (1) it is permitted by regulations and (2) the Human Tissue Authority is satisfied that the specified conditions are fulfilled. For discussion of s 33 and the relevant regulations see Pattinson 2020, 461–464.

[122] Following the model implemented by the regulations enacted under the 2004 Act, whereby a panel of three is specified for particularly controversial types of living donation procedures: see Pattinson 2020, 461–464.

[123] See Office of the Parliamentary Council 2015.

[124] www.legislation.gov.uk/ukpga/2008/22/notes/contents.

My document displays three notable departures from current practice, all of which could be implemented easily by the government when putting this (and other Bills) before Parliament. The first is that it refers to an extensive public engagement and consultation process prior to the issuing of the White Paper and the Bill. Consultation documents are often issued to support significant legislative plans, but Themis' government would adopt a far more extensive process, designed to engage with all sections of society. In the Explanatory Notes below, and in the those in chapter 5, this is referred to as the Policy on Public Engagement and Consultation. The second departure from current practice involves a commitment to ensuring that the 1990 Act appears in its final amended form on legislation.gov.uk in accordance with a new policy on timing, referred to as the Policy on Public Availability of Acts of Parliament. At present, where complex legislation is amended it often takes some time for that legislation to appear online in its final form. Until this happens, those wishing to read the amended legislation in its final form often need to use commercial databases such as Westlaw. Themis' government would seek to change this practice. She would seek to ensure that it is possible to download a PDF of the amended 1990 Act, as it will be after it the new Act comes into effect, no later than two weeks after the new Act receives Royal Assent. She will also ensure that the 1990 Act appears in its amended form on legislation.gov.uk on the day that the relevant changes take effect. The third departure from current practice is that the Bill supplements its long title with a preamble setting out its governing principles (para 11). This seeks to ensure that future legislative interpretation is aided by a parliamentarily approved declaration of the Act's principles, in a similar way to the recitals of EU legislation.

3.6.2. Explanatory Notes to Bill

HUMAN FERTILISATION AND EMBRYOLOGY (HERITABLE GENOME EDITING) BILL

EXPLANATORY NOTES

What these notes do

These Explanatory Notes relate to the Human Fertilisation and Embryology (Heritable Genome Editing) Bill as introduced in the House of Commons on 1 August 2022 (Bill 1).

- These Explanatory Notes have been prepared by the Department of Health and Social Care in order to assist the reader of the Bill and to help inform debate on it. They do not form part of the Bill and have not been endorsed by Parliament.
- These Explanatory Notes explain what each part of the Bill will mean in practice; provide background information on the development of policy; and provide additional information on how the Bill will affect existing legislation in this area.
- These Explanatory Notes might be read alongside the Bill. They are not, and are not meant to be, a comprehensive description of the Bill.

Overview of the Bill

1 The Bill amends the law relating to assisted reproduction to take account of recent developments in biomedical research, treatment and practice. It amends many of the provisions of the Human Fertilisation and Embryology Act 1990, but the main features of the existing model of regulation are retained.

2 The following terms are used throughout the Explanatory Notes

DNA	Deoxyribose Nucleic Acid (genetic material)
Heritable genome editing	Modifying the DNA possessed by human embryos, gametes or gamete precursor cells with the aim of then establishing a successful pregnancy with the edited embryo
HFEA	Human Fertilisation and Embryology Authority
The 1990 Act	The Human Fertilisation and Embryology Act 1990
The 2008 Act	The Human Fertilisation and Embryology Act 2008

3 The Bill amends the 1990 Act to enable the HFEA to licence specific uses of genetic testing and genome editing technology.

4 To assist the reader of the Bill, the Department of Health and Social Care has produced an illustrative consolidated text of the 1990 Act as amended. This shows the effect of the amendments made by the Bill. The text has no official status. The final form of the amended 1990 Act will be available after enactment of this Bill in accordance with the *Policy on Public Availability of Acts of Parliament.*

Policy background

5 This Bill fulfils the Government's commitment to ensuring that UK law takes full account of recent developments in the field of human genetics and assisted reproduction. These include significant advances in the ability to edit the DNA possessed by embryos, gametes and gamete precursor cells so as to modify the traits of any resulting child (heritable genome editing). Using this technology, it

is now possible for a child to be born with genetic immunity to coronaviruses, enhanced vision or a selected eye colour.

6 The Department of Health and Social Care consultation entitled *The Future of Genetics in Human Reproduction* sought views on policy proposals to address these developments. These proposals included permitting heritable genome editing in specific circumstances, ensuring that no anticipated forms of heritable genome editing are unregulated and widening the purposes for which the DNA of embryos may be lawfully tested. These proposals require new legislation.

7 The process leading up to the Bill has followed the *Policy on Public Engagement and Consultation*. Over twenty thousand individual responses were received from a wide range of organisations and professional bodies as well as the general public. In addition to these responses to the consultation, over 50 workshops and engagement events were held with individuals from groups identified as likely to be particularly affected by or concerned about these developments. The Government took account of these views when publishing the White Paper: *Review of the Human Fertilisation and Embryology Acts: Proposals for revised legislation to address heritable genome editing*. This Bill implements the proposals in the White Paper.

Legal background

8 The 1990 Act was enacted to regulate the creation, keeping and use of embryos outside the human body and the storage and use of gametes to create embryos. The 2008 Act amended many of the provisions of the 1990 Act but retained the main features of the pre-existing model of regulation.

9 The 1990 Act, as amended by the 2008 Act, prohibits certain activities from being carried out without a licence or, in some cases, a third party agreement with a licence-holder. Other activities are subject to an absolute prohibition. Licences can be granted for the purpose of fertility treatment, for storage and for research. The 1990 Act imposes mandatory conditions for each type of licence and enables other conditions to be imposed. Activities under the 1990 Act are overseen by the HFEA, a statutory licensing authority.

10 The policy background section of these Notes explains the government's commitment to amending specific provisions of the 1990 Act (see paragraphs 5 to 7 of these Notes).

Commentary on provisions of Bill

Part 1: Amendment of the Human Fertilisation and Embryology Act 1990

Clause 1: The preamble

11 Clause 1 provides a preamble to the Bill comprising a set of principles to explain and justify its provisions:

- The Bill seeks to regulate all heritable genome editing.
- The purposes for which a licence may permit heritable genome editing of embryos must not extend beyond the purposes for which a licence may permit the testing of the nuclear or mitochondrial DNA of embryos.
- Heritable genome editing may only be undertaken where the procedure and its likely consequences accord with the best interests of any child who might be born as a result.
- Heritable genome editing potentially only accords with the best interests of any child who might be born as a result where it is likely to increase the abilities of

that child to successfully achieve all of its potential future purposes or a wide set of its potential future purposes.

Clause 2: Prohibitions in connection with embryos and gametes

12 Clause 2 amends section 3 of the 1990 Act to empower the HFEA to licence heritable genome editing on embryos and gametes. Section 3(2) of the 1990 Act prohibits the placing in any woman of any embryo other than a "permitted embryo" or any gametes other than "permitted eggs" or "permitted sperm". Regulations are permitted under section 3ZA(5), which was inserted by the 2008 Act to address mitochondrial replacement techniques. Clause 2 introduces a further exception to the definitions of permitted eggs, permitted sperm and permitted embryos in section 3ZA.

13 This clause introduces a new subsection and a new section into the 1990 Act. Both new provisions provide for regulation-making powers.

14 New section 3ZA(5A) provides for an additional situation where regulations may provide that a gamete can be a permitted gamete even though its nuclear or mitochondrial DNA has been altered and an embryo can be a permitted embryo even though the nuclear or mitochondrial DNA of one or more of its cells has been altered. This new subsection provides for a regulation-making power to permit alteration of the DNA of a gamete or embryo where it is undertaken by a licensed clinic and approved by the HFEA. The HFEA approval panel must be satisfied that the conditions specified in both this subsection and the regulations are fulfilled. The HFEA must, in particular, be satisfied that the proposed genome editing is a suitably safe and reliable means of increasing the abilities of the child who could be born from the modified gamete or embryo to successfully achieve all of its future purposes or a wide set of its future purposes.

15 New section 35C is inserted into the 1990 Act to require the HFEA to submit an annual report to the House of Commons on all heritable genome editing and its social effects. This section also provides for a regulation-making power to enable specification of the methods by which social effects are to be measured and recorded.

Clause 3: Prohibitions in connection with germ cells

16 Clause 3 amends the 1990 Act to ensure that a potential means of deliberately genome editing gametes and their precursors falls within the Act. The purpose of this clause is to ensure that a licence would be required if a sperm precursor were genome-edited and returned to the testes (where the recipient has been sterilised in the meantime to remove other sperm) so that the conception occurs with a partner through unassisted reproduction.

17 This clause amends section 3A which covers prohibitions in connection with germ cells.

18 New section 3A(1A) prohibits placing in a man any germ cell whose nuclear or mitochondrial DNA has been altered, except in pursuance of a licence and with the approval of the HFEA. The definitions in section 3A(2) are expanded so that "male germ cells" includes cells of the male germ-line at any stage of maturity.

Clause 4: Other prohibitions in connection with heritable genome editing

19 Clause 4 amends the 1990 Act to ensure that other potential means of heritable genome editing fall within the Act. In particular, the possibility that genome

editing reagents could be successfully administered to the ovum in the fallopian tubes or uterus shortly before or after unassisted fertilisation.

20 New section 35D makes it an offence to intentionally administer or supply for self-administration heritable genome editing reagents except in accordance with a licence from the HFEA.

Clause 5: Licences for embryo testing

21 Clause 5 adds two provisions to Schedule 2 of the 1990 Act to extend the purposes for which embryo testing can be licensed.

22 Embryo testing can involve invasive procedures such as embryo biopsy, involving removal of a cell or cells from the embryo for subsequent analysis. The effect of new paragraph 1ZA(1)(f) is that the testing of an embryo can be authorised to establish whether the embryo has genes associated with the 'specified functional abilities' of any resulting child. New section 1ZC defines the specified functional abilities as those that relate to all of its potential future purposes or a wide set of its potential future purposes, where a licence could be granted under the Act to permit editing the DNA of the embryo to improve or increase those future abilities.

4

Ectogestation

4.1. Introduction

In 2017, researchers in the United States announced a significant development in womb replacement technology.[1] They had removed premature lamb fetuses by caesarean section and put them into 'biobags'. Each biobag was filled with a substitute amniotic fluid, which was continually exchanged to prevent infection. Each fetus' umbilical cord was connected to a pumpless oxygenator circuit in which the blood flow was driven by the fetal heart. The lambs were extracted from the womb at between 15 and 17 weeks of the full 21-week gestation period and supported in biobags for up to four weeks. This is the equivalent of extracting a human fetus at 22 to 24 weeks of the full 40-week gestation period.[2] Although some of the biobag fetuses experienced complications, many had normal growth and lung development. One of the lambs remained healthy more than a year later.

Haldane coined the term 'ectogenesis' in 1923 for human development outside the maternal body.[3] The lamb fetal experiments were a major step, but the technology still has a long way to go before it can enable a human to be conceived and fully gestated outside the body (*full ectogenesis*) or, like the lamb fetuses, gestated outside the body after initial but incomplete gestation in the womb (*partial ectogenesis/ectogestation*).[4] This chapter will first examine the current science (4.2), before considering the challenges the technology could pose to the interpretation and application of existing legal rules, categories and doctrines (4.3). The chapter will then present an imagined scenario for the future of the technology in which partial ectogestation has been successfully applied to humans (4.4). This will be followed by an application of the PGC (4.5) and a hypothetical appeal case in which judicial consideration is given to activities arising within my imagined future (4.6).

[1] See Partridge 2017. See also reports elsewhere: Hamzelou 2017 and Devlin 2018.

[2] The head of the biobag team has claimed that neonates at this stage 'have only a 10 per cent chance of survival' (Flake, as quoted in Hamzelou 2017). Cf 4.2, below.

[3] See Haldane 1923, esp 64, 65 and 66.

[4] This usage of 'ectogestation' derives from Kingma & Finn 2020 and Stefano et al 2020. There is a third option: partial ectogenesis with no ectogestation (where creation takes place outside the body, but all gestation takes place in the womb, such as in standard IVF).

4.2. Ectogenesis and Ectogestation

The last century has seen many significant advances in the technology for developing the early human outside the body. Initially, the focus was on ensuring the survival of premature neonates. Incubators have been used since the early twentieth century to create a controlled environment in which pre-term births and sick neonates can be monitored and assisted.[5] Subsequent developments in neonatal care have included use of mechanical ventilation since the 1980s (to help neonates breathe, especially those born pre-term with underdeveloped lungs) and the administration of steroids to those at risk of giving birth prematurely since the late 1990s.[6] The cumulative effect of such innovations is that premature neonates given state-of-the-art neonatal care now have a much greater chance of survival. One comparison of cohorts of extremely pre-term births (between 22 and 25 weeks' gestation) in England from 1995 and 2006 reported a 13% increase in survival to discharge from hospital (from 40% to 53%).[7] There are now even reported instances of neonates as young as 21 weeks' gestation surviving.[8] But survival rates for extremely premature neonates remain low and many of those who do survive experience severe long-term complications, such as brain damage and lung disease.[9] There are, however, significant variations between neonatal clinics. At the top end, 26% of infants born at 22–23 weeks and admitted to a particular neonatal clinic in Cologne, Germany in a five-year period had survived without complications.[10]

There have also been significant technological advances at the conception-end of human development. Louise Brown, the first IVF baby, was born in July 1978. IVF, or to give it its full name, *in vitro* fertilisation, involves the creation of an embryo outside the body. For nearly three decades embryos created in this way could only be kept alive in culture for seven to nine days. But, in 2016, two teams successfully cultured human embryos to 13 days, before destroying them to comply with regulatory requirements.[11]

At first sight, it seems that full ectogenesis (conception and gestation entirely outside the body) is just a matter of closing the gap between what is already possible with very early embryos and premature neonates. Many have pointed out that the gap is closing[12] and we shall see in 4.2.1 that this seems to be a continuing trajectory. But much is still not understood about the precise features of a normal human pregnancy from the implantation of the very early embryo into the uterus

[5] See peopleshistorynhs.org/encyclopaedia/premature-birth-and-the-nhs.
[6] See Glass et al 2015, 1339.
[7] See Costeloe et al 2012.
[8] See Bilger 2020 (reporting survival of an infant at 21 weeks and 0 days' gestation) and Ahmad et al 2017 (infant at 21 weeks and 4 days' gestation).
[9] See eg Costeloe et al 2012; Moore et al 2012; Glass et al 2015.
[10] See Mehler et al 2016. The data was from 1 January 2010 to 31 December 2014.
[11] See Deglincerti et al 2016 and Shahbazi et al 2016.
[12] See eg Singer & Wells 1984, 132 and Coleman 2004, 45.

wall (at the blastocyst stage) to birth,[13] which triggers transition from reliance on the placenta for oxygen and nutrients to reliance on the lungs and mouth/gut.[14]

Romanis has argued that there are important conceptual differences between standard gestation in the womb, 'artificial womb technology' (AWT) and 'neonatal intensive care' (NIC).[15] She argues that it is therefore potentially confusing and misleading to refer to the subjects in AWT (such as in the biobag) as either fetuses or neonates. Accordingly, Romanis coins the term the 'gestateling' for 'a human being in the process of ex utero gestation exercising, whether or not it is capable of doing so, no independent capacity for life'.[16] Romanis thereby distinguishes the fetus, gestateling and neonate, and argues that the gestateling is 'more ontologically similar' to the fetus than the neonate.[17]

Kingma and Finn support these conclusions but argue that Romanis has failed to provide an adequate conceptual account of these distinctions. They argue, for example, that it is false to claim that the gestateling exercises 'no independent capacity for life', because fetuses 'sustain their own independent circulation/heartbeat, which the recent technological developments directly exploit'.[18] So, AWT merely requires '*less* independence than NIC', which calls for an account of where on the support-continuum these two technologies are to be distinguished.[19]

Kingma and Finn support the distinction between AWT and NIC and the claim that gestatelings are more like fetuses than neonates. They argue that fetuses and neonates differ in more than their locations (in or outside the maternal body), because they 'have different physiological and physical characteristics'.[20] One notable example is that 'fetuses do not breathe but oxygenate their blood via the placenta' and have correspondingly different cardiovascular systems.[21] Such physiological and physical differences enable an account to be given of the distinction between AWT and NIC: the former ('ectogestation') supports the 'fetal physiological system', whereas the latter ('neonatal incubation') supports 'the physiological blue-print of a neonate'.[22] While a gestateling is more like a neonate in terms of its location, it is more like a fetus in terms of its physiology.[23]

The helpful insights of Romanis, Kingma and Finn do not (nor are they meant to) answer the underlying moral questions. As I argued in chapter 2 and will

[13] On the initial development of the embryo in utero see eg Chen & Chrisholm 2017 and Zernicka-Goetz 2017.

[14] See Stefano et al 2020, 381 (n47).

[15] Romanis 2018, 751. See also Romanis 2020a, 97–98.

[16] Romanis 2018, 753. See also Romanis 2020a, 98; 2020b, 398 (n 85); 2020c, 347 (n 32).

[17] Romanis 2018, 753 and Romanis 2020a, 98. Romanis refers to the fetus (as opposed to the embryo and fetus), because she is focused on partial ectogestation. An early (embryonic) gestateling would be even further away from a breathing neonate than a later (fetal) gestateling.

[18] Kingma & Finn 2020, 357.

[19] Kingma & Finn 2020, 357 (original emphasis).

[20] Kingma & Finn 2020, 354.

[21] Kingma & Finn 2020, 358.

[22] Kingma & Finn 2020, 361.

[23] This liminal status leads De Bie and co-authors to offer the alternative terminology of the 'fetal neonate' or 'fetonate': see De Bie et al 2022.

develop below, the moral status of the developing human is determined by the extent to which it displays the behavioural and physical characteristics associated with agent-behavers. Those characteristics are not coterminous with classification as a fetus, gestateling or neonate on either of the accounts above. As Kingma and Finn recognise, an extremely premature neonate, 'barely clinging to life' in neonatal intensive care, would display far less physical, physiological and cognitive development than a late-term fetus 'about to emerge into healthy, screaming babyhood'.[24] As readers will be aware, moral status is only one factor in the moral equation and location is directly relevant to the interests of the pregnant person.[25]

4.2.1. The Biobag, EVE and the Weizmann Process

In 2019, another team of researchers announced that they had successfully maintained even younger lamb fetuses in a womb replacement, which they referred to as an 'ex vivo uterine environment' (EVE).[26] The subjects were removed at 95 days' gestation and placed inside EVE for five days. By way of comparison, the youngest put into the biobag was at 106 days' gestation and previous experiments using EVE had removed subjects at 111–115 days.[27] The later EVE subjects were euthanised at 100 days and compared to a control group of fetuses removed from the womb and euthanised immediately at 100 days' gestation. Seven of the eight research subjects survived all five days of EVE therapy and were reported to be just as healthy and developed as the control group.

Some media outlets reporting the biobag research in 2017 predicted that human trials could be only three years away.[28] But other reports cited the head of the biobag research team (Alan Flake) as estimating that human trials were *at least* three years away.[29] It was at the time likely that human trials were much further away because the biobag and EVE experiments involved very small numbers of non-human animals for only short durations.[30] In 2020, the head of the EVE research team (Matthew Kemp) is quoted as saying: 'Anyone who tells you they are going to be doing this in two years either has a wealth of data that is not in the public domain or is being a bit sensationalist.'[31] Kemp goes on to point out that the experiments to date have involved healthy lamb pregnancies, but the first likely application to humans would be to a 'very sick' fetus at the equivalent gestational age – 21 to 22 weeks, in the case of the EVE experiments from 2019.

[24] Kingma & Finn 2020, 358.

[25] I will use the term 'the pregnant person' to recognise that some of those who are pregnant do not identify as women. Since, however, UK legislation uses the term 'the pregnant woman', I revert to that term when examining the details of that legislation.

[26] See Usuda 2019 et al.

[27] See Usuda et al 2017 (those subjects were maintained inside EVE for one week).

[28] See eg Gregory 2017: 'Scientists believe it could be ready for human trials in three years'.

[29] See Couzin-Frankel 2017.

[30] See Romanis 2020b, 394.

[31] Kleeman 2020.

Animal experiments have also continued to push the boundaries of *ex utero* development of the early embryo. In 2021, Jacob Hanna and his team at the Weizmann Institute of Science reported that they had developed a two-step process for growing mouse embryos outside the womb for six days, which is around a third of their 20-day gestation.[32] The first stage involved growing embryos, from just after the point at which they would have implanted into the uterine wall, in a special medium in a laboratory dish. This stage lasted around two days, during which the early embryos attached to this medium as they would to the wall of the uterus. The second stage involved culturing the embryos in tiny rotating bottles in which they were bathed in continually mixing nutrients. During this stage the embryos formed early organs – referred to in their article in *Nature* as 'advanced organogenesis in culture'.[33] The externally developing embryos were periodically compared to embryos removed from pregnant mice at the relevant time, which indicated that the *ex utero* embryos were developing normally.

Technologies such as the biobag, EVE and the Weizmann process[34] are developing alongside technologies designed to enable or assist gestation *in utero*: assisted gestative technologies. Among the most recent of these is uterine transplantation. The first live-birth following transplantation of a womb from a living donor occurred in Sweden in 2014.[35] The first live-birth after uterine transplantation from a deceased donor occurred in Brazil in 2018.[36] There is ongoing research into the creation of a bio-engineered womb from stem cells for future uterine transplantation, which would avoid the need to remove a womb from a living or deceased donor.[37] Assisted gestative technologies, however, raise different kinds of societal and regulatory challenges to those presented by ectogestation.

4.2.2. Challenges and Opportunities

Public perception of human gestation outside the body has been marred by dystopian depictions, such as the 'hatchery' in Aldous Huxley's *Brave New World*.[38] Leaving fictional dystopias aside, plausible future technological developments in this area are likely to be disruptive to many societal expectations and regulatory compromises. Birth, for example, triggers a change of legal status (see 4.3.5) and most of us celebrate our *birth*days throughout our lives.

[32] See Aguilera-Castrejon et al 2021 and Weizmann Institute of Science 2021.
[33] Aguilera-Castrejon et al 2021, 3.
[34] See also the recent creation of blastoids (blastocyst-like structures produced outside the body): Niemann & Seamark 2021.
[35] See Brännström et al 2015. This was widely reported by the media at the time: see eg BBC 2014.
[36] See Wise 2018.
[37] See Brännström 2017.
[38] See Huxley 1932.

Disruptive technologies often evoke a family of psychological phenomena commonly referred to as 'status quo bias'.[39] By this I refer to the prevalent psychological preference for an option that preserves the status quo, which often leads to that option being prematurely judged to be better. Bostrom and Ord have offered a test to determine whether our thinking betrays resistance to change without good reason, which they call the 'reversal test':

> When a proposal to change a certain parameter is thought to have bad overall consequences, consider a change to the same parameter in the opposite direction. If this is also thought to have bad overall consequences, then the onus is on those who reach these conclusions to explain why our position cannot be improved through changes to this parameter. If they are unable to do so, then we have reason to suspect that they suffer from status quo bias.[40]

Applied to full ectogenesis (where development is outside the body from the start), the reversal test asks us to consider whether, if external gestation were what usually occurred, we would be willing to bring about womb gestation. If we would be equally reluctant to permit change in the reversed scenario, then the status quo bias could be influencing our thinking and we are, in effect, assuming the existing position to be optimal. In fact, it seems to me that if external gestation were our biological starting point, few would be arguing in favour of modifying the human body to enable womb gestation and vaginal delivery. Indeed, theorists such as Kendal and MacKay welcome the prospect of full ectogenesis as a means of liberating society from oppressive assumptions about the function of women.[41]

Partial ectogestation (ectogestation after initial development in the womb) is unlikely to evoke the status quo bias, because it is likely to be perceived as analogous to existing neonatal care. Yet, as we saw in the previous section, partial ectogestation is not technologically the mere extension of neonatal care, because a gestateling is closer to a fetus than a neonate in terms of its development and the type of support it requires.

The successful application of partial ectogestation to the developing human would be relevant to 'viability'. This is pertinent because viability, understood as attainment of a particular threshold for survival outside the womb, has been offered as the justification for distinguishing legal from illegal abortion. Famously, the US Supreme Court in *Roe v Wade* held that only after viability could the state's interest in protecting fetal life override the pregnant woman's constitutional right to privacy.[42] *Roe* was overruled nearly 50 years later.[43] Viability remains relevant to the law of this jurisdiction. As we shall see below, the Infant Life (Preservation) Act 1929 protects a fetus from intentional termination once it is 'capable of being born alive'. The Abortion Act 1967 was originally subject to the 1929 Act,

[39] See eg Samuelson & Zeckhauser 1988; Bostrom & Ord 2006.
[40] Bostrom & Ord 2006, 664–665.
[41] See Kendal 2015 and MacKay 2020. Cf Cavaliere 2020.
[42] (1973) 410 US 113, esp 163–164.
[43] *Dobbs v Jackson Women's Health Organization* (2022) 945 Ff 3d 265.

so termination under its provisions was initially limited by the 'capable of being born alive' threshold.[44] As a result of amendment by the Human Fertilisation and Embryology Act 1990, the grounds for abortion in the 1967 Act are no longer subject to this threshold.[45] Nonetheless, the first of the amended 1967 Act's four grounds for abortion is limited to 24 weeks' gestation, which was considered by Parliament to capture a gestational point suitably connected to the likelihood of fetuses surviving outside the womb.

Multiple thresholds of viability are available for consideration, including the stage at which survival outside the womb has been shown to be: feasible; the outcome for a given percentage (say 50 or 80 per cent) of a population; likely without disability or at least without severe disability; or likely without the need for specific types of medical intervention.[46] However it is measured, viability is not static. It will vary according to access to facilities and technological developments in neonatal care and ectogestation. Glass and co-authors, for example, define viability as the gestational age at which there is a 50 per cent chance of survival outside the body, which they identify as currently around 23 to 24 weeks in high-income countries and closer to 34 weeks in low- and middle-income countries.[47] The lower the selected threshold, the sooner future developments in partial ectogestation could affect viability. Simonstein has argued that the realisation of full ectogenesis could render 'viability … possible at all times from the beginning of a pregnancy'.[48]

Granting moral status to the fetus renders viability relevant to the moral permissibility of abortion. That's because the case for abortion is then a case for expulsion in the interests of the pregnant individual without automatically supporting termination of the fetus' life. Their comparative status then matters because the burden of the process for removal from the womb for the pregnant individual is almost inevitably increased if it is performed in such a way as to maximise the fetus' chances of survival. This is an issue to which I will return when applying the PGC, below.

4.3. The Boundaries and Uncertainties of the Current Law

Ectogenesis has the potential to challenge current regulatory distinctions and boundaries. Existing regulatory distinctions are drawn according to location

[44] s 5, 1967 Act, as originally enacted. See *Rance v Mid-Downs HA* [1991] 1 QB 587.

[45] s 5(1), 1967 as substituted by s 37(4), 1990 Act. Cf Romanis 2020a, 110 ('the Abortion Act 1967 specifies that the fetus in uterus is "capable of being born alive" from 24 weeks gestation') and 114 ('The Abortion Act 1967 … stipulated that a fetus was assumed *capable of being born alive* at 24 weeks', original emphasis).

[46] See Stefano et al 2020, esp 377.

[47] See Glass et al 2015, 1337 and 1338.

[48] Simonstein 2006, 362.

during human development: outside the body before implantation, in the womb during gestation and outside the body after birth. Developments in medical science could potentially render removal and termination of a fetus separable, and create an entity (a gestateling) that fits into no existing legal category.

This section examines legal categorisation and consequences concerning embryos (4.3.1), miscarriage (4.3.2), the capacity to be born alive (4.3.3), termination of pregnancy (4.3.4) and being born alive (4.3.5).

4.3.1. Human Fertilisation and Embryology Act 1990

Full ectogenesis is currently unlawful in the United Kingdom, because an embryo cannot be implanted or used for research beyond 14 days from the start of its creation. More specifically, the Human Fertilisation and Embryology Act 1990 (the 1990 Act) makes it a criminal offence to keep or use an embryo 'after the appearance of the primitive streak' or 14 days, whichever is earlier.[49] It may be frozen or used before this threshold in accordance with a storage, treatment or research licence granted by the Human Fertilisation and Embryology Authority (the HFEA). It follows that if the primitive streak were to appear earlier than 14 days, the embryo would then need to be destroyed. Primary legislation would be required to permit research into continued ectogenesis beyond this threshold.

Below the statutory threshold, we have seen that ectogenesis requires a licence from the HFEA. The 1990 Act prohibits, in particular, all uses of embryos outside the body unless specifically licensed within its terms (section 3(1A)). The Act's definition of an embryo was amended by the Human Fertilisation and Embryology Act 2008, so that it now encompasses any method of creation: under section 1(1) an embryo means 'a live human embryo', including an egg 'in the process of fertilisation or … undergoing any other process capable of resulting in an embryo'. This definition means that the 1990 Act's prohibitions in connection with embryos (including the above time limit) cannot be evaded by creating an embryo using a cloning technique. But the tautologous use of the very term being defined also means that the Act does not itself identify when a developing human is no longer an embryo and thus free from the time limit for keeping or using it outside the body. That is not to suggest that there is any scope for construing the term so that it ceases to be an embryo if temporarily transferred to the womb before continued ectogenesis.[50] In such a case, it would remain an embryo and the primitive streak/14-day limitation would apply. Rather, the point is that there is some scope for debate as to when an early human that has been developing in the womb can (after removal) be kept or used outside the body without engaging the Act's

[49] s 3(3)(a), read with s 3(4).

[50] The Act expressly deals with keeping and using embryos outside the body: s 3(1A). Only the prohibitions in connection with creation outside the body exclude 'embryos taken from a womb': s 1(2)(b).

prohibitions. The interpretative options permitting at least some forms of ectogestation are explored in the hypothetical case below (4.6.2).

The 2016 experiments that extended the period for which it is currently feasible to keep a human embryo alive outside the body (outlined in 4.2) have put pressure on the international adoption of the so-called 14-day rule. The International Society for Stem Cell Research (ISSCR), which is the largest global professional organisation of stem cell scientists, revised its guidelines in May 2021.[51] The guidelines concede that culturing human embryos beyond formation of the primitive streak or 14 days is 'currently not technically feasible'.[52] But add that embryo culture systems are evolving and future research at or beyond the regulatory threshold are 'crucial' for improving understanding of infertility, IVF, pregnancy loss, some developmental disorders and the development of stem cell-based embryo models for future research. The guidelines recommend that if 'broad public support' can be achieved and regulatory structures adopted to ensure appropriate scientific and ethical oversight, then scientific objectives could, in principle, now 'necessitate and justify' culturing human embryos beyond 14 days.[53] Given the United Kingdom's status as a leader in embryo research and its previous willingness to relax regulatory restrictions in light of scientific developments,[54] it would seem to be only a matter of time before the United Kingdom's 14-day rule is relaxed.

Complexities for partial ectogestation are also raised by the law's reliance on terms such as 'miscarriage' and 'born alive'.

4.3.2. Offences against the Person Act 1861

The starting point for the law applying to abortion comprises two offences in the Offences against the Person Act 1861. Section 58 makes it a criminal offence, punishable by up to life imprisonment, to unlawfully and intentionally attempt to procure a 'miscarriage'. Section 59 makes it an offence to unlawfully supply drugs or other instruments knowing that they are intended for use in procuring a 'miscarriage'.

The 1861 Act does not define key terms such as 'unlawfully' or 'miscarriage'. As a result, interpretative possibilities arise with regard to its application to the transfer and continued gestation of a fetus in an ectogestative device. Three key questions are: Is removal from the pregnant person for this purpose prohibited by section 58? Is removal from an ectogestative device prohibited by section 58? If the procedure is prohibited by section 58, is a defence available under the Abortion Act 1967?

[51] See ISSCR 2021.
[52] ISSCR 2021, 12.
[53] See ISSCR 2021, 13 (recommendation 2.2.2.1).
[54] See eg the discussion of the Human Fertilisation and Embryology (Mitochondrial Donation) Regulations 2015/572 in 3.3.2.

The meaning of 'miscarriage' has been considered by the lower courts twice. In *Dhingra*, Wright J (sitting in the Crown Court) held that 'miscarriage' related to expulsion after the fertilised egg has become implanted into the womb and therefore dismissed a charge against a doctor under section 58 for inserting an intrauterine device (IUD) for contraceptive purposes.[55] In *Smeaton*, Munby J rejected the Society for the Protection of Unborn Children's (SPUC's) claim that allowing the sale of a morning-after pill without prescription contravened the 1861 Act.[56] He held that the term 'miscarriage' was to be interpreted as an 'ordinary English word', according to how it is '*currently* understood' and 'in the light of the best current scientific and medical knowledge'.[57] Applying this, Munby J held that miscarriage is to be understood as the 'termination of an established pregnancy, and there is no established pregnancy prior to implantation'.[58] The implication being that 'carriage' requires the fertilised egg to have been implanted and the morning-after pill prevents implantation, so does not involve bringing about a miscarriage.[59] Further, his Lordship noted, SPUC's arguments would have serious implications for those using any form of contraception that prevents the implantation of a fertilised egg.[60]

Munby J was not, of course, considering partial ectogestation. At first sight, transfer into an ectogestative device would seem to involve procuring a miscarriage, even if the technology had developed to the point where survival in such a device had become likely. After removal from the womb and severing of the umbilical cord, there is no longer 'an established pregnancy' as the fetus is no longer being carried in the body. On this interpretation, section 58 prohibits intentional removal from the womb but not intentional removal from an ectogestative device. The Act therefore requires a defence for the former but not the latter.

Alghrani and Brazier offer a slightly different view. They argue that the 1861 Act envisaged miscarriage as 'a process inevitably designed to kill the fetus', whereas partial ectogestation 'offers a chance of life'.[61] Interpretative options arise, and will be considered because section 58 prohibits an 'unlawful act' performed with the 'intent' to procure a 'miscarriage'. Alghrani and Brazier go on to point out, however, that since fetal death is 'virtually certain [at 19 weeks], such an exercise in statutory interpretation of the 1861 Act may not recommend itself to the courts'.[62] Alghrani reiterates these thoughts in her later book, noting that survival of transfer at such an early gestative stage is currently so unlikely that 'it could be argued that fetal death was virtually certain, and thus contrary to the 1861 statute'.[63]

[55] *R v Dhingra* (1991) unreported but quoted extensively in *R (Smeaton) v Secretary of State for Health* [2002] EWHC 610.
[56] [2002] EWHC 610.
[57] [2002] EWHC 610, [350] (original emphasis).
[58] [2002] EWHC 610, [17].
[59] [2002] EWHC 610, esp [18] and 353.
[60] [2002] EWHC 610, [395].
[61] Alghrani & Brazier 2011, 75. These words are reproduced in Alghrani 2018, 147.
[62] Alghrani & Brazier 2011, 75.
[63] Alghrani 2018, 147.

Once successful partial ectogestation has been shown to be feasible with a human fetus of the relevant gestational age, interpretative options arise from Munby J's insistence that the 1861 Act's wording be given its current meaning in light of the best current scientific and medical knowledge. One option is that suggested by Alghrani and Brazier: 'miscarriage' could be understood as *termination of pregnancy by fetal death.* On this interpretation, the *mens rea* for the section 58 offence cannot be established where the fetus is removed from the womb with the intention that its gestation continues in an ectogestative device. In these circumstances, no defence would be required by section 58 for removal from the womb or for later removal from the ectogestative device (because the pregnancy would be regarded as lawfully terminated at the point of removal from the womb). Another option arises if miscarriage came to be understood as *termination of carriage* with transfer to an ectogestative device being regarded as continued carriage. Accordingly, removal from the womb for this purpose would not require a defence to the section 58 offence but a defence would be required for later removal from the ectogestative device.

Further issues arise from all three interpretations. The *first interpretation* would require a defence to section 58 for removal from the womb for the purpose of continued ectogestation. But the defences in the Abortion Act 1967 are not readily applicable, even if ectogestation accords with the will of the pregnant woman and best protects the fetus' interests (see 4.3.4). The *second interpretation* requires no defence to section 58 for removal from the womb or the ectogestative device. But Romanis has presented three objections:

(i) the 1861 Act does not expressly refer to fetal death (in contrast to the Infant Life (Preservation) Act 1929 Act's reference to child destruction, on which see 4.3.3);
(ii) section 58 refers to methods for procuring miscarriage going beyond those that cause damage to the fetus ('any poison or other noxious thing ... *or other means whatsoever*'); and
(iii) the condition of the fetus is not the primary concern of section 58, because the offence is made out against a person other than the pregnant woman even if she was not actually pregnant.[64]

The *third interpretation* is the least plausible. It would also require a defence to section 58 for removal from an ectogestative device, yet the Abortion Act 1967 only applies to the termination of pregnancy.

The proper interpretation of the 1861 Act is considered in the hypothetical case below (4.6.2).

[64] See Romanis 2020c, 358.

4.3.3. Infant Life (Preservation) Act 1929

Since killing a fetus during childbirth might not be considered procurement of a miscarriage, Parliament created the offence of 'child destruction'. More specifically, section 1(1) of the Infant Life (Preservation) Act 1929 provides that any person who intends to destroy the life of a child 'capable of being born alive' commits an offence, unless the act was done 'in good faith for the purpose only of preserving the life of the mother'. This thereby imports a viability threshold into the law, and section 1(2) went further by providing for an evidential presumption that a 28-week fetus is capable of being born alive. Before 28 weeks the prosecution would need to establish that the fetus was capable of being born alive without the assistance of an evidential presumption.

The 1929 Act asks, in effect, a counter-factual question: if the fetus had been given the opportunity, would it have been capable of being born alive at that time? In *C v S*, the Court of Appeal held that a particular 18–21-week fetus would not have been capable of breathing either naturally or artificially, and so was not 'capable of being born alive' under the 1929 Act.[65] In *Rance v Mid-Downs HA*, Brooke J held that a child was capable of being born alive within the meaning of the Act when it possessed the attributes needed to breathe 'through its own lungs alone, without deriving any of its living or power of living by or through any connection with its mother'.[66]

If a fetus would, without the defendant's intervention, have been likely to survive removal and transfer to a neonatal device, then it is capable of being born alive in the sense articulated by Lord Donaldson in *C v S*.[67] At the moment, a less developed fetus that is removed and transferred to an ectogestative device (such as the biobag and EVE) would not be likely to survive, so could not be regarded as capable of being born alive at the point of removal. If the technology develops to the point where a gestateling is likely to survive in an ectogestative device, then things become more complex. A gestateling in the biobag, EVE or similar ectogestative device would continue to receive oxygen through the umbilical cord, rather than by breathing. It would not be capable of breathing until it developed to the point at which it could be removed from the ectogestative device. Thus, *if* being born alive requires breathing outside the maternal body, then a gestateling has not been born alive; and an early fetus that can only survive outside the body in an ectogestative device (as opposed to a neonatal device) cannot be regarded as capable of being born alive. Yet, contrary to appearances and for reasons to be examined in 4.3.4, *C v S* and *Rance* might be regarded as inconclusive on whether breathing is required to be born alive.

A further question arises as to whether the *mens rea* of the section 1(1) offence – the '*intent* to destroy' its life by 'any *wilful* act' – would be satisfied where the

[65] [1988] QB 135.
[66] [1991] 1 QB 587, 621.
[67] The potential differences between the judgments in *C v S* and *Rance* are explored in 4.3.5, below.

purpose is not to kill the fetus but to transfer it to an ectogestative device. At the current time, the chances of survival are so low that removal and transfer would make death a virtually certain consequence, and it is well established that intent can be inferred by a jury from the conclusion that the outcome was known to be a virtual certain consequence.[68] If ectogestative technology were to develop, however, removal and transfer could be conducted with the deliverable purpose of maintaining its life. The *mens rea* of the offence could then be absent even if the fetus is capable of being born alive and is killed during the process.

4.3.4. Abortion Act 1967

The Abortion Act 1967, as amended by the 1990 Act, provides that no offence is committed under the 1861 or 1929 Acts when a pregnancy is terminated in accordance with its provisions. The pregnancy must be terminated by a registered medical practitioner and two medical practitioners must have certified in 'good faith' that at least one of the Act's grounds for lawful termination have been satisfied.[69]

The first ground in the 1967 Act permits termination until the 24th week on therapeutic and social grounds: where the continuance of the pregnancy involves risk, greater than termination, of physical or mental injury to the pregnant woman or any existing children of her family (section 1(1)(a)). This is widely referred to as the 'social ground'. Notice that it has two limbs: the comparative risk to the pregnant woman and the comparative risk to any existing children in her family. Most abortions in England and Wales are performed under the first limb: 98% in 2021 with only 0.4% under the second limb.[70] The first limb is generally regarded as satisfied, at least within the first 12 weeks, by the inherent risks of pregnancy.[71] But removal for the purposes of ectogestation differs from standard medical termination of an early pregnancy. The experiments with the biobag and EVE involved removal of a fetus by caesarean section. This is a major operation involving cutting through the abdominal wall. It exposes pregnant patients to risks of haemorrhage, infection and damage to their abdominal organs: 5–9% of caesareans lead to serious side-effects and the risk of maternal mortality is between 2 and 11 times higher than for vaginal delivery.[72] A caesarean will also often require delivery of any future child in the same way and leave a scar.[73] What is more, the risk of serious complications is even greater if undertaken mid-gestation – it requires the

[68] See *R v Woollin* [1999] 1 AC 82, 96 (Lord Steyn).
[69] s 1(1). One certification suffices where the termination is 'immediately necessary to save the life or to prevent grave permanent injury to the physical or mental health of the pregnant woman': s 1(4).
[70] See DHSC 2022.
[71] See Laurie, Harmon & Dove 2019, 9.62 and Pattinson 2020, esp 247–248. See also WHO 2012, 113 (medical abortion up to 9 weeks) and 114 (medical abortion between 9 and 12 weeks).
[72] See Michalowski 1999, 122.
[73] See Robertson 1983, 454.

opening up of the upper part of the uterus, rather than just the lower section as would usually occur at or near term.[74] Thus, the risk to the pregnant person from a mid-gestation caesarean would be very likely to outweigh the risk from continued pregnancy, preventing reliance on the first limb of section 1(1)(a).[75]

Abortion is also permitted up to birth to save the life of the woman, to prevent 'grave permanent injury' to the physical or mental health of the pregnant woman, or where there is a 'substantial risk' that the child would be born 'seriously handicapped' (section 1(1)(b)–(d)). In 2021, the first two of these grounds together accounted for only 0.009% of abortions in England and Wales and the fetal abnormality ground accounted for only 1.6%.[76] Complications arise if these provisions are to be invoked to support removing a fetus to complete its gestation in an ectogestative device. If that removal would otherwise be contrary to the 1861 or 1929 Acts, then these grounds would need to support removal undertaken in a way that maximises fetal survival even though removal by standard surgical abortion would be likely to pose fewer risks to the life and physical health of the pregnant woman. Consider the complexities raised for each of these three provisions in turn. The chosen procedure would hinder the termination judged to be 'necessary' to prevent grave permanent injury to the physical or mental health of the pregnant woman, as per section 1(1)(b). It might not reduce the risk to the life of the pregnant woman in comparison to her continued pregnancy (as per section 1(1)(c)) and, even if it did, it would be likely to pose a greater physical risk to her life over standard surgical abortion. Finally, the chosen procedure would not ordinarily be addressed to preventing the birth of a child with 'such physical or mental abnormalities as to be seriously handicapped', as per section 1(1)(d).[77]

What about the possibility of relying on these grounds if removal from an ectogestative device requires a defence to the offences in the 1861 and 1929 Acts? With the exception of the second limb of the first ground (the comparative risk to 'any existing children of her family') and the fourth ground (the risk of 'physical or mental abnormalities'), the grounds for termination of pregnancy require risk to the life or health of the individual carrying the fetus ('the pregnant woman'). The fourth ground requires consideration of the traits that would be displayed by the child if it were 'born'. Thus, the 1967 Act assumes the fetus to be developing inside the body of a pregnant individual and makes no reference to continued gestation outside of that body. Section 1, after all, provides for the 'medical termination of *pregnancy*', rather than the medical termination of *gestation*.

Again, these issues are considered in the hypothetical case below (4.6.2).

[74] See NCOB 2006, 67 (n 5) and Stefano et al 2020, 283 (n 49).

[75] See Alghrani & Brazier 2011, 75.

[76] See DHSC 2022. There were 214,256 abortions for residents of England and Wales, of which only 20 were performed under the first of these grounds (alone or with other grounds) and 836 were performed under the second.

[77] I 'say' ordinarily' to leave open the possibility that partial ectogestation might, in some future circumstances, present opportunities for treatment options not available if the fetus continues *in utero*.

4.3.5. The Born Alive Threshold

A living human child is protected by the law of murder and manslaughter. It will suffice if injury is deliberately or grossly negligently inflicted in the womb as long as it causes death after the child is born alive.[78] Similarly, a civil action can be brought in the name of a child that has been born alive with disabilities as a result of negligently inflicted injuries in the womb.[79] Such legal rights and protections are said to 'crystallise' at the point of being 'born alive', before which the fetus is said not to be a 'legal person'.[80]

Two types of case have come before the courts: those where the interests of the fetus are directly pitted against those of the pregnant woman, and those where fetal and maternal interests are aligned on the specific facts. The *first type* of case includes those where (a) the putative father seeks to prevent a woman from terminating her pregnancy,[81] (b) it is claimed that the pregnant woman's conduct during pregnancy is harming or has harmed the fetus[82] and (c) the pregnant woman refuses to consent to a caesarean section, or other invasive treatment in late pregnancy, considered by doctors to be in the fetus' interests.[83] The *second type* of case includes those (i) where a tortious action is being brought in the name of the fetus or later child against a third party for allegedly causing harm to the claimant when in the womb[84] or (ii) a prosecution is brought against a third party for allegedly causing harm to the fetus or later child when in the womb.[85]

The crystallising effect of being 'born alive' stems from several pragmatic concerns. First, it generally operates as a clear and easily identifiable threshold. As Romanis points out, 'it is usually easy to observe life in the new born without complex diagnostic tools' and 'before the advent of techniques likes ultrasound, [birth was] the most reliable confirmation that a developing human existed'.[86] Secondly, this threshold enables judges to avoid dealing with a direct conflict between the legal rights granted to the fetus and the pregnant person. Even in

[78] *AG's Reference (No 3 of 1994)* [1998] AC 245.

[79] Congenital Disabilities (Civil Liability) Act 1976 and *Burton v Islington HA* [1993] QB 204.

[80] On 'crystallisation' see *C v S* [1988] QB 135, 140 (Heilbron J at first instance); *Burton v Islington HA* [1993] QB 204, esp 215 (Phillips J at first instance and Dillion LJ in the Court of Appeal, citing with approval dicta from the Australian case of *Watt v Rama* [1972] VR 353).

[81] *Paton v BPAS* [1979] QB 276; *C v S* [1988] 1 QB 135.

[82] *Re F (in utero)* [1988] Fam 122 (application to make the fetus a ward of court – discussed below); *D (a minor) v Berkshire County Council* [1987] 1 All ER 20 (application to take a child into care having regard to the mother's drug use during pregnancy).

[83] eg *Re MB* [1997] 2 FLR 426; *St George's Healthcare NHS Trust v S* [1999] Fam 26. A recent case has considered the refusal of transportation to hospital for birth due to agoraphobia: see *A NHS Foundation Trust v An Expectant Mother* [2021] EWCOP 33 and the discussion in Neal 2021.

[84] *Rance v Mid-Downs HA* [1991] (action against a health authority and doctor for negligently failing to diagnose the child's disability when a fetus); *Burton v Islington HA* [1993] QB 204 (action against Health Authority for alleged negligence during pregnancy resulting in birth with numerous disabilities).

[85] *AG's Reference (No 3 of 1994)* [1998] AC 245 (discussed below).

[86] Romanis 2020a, 100.

the second type of case, where the interests of the pregnant person and the fetus happen to be aligned on the facts, any rights granted to the fetus could potentially misalign their interests or create a direct conflict in other cases. As Alghrani and Brazier put it, 'The major issue at stake is the woman's control of her body.'[87]

Re F (in utero) is an example of the first type of case (category (b)).[88] In this case, the Court of Appeal refused to make a fetus a ward of court to protect it from its mentally disturbed, nomadic carrier. A crucial reason for concluding that the fetus lacked the legal personality necessary to make it a ward of court was said to be that any other conclusion was 'bound to create conflict between the existing legal interests of the mother and those of the unborn child and that it is most undesirable that this should occur'.[89]

AG's Reference (No 3 of 1994) is an example of the second type of case (category (ii)).[90] This was a case in which the House of Lords had to consider whether the crimes of murder or manslaughter could be committed where unlawful injury was inflicted on a fetus *in utero* or on the person carrying the fetus. Lord Mustill (with whom their Lordships agreed) declared that

> it is established beyond doubt for the criminal law, as for the civil law … that the child en ventre sa mère [*in utero*] does not have a distinct human personality, whose extinguishment gives rise to any penalties or liabilities at common law.[91]

His Lordship reasoned that the fetus was

> an organism *sui generis* lacking at this stage the entire range of characteristics both of the mother to which it is physically linked and of the complete human being which it will later become.[92]

The House of Lords concluded that only once the child has been 'born alive' could prenatal injuries support criminal liability for homicide or grievous bodily harm.

The reasoning in the *AG's Reference* case (to the effect that the fetus has legal status but lacks the full rights attributable to possession of legal personality) was reiterated by the Court of Appeal when considering the refusal of treatment in late pregnancy. In *St George's Healthcare*, Judge LJ declared: 'Whatever else it may be a 36-week foetus is not nothing: if viable it is not lifeless and it is certainly human'.[93] Yet, a woman who satisfies the standard adult test for legal capacity has the right to refuse treatment for herself or her fetus, because: 'Of themselves the perceived needs of the foetus did not provide the necessary justification' for restricting the pregnant woman's autonomy.[94] While (in this case in the High Court and in other cases) the courts have displayed a noticeable willingness to rule that the pregnant

[87] Alghrani & Brazier 2011, 55.
[88] [1988] Fam 122.
[89] [1988] Fam 122, 137 (May LJ).
[90] [1998] AC 245.
[91] [1998] AC 245, 261.
[92] [1998] AC 245, 255–256.
[93] [1999] Fam 26, 45.
[94] [1999] Fam 26, 50.

woman before the court happens to fail the capacity test,[95] the Court of Appeal's reasoning affirms that any legal interests possessed by the fetus cannot formally override those of the legal person in whose body it resides until it has been separated as a result of being born alive.

The moment of birth has other legal consequences. The Birth and Deaths Registration Act 1953 requires registration of the 'birth of every child born in England and Wales' with different particulars applying for 'live-births' and 'still-births' (section 1(1)). A live-birth is defined to mean 'the birth of a child born alive' (section 41). A still-born child is defined in the same section as one that 'has issued forth from its mother' after the 24th week of pregnancy and 'which did not at any time after being completely expelled from its mother breathe or show any other signs of life'. It follows that a very early human could be expelled from the womb without it becoming registrable as either a live-birth or a still-birth: where it displays no signs of life following miscarriage before the 24th week of pregnancy. This Act raises some interesting questions, because if the technology develops to the point whereby a gestateling can be placed into an ectogestative device (as opposed to a neonatal incubator) and survive, it would not 'breathe' through its lungs (it would receive umbilical oxygenation) but it would display other signs of life.

The relevance of breathing to being 'born alive' was directly considered in *C v S* and *Rance v Mid-Downs HA*, as mentioned in 4.3.3. Lord Donaldson in *C v S* considered a child not to be capable of being born alive under the 1929 Act 'if incapable of breathing either naturally or with the aid of a ventilator'.[96] Brooke J in *Rance v Mid-Downs HA* expressed himself differently, declaring that a child was capable of being born alive within the meaning of the Act only when it had the capacity to breathe 'through its own lungs alone, without deriving any of its living or power of living by or through any connection with its mother'.[97] Brooke J's could be read as setting a higher threshold, whereby the words 'own lungs alone' are taken to exclude breathing with the support of a ventilator. In my view, however, Brooke J was merely intending to exclude the derivation of oxygen from 'any connection with its mother', because children and adults breathing on ventilators are unequivocally regarded as alive unless and until they suffer cardiovascular or brain stem death.[98] In any event, *C v S* was a decision of the Court of Appeal.

Yet, could these two cases be regarded as inconclusive on whether breathing is required at all to be born alive? Both decisions were decided prior to any realistic prospect of partial ectogestation. *C v S* was decided *ex tempore* with full reasons to

[95] See further Pattinson 2018, 153–157 and Pattinson 2020, ch 5.
[96] [1988] QB 135, 151.
[97] [1991] 1 QB 587, 621.
[98] See also Alghrani & Brazier 2011, 72 (who express the opinion that Lord Donaldson's view 'represents the current law') and Romanis 2020a, 110 (who argues that any other view leads to 'illogical conclusions').

be given later, which did not occur in light of leave to appeal being declined by the House of Lords.[99] This question is addressed in the hypothetical appeal in 4.6.2.

The legal significance attached to 'birth' presents complex questions beyond the issues raised by future ectogestation. In 2016, it was reported that a baby in Texas, United States had been 'born twice'.[100] During Margaret Boemer's pregnancy it was discovered that her fetus had a large tumour on its tailbone that was diverting the blood supply and putting strain on its heart. Innovative surgery was performed at 23 weeks and five days' pregnancy, during which the fetus was surgically removed from the womb for 20 minutes (while remaining attached to the umbilical cord) and afterwards placed back into the womb to continue gestating. LynLee Boemer was later delivered healthy at 36 weeks via caesarean section.

Romanis argues that complexities are raised by a conclusion either way on whether the fetus' temporary removal from the womb for surgery amounts to its being born alive.[101] If it does, Romanis argues, it would seem to mean that the fetal-operatee has legal personality that is not lost until its death.[102] That would grant the fetal-operatee legal rights (both during surgery and when later returned to the womb) that exceed those granted to other fetuses at the same stage of development. If its temporary removal does not amount to it being born alive, then during the surgery it lacks the criminal and civil law protection granted to legal persons for negligently inflicted harm. It would also need to be explained what is different about its removal for surgery as opposed to its later delivery, especially since the case law indicates that a baby can be legally born alive even when still attached by the umbilical cord.[103] The hypothetical judgment in 4.6.2 is sensitive to these issues.

4.4. A Future Scenario

We have seen that ectogestative research is still in its early stages, currently focused on small samples of non-human animals and taking place in countries other than the United Kingdom (see 4.2). Extensive research is still required and the first experiments on humans are far more likely to benefit future fetuses than those first subjects.[104] My scenario envisages significant developments in both non-human and human partial ectogestative technology and, crucially, its move into clinical application. It thereby evades Singer and Wells' 'catch-22' situation, whereby it is declared unethical to use the technology on humans until it is sufficiently safe, and it is not sufficiently safe until it has been used on humans.[105] Instead, my scenario

[99] [1988] QB 135, 152.
[100] See Scutti 2016.
[101] See Romanis 2020a.
[102] See Romanis 2020a, 104–105.
[103] See *R v Crutchely* (1837) 7 Car & P 814 and *R v Trilloe* (1842) Car & M 650, discussed in Romanis 2020a, 106. These cases noticeably predate the Infant Life (Preservation) Act 1929.
[104] See Romanis 2020b, 393.
[105] See Singer & Wells 1984, 145.

is focused on a situation in which the technology has already been shown to be clinically effective in two other jurisdictions. I envisage a situation in which there are four children who are the products of successful ectogestation after removal from the womb at between 21 and 23 weeks of pregnancy: two in China and two in Sweden. I have named these countries for ease of reference in the judgment below and, to repeat myself, I should not be taken to be making predictions as to the likely future of the technology. The first genome-edited humans were born in China and the first live-birth following transplantation of a womb from a living donor occurred in Sweden, but these are completely different technologies and the animal experiments outlined earlier took place in the United States (the biobag experiments), Australia (the EVE experiments) and Israel (the Weizmann experiments).

Any future success is likely to build upon failure. If I were to engage in crystal ball gazing, I would predict that any successes in human partial ectogestation will be preceded by many fetal deaths. The primary purpose of this book is, however, to apply contextual legal idealism to situations where biomedical developments have left existing law behind, so for the purposes of this chapter I will simply specify that biomedical science has reached the point where there have been twice as many successful clinical applications as failures.

Many criticisms have been legitimately directed at the United Kingdom for being slow to properly equip its regulatory framework for future developments in human reproduction. It notably took over a decade for the UK to enact the Human Fertilisation and Embryology Act 1990 in response to the birth of Louise Brown, the first IVF baby. When the 1990 Act was amended in 2008 by an Act with the same title, academics noted that the UK's approach was largely to focus on what had already occurred, rather than to prepare for what was coming next.[106] But, despite this, the UK was still at the vanguard of countries legislating in this area in 1990 and the 2008 Act did provide for the secondary legislation that would later permit mitochondrial replacement therapy, making the UK the first country in the world to do so (see 3.3.2). This leads me to suggest that another unlikely feature of my scenario is that it envisages a situation in which the UK has failed to enact any legislation in response to partial ectogestation reaching the point of successful clinical application. Nonetheless, the hypothetical case below (4.6) is addressed to the law as it is at the time of writing this chapter, while imagining a context in which biomedical science has moved on.

4.5. Application of the PGC

Chapter 2 examined the justification and application of the PGC. This is a categorical moral principle requiring agents to act in accord with the generic rights

[106] See eg Alghrani 2009 and 2018.

possessed by all agents. The *generic rights* are claim-rights under the will conception of rights to whatever is needed to act at all or with general chances of success: will-rights to the *generic needs*.

Since the PGC is categorical and it is not strictly possible to know whether another is an agent, all others must be treated according to strict moral precaution (2.3.1). It follows that those others who display sufficient characteristics and behaviour to be meaningfully treated as agents (*agent-behavers*) must be treated as possessing generic rights. Those others who display only some of the characteristics and behaviour expected of agents (*partial agent-behavers*) must be treated as possessing interest-rights to the generic needs. Where there is a conflict of duties, agent-behavers have full moral status and partial agent-behavers have lower moral status. This lower moral status is proportionate to the closeness to being an agent-behaver. This is because the closer a partial agent-behaver is to being an agent-behaver, the fewer or less implausible speculative hypotheses are needed to explain why it does not display the characteristics and behaviour expected of an agent.

A healthy human embryo or fetus is a partial agent-behaver with a feasible developmental pathway or trajectory for becoming an agent-behaver. It is, in this sense, a potential agent-behaver. But its increased status (over a partial agent-behaver that is equivalent save for the absence of such a developmental trajectory) is not due to treating potentiality as actuality. It is due to its comparatively greater closeness to being an agent-behaver. For this reason, Holm and Coggon display misunderstanding when they criticise this precautionary thesis on the basis that 'it is not clear that general potential to become an agent has any bearing on something's being an agent'.[107] It is true that potentially being X is not equivalent to being X, whether X is 'being an agent' or 'being an agent-behaver'. But the claim being made is very different: it is that potential to become an agent-behaver – in the sense of a feasible developmental pathway to becoming an agent-behaver in the future – has a bearing on closeness to being an agent-behaver. A germinating acorn is not an oak tree; but it is closer to being an oak tree than a tomato seed is to being an oak tree.

Since the moral status of the developing human is proportional to its closeness to being an agent-behaver, it follows that, all things being equal, the fetus is entitled to greater protection than an embryo and a late fetus is entitled to greater protection than an early fetus. Granting moral status to the fetus renders its ability to survive outside the womb – its *viability* – relevant to the moral assessment of abortion (see 4.2.2). The comparative status of the pregnant individual and the fetus then matters, because the burden of the process for removal from the womb for the pregnant individual is almost inevitably increased if it is performed in such a way as to maximise the fetus' chances of survival. The partial ectogestation experiments using the biobag and EVE involved removal of a fetus by caesarean section. This is a major operation carrying significant risks that are magnified if the procedure is undertaken mid-gestation. Premature expulsion by vaginal delivery is sometimes

[107] Holm & Coggon 2008, 302.

compatible with fetal survival, but only at a later stage, because it is likely to trigger transition from fetal to neonate circulation and digestion, so the emerging human would be likely to require neonatal care, rather than ectogestation. In any case, maximising the chances of survival for the emerging human during premature labour is likely to require additional interventions not directed to the interests of the pregnant patient, such as transfer to a neonatal facility and intramuscular injections of steroids.[108] The continued existence of biological offspring due to unwanted partial ectogestation could also have (difficult to predict) social and psychological consequences for the biological parents.[109] Thus, even if partial ectogestation becomes clinically feasible, it could not become a precondition for the termination of pregnancy unless the fetus' moral interests override those of the pregnant patient.

Elsewhere I have considered the moral relevance of qualitatively different levels of displayed behaviour and characteristics.[110] Bricks and tables cannot meaningfully be granted even interest-rights, because they exhibit none of the behavioural capacities of agent-behavers.[111] Bacteria and other very simple organisms can meaningfully be granted interest-rights but protecting even their most basic presumed generic needs (their lives) would threaten the lives of all others. Thus, in practice, those rights must be presumptively regarded as overridden by *any* generic need of an agent-behaver. The developing fetus initially has only a marginal status but that status increases with gestational development. Neural and brain developments are of significantly greater relevance than, say, developments to the respiratory or digestive system. The person within whose body a fetus is gestating will almost invariably have greater moral status and will usually be an agent-behaver. Balancing PGC-relevant considerations here is complex, but the most plausible conclusion is that even just before birth, *all* the basic generic needs of a pregnant agent-behaver should be presumptively treated as at least as valuable as the fetus' life.[112]

In many situations, the pregnant agent-behaver will be properly considered to be *competent* to make decisions with regard to what is to happen to her body.[113] If that is the case, then she may waive her own generic rights and thereby permit partial ectogestation irrespective of any additional burdens it places upon her body. Since those additional burdens usually involve basic generic harm and priority is to be given to the pregnant person's basic generic needs over those of the fetus, partial ectogestation cannot be required against her competent will. It also follows

[108] See Stefano et al 2020, 283 (n 53).
[109] See eg Räsänen 2017 for three arguments for a right to the death of a fetus and criticisms of those arguments in Kaczor 2018 and Blackshaw & Rodger 2018.
[110] See Pattinson 2002, 71–75.
[111] See also Beyleveld & Pattinson 2010, 262–363.
[112] See also Rodrigues & van den Berg 2012, 153–154.
[113] On competence, see Pattinson 2018, 77–81.

that when dealing with an agent-behaver who lacks competence to make a decision of this type, removing the fetus to protect her basis generic needs need not, in many circumstances, require a removal procedure designed to maximise the fetus' chances of surviving removal. But future developments in partial ectogestation will, by enabling separation of fetal removal from fetal death, extend the circumstances in which termination in mid- to late pregnancy is justifiable even when not seeking to avoid basic generic harm to the pregnant person from the continued pregnancy.

Beyond these points, the nature of the *indirect application* of the PGC is such that there could be many defensible differences in regulatory responses in different jurisdictions (see 2.3.2). The hypothetical case below is presented within the future scenario outlined in 4.4. It does not raise many of the issues that would be relevant to a full ethical and legal discussion of ectogestation. It involves a situation in which the PGC would permit the pregnant woman in question to access ectogestative technology, yet the positive law is outdated and does not explicitly permit direct consideration of many of the relevant moral variables. My judge focuses on delivering an outcome that best accords with her competent and good faith attempt to give effect to the PGC in the context in which she operates.

4.6. Hypothetical Case

This chapter considers a hypothetical application for a declaration to confirm the lawfulness of removing a fetus from the womb at 22 weeks for the purpose of transferring it into an ectogestative device. The imagined case is referred to as *Re B*.

4.6.1. Explanation of the Scenario

By its nature, an imagined case could come before any level of court. It seems to me, however, that the complexities presented by the existing law are such that a future case would be unlikely to be regarded as satisfactorily addressed by a decision at first instance. I was therefore tempted to imagine this case arising before the UK Supreme Court, but on reflection concluded that the judgment could better illustrate the application of contextual legal idealism if it were presented as a judgment of the Court of Appeal of England and Wales. Setting the case at this level requires my imaginary judge to deal with previous decisions that cannot be formally overruled within the judicially declared parameters of the doctrine of precedent. Previous cases have routinely declared that all courts below the highest appeal court are bound by its decisions[114] and the Court of Appeal's decisions bind

[114] On the highest appeal court see *Practice Statement (Judicial Precedent)* [1966] 1 WLR 1234 (declaring willingness to depart from *London Tramways Company v London County Council* [1898] AC 375) and *Austin v Southwark LBC* [2010] UKSC 28, esp [25]. See also *Willers v Joyce* [2016] UKSC 44, esp [5].

the court itself (with narrow exceptions) and all courts below.[115] While *stare decisis* does not, in practice, operate as a set of absolute rules, it can challenge a judge to explain and justify her interpretation and response to previous decisions.[116]

My judge is referred to below as Lady Athena, Master of the Rolls. In line with my analysis above, her task will be to ensure that interpretative and developmental options are utilised to grant an appropriate level of protection to both the pregnant individual and the fetus/gestateling. Since existing rules and rulings constrain the range of legal principles that may be discerned from the law, some options that would have been available to an appeal court in the past or would now be available to Parliament are not readily available to Lady Athena. One example concerns the direct alignment of the language of legal status with the PGC. In *Revisiting Landmark Cases in Medical Law*, I considered the options that were available to earlier appeal courts and made the case for a different approach to that adopted in the appeal before the House of Lords in *Airedale NHS Trust v Bland*.[117] In my revisiting of *Bland*, Lady Athena held that an adult patient in a 'permanent vegetative state' has a legal status less than that of a patient who displays evidence of ability to feel pain, so the legal test to be applied when determining the lawfulness of withdrawing life-sustaining care to such a patient should weigh overall interests, rather than adhere to the patient's best interests alone.[118] I also considered the case for granting a lower legal status to one of the twins in *Re A*, a case involving the lethal separation of conjoined twins.[119] The actual decisions in these cases achieved a consistent result but adhered to the language of full legal status, and the actual reasoning in *Bland* is now firmly embedded in the law, thereby constraining the options open to Lady Athena in the hypothetical appeal below.

In practice, if prospective partial ectogestation were to come before a court, many interested bodies would seek to present submissions. But addressing this complexity in the judgment below would require both consideration of issues beyond those examined in this chapter and guesswork as to which bodies would seek to present submissions or would come into existence as a result of the arrival of ectogestative advances in other countries. Some educated predictions could be made on the basis of the legislation on which declarations would be sought. I would, for example, predict that submissions would be made by the Secretary of State for Health and Social Care or even the Human Fertilisation and Embryology Authority. I have, however, chosen to keep matters simple and advance legal arguments as if presented by only two legal teams: counsel on behalf of an anonymous NHS Trust and counsel on behalf of the Official Solicitor. The possibility of the Official Solicitor acting as amicus curiae is suggested by previous cases.[120]

[115] *Davis v Johnson* [1979] AC 264, 324 and 328 (approving *Young v Bristol Aeroplane* [1944] KB 718) and *RJM* [2008] UKHL 63.
[116] See further 2.4.2 and Pattinson 2018, ch 6 (6.2).
[117] [1993] AC 789 (hereafter *Bland*).
[118] See Pattinson 2018, ch 4 (esp 4.5).
[119] [2001] Fam 147 and Pattinson 2018, 6.4.1.
[120] See, in particular, *Re F (in utero)* [1988] Fam 122, 124 and *C v S* [1988] QB 135, 147.

Similarly, the NHS Trust is no more than an imaginary applicant – an application of this type would perhaps be more likely to be privately funded and brought by a private provider. Also, again driven by a desire to avoid distracting complexity, I have departed from the usual judicial practice of referring to counsel by name.

The facts specified in the case below build on my future scenario on developments in ectogestative science. I have provided a brief backstory in which a court application could be plausibly triggered. To provide time for the clinical team to make the necessary arrangements and for the case to be fully argued, my backstory is one in which a decision is not required in an emergency presented by the imminent death of the fetus or pregnant woman. It is nonetheless intended to be a situation in which it is plausible that a clinical team would be willing to assist the pregnant woman and therefore involves an element (namely, a prior rape) that is not in any way relevant to Lady Athena's reasoning. It is also assumed, as stated in paragraph 8 in the judgment below, that various extraneous legal matters were satisfactorily addressed at first instance.

I have adopted various stylistic features below that accord with recent law reports, particularly with regard to punctuation and referencing. In this vein, the judgment departs from the etymologically correct spelling of 'fetus', because case reports more typically spell it with an 'o' or diphthong.[121] Further, this judgment continues my practice of using names from Greek mythology: Apollo J is the name given to the judge in the High Court.[122]

[121] On the case for preferring 'fetus' (which is now also standard practice in the medical literature), see Williams 1994, 71 (n 1), and Grace 1999, 57.

[122] Apollo was one of the children of Leto, a Greek goddess of motherhood.

4.6.2. Re B (Court of Appeal)

Lady Athena MR

Introduction

1. B became pregnant as a result of being raped. She does not want to be pregnant but is ethically opposed to the termination of early human life. She has identified what she hopes is a way out of her dilemma. Elsewhere, foetuses at 21 weeks have been successfully removed from the womb and gestated outside the body (a process known as "partial ectogestation"). B has found a clinical team in this country willing to continue the gestation of her foetus in what they refer to as the Advanced Ectogestative Device or Aed (which is intended to be pronounced like "aide"). That clinical team are, however, only willing to assist B once her pregnancy has reached 22 weeks' gestation and then only if the lawfulness of what is proposed is confirmed by a court declaration.
2. B and the NHS Trust at which the procedure would be performed brought an application seeking declarations to the effect that the procedure would be lawful if undertaken at 22 weeks of pregnancy. B was 10 weeks into her pregnancy at the time of that first hearing. The matter came before Apollo J, who invited the Official Solicitor to instruct counsel as amicus curiae. Apollo J made various declarations and concluded that what is proposed is unlawful. This appeal has been brought by the applicant NHS Trust.
3. For the reasons I detail below, I would allow this appeal. In my judgment, the proposed procedures could be lawfully performed and various declarations made by Apollo J should be set aside.

The facts

4. It is common ground that B's pregnancy was in the tenth week at the time of the hearing before Apollo J and in its 12th week at the time of the hearing before this Court. There is more than one way of measuring the duration of a pregnancy. The convention is to treat the first day of the woman's last menstrual period as the start date, which generally errs on the side of caution, as a pregnancy will usually have started two weeks later. This convention is routinely adopted by clinicians for the purposes of calculating time limits under the Abortion Act 1967 and the Births and Deaths Registration Act 1953, which is a practice endorsed by this Court in *R (BPAS) v Secretary of State for Health and Social Care* [2020] EWCA Civ 355. The clinical team are satisfied that the evidence supports its application to B's pregnancy.
5. Ectogestative devices of the type proposed here have been successfully used in other jurisdictions. The first beneficiary of this technology is a child who successfully transitioned from ectogestative to standard neonatal care in China over six months ago and continues to develop in accordance with expectations for a child of her age. Since that time a further three children have successfully emerged from ectogestation: another in China and two others in Sweden. There are therefore four children who are the products of successful partial ectogestation, removed from the womb at between weeks' 21 and 23 of pregnancy. The team proposing to undertake the procedure in this case is to be assisted by the leader of the Swedish team and consider it to be more reliable at 22 weeks than earlier.

6. This is new technology and not all attempted partial ectogestation has been successful. The first successful use was preceded by two unsuccessful attempts to utilise ectogestation and the second attempt in Sweden was similarly unsuccessful. In contrast to the case before this Court, however, previous transfers of a foetus to an ectogestative device have taken place in emergency situations in which the alternative was foetal death. The evidence, accepted by Apollo J and not questioned before this Court, is that the chances of B's foetus surviving are significantly higher on account of removal being elective rather than conditioned by an emergency. There is, however, no way to eliminate the risk that the procedure will fail, because the foetus will be only just over halfway through a full gestative term of 40 weeks.

Apollo J's declarations

7. Apollo J considered "the application of legislation enacted in the nineteenth and twentieth centuries to procedures that would have been considered science fiction at the turn of this century". He concluded that the proposed removal of the foetus at 22 weeks for transfer into an ectogestative device was unlawful and made several declarations. This appeal is concerned with the four declarations below.

   (1) What is proposed does not involve keeping or using an embryo outside the body, contrary to section 3 of the Human Fertilisation and Embryology Act 1990 *(the 1990 Act)*, as amended by the Human Fertilisation and Embryology Act 2008.
   (2) What is proposed involves unlawfully and intentionally attempting to procure a miscarriage, contrary to section 58 of the Offence against the Person Act 1861 *(the 1861 Act)*.
   (3) What is proposed does not give rise to a defence under section 1 of the Abortion Act 1967 *(the 1967 Act)*, as amended by the 1990 Act.
   (4) If what is proposed were to take place, the foetus at the relevant time would not become a "legal person" by virtue of being "born alive" at the point of its transfer into the ectogestative device.

8. No appeal is sought with regard to the judge's additional declarations on obtaining regulatory approval for use of the Aed, B's capacity to provide suitably informed consent and various other matters. Before addressing the four declarations listed above, I will first consider the principles of statutory interpretation.

Interpreting legislation

9. It is, as Lady Arden and Lord Burrows stated in *Rittson-Thom v Oxfordshire CC* [2021] UKSC 13 at para 9, a "well-settled view that the courts should adopt a purposive approach to statutory interpretation where possible". The previous cases include two decisions of the House of Lords on the proper interpretation of the 1990 Act: *R (On the Application of Bruno Quintavalle) v Secretary of State for Health* [2003] UKHL 13 and *R (On the Application of Josephine Quintavalle) v HFEA* [2005] UKHL 28. In the first of these cases, Lord Bingham at para 8, held:

   > "The court's task, within the permissible bounds of interpretation, is to give effect to Parliament's purpose. So the controversial provisions should be read in the context of the statute as a whole, and the statute as a whole should be read in the historical context of the situation which led to its enactment."

   Lord Steyn, who expressed himself similarly at para 21, explicitly asked at para 22 "whether it is appropriate to construe the 1990 Act in the light of the new scientific knowledge". It was appropriate, his Lordship reasoned, because an aim of the 1990 Act was to be "always speaking", rather than merely to deal "with a particular grievance or problem". His Lordship concluded that the 1990 Act was to "be construed in the light of contemporary scientific knowledge". Thus, Parliament's purposes are to be identified by reference to the statute as a whole and the context of its enactment may require its provisions to be read broadly in the light of subsequent scientific developments.

10. In my view, identifying the purposes of a statute requires discernment of the principles that explain and justify its provisions. Where there is a complex web of overlapping legislation, the discerned principles are those that explain and justify these statutes as a whole. The three statutes relevant to this appeal are directly linked: the 1990 Act amends the 1967 Act, which provides defences to the relevant offences in the 1861 Act.

Question 1: Does what is proposed involve keeping or using an embryo outside the body after 14 days or the development of the primitive streak, contrary to section 3 of the 1990 Act?

11. This question concerns the proper interpretation of sections 1 and 3 of the 1990 Act, as amended:

"*Meaning of 'embryo'* …

(1) In this Act …—

(a) embryo means a live human embryo …, and
(b) references to an embryo include an egg that is in the process of fertilisation or is undergoing any other process capable of resulting in an embryo.

…

(3) This Act, so far as it governs the keeping or use of an embryo, applies only to keeping or using an embryo outside the human body. …

Prohibitions in connection with embryos

3. …

(1A) No person shall keep or use an embryo except—

(a) in pursuance of a licence, or
(b) in the case of—
  (i) the keeping, without storage, of an embryo intended for human application, or
  (ii) the processing, without storage, of such an embryo, in pursuance of a third party agreement.

…

(3) A licence cannot authorise—

(a) keeping or using an embryo after the appearance of the primitive streak,

…

(4) For the purposes of subsection (3)(a) above, the primitive streak is to be taken to have appeared in an embryo not later than the end of the period of 14 days beginning with the day on which the process of creating the embryo began, not counting any time during which the embryo is stored."

12. Counsel instructed by the Official Solicitor points out that the enactment of the 1990 Act was stimulated by the report of the Committee of Inquiry into Human Fertilisation and Embryology, which was chaired by Baroness Warnock and published in 1984 (Cmnd 9314). That report stated that its underlying view was that "the embryo of the human species ought to have a special status" and should accordingly be "afforded some protection in law" (para 11.7). It went on to express the view that the technology for "developing embryos in an artificial environment (ectogenesis)" was "well into the future" and "our recommendation is that the growing of a human embryo *in vitro* beyond fourteen days should be a criminal offence" (para 12.7).
13. The principle that the human embryo ought to be accorded some legal protection on the basis of its special status is embedded in the 1990 Act. The Act's long title provides a list of its purposes, including: "to make provision in connection with human embryos and any subsequent development of such embryos" and "to prohibit certain practices in connection with embryos and gametes". The Warnock Report's recommendation of a 14-day limit on the growing of a human embryo outside the body is given effect by section 3. More specifically, section 3(3), read with 3(4), prohibits keeping or using embryos after the appearance of the primitive streak or 14 days, whichever is earlier. By virtue of section 1(3), this prohibition only applies to "keeping or using an embryo outside the human body".
14. Section 3 is thus explained and justified by the principle that the embryo's status is such that it may only be subject to interventions and development outside the body before the appearance of the primitive streak or 14 days (hereafter the specified threshold). At the time, embryos could only survive in culture for seven to nine days. The special status of the embryo was considered to be incompatible with future *in vitro* development of an embryo beyond the specified threshold. It was not considered to require additional legal protection for the embryo inside the body, which can be explained and justified on the basis that an embryo inside the womb is indirectly protected by the pregnant person's legal rights and directly protected by the 1861 Act and the Infant Life (Preservation) Act 1929.
15. The ambit of section 3 turns on what is meant by an "embryo", which section 1(1) defines to mean "a live human embryo". This definition was considered by the House of Lords in the *Bruno Quintavalle* case [2003] UKHL 13. This case was decided before the 1990 Act was amended by the 2008 Act and was concerned with whether an embryo within the 1990 Act could be created by a process other than by fertilisation. Lord Millet's analysis, at para 45, remains pertinent:

    > "... I can turn to the wording of section 1(1). The definition in para (a) is in part circular, since it contains the very term to be defined. It assumes that the reader knows what an embryo is. The purpose of the opening words of the paragraph is not to define the word 'embryo' but rather to limit it to an embryo which is (i) live and (ii) human. These are the essential characteristics which an embryo must possess if it is to be given statutory protection."

16. The amendment of the 1990 Act in 2008 introduced no provision explicitly stating when a living human embryo becomes another type of living human entity.
17. There are three options for which some support may be offered as to when a developing human ceases to be an embryo: (i) when it implants into the uterus,

(ii) when it is clinically considered to be a foetus, or (iii) when it is born alive. Apollo J declared that section 3 did not apply to what is proposed on the basis that a human entity ceases to be an embryo at the point at which it implants into the uterus. The judge held that the purpose of the 1990 Act was to make provision for otherwise unregulated activities in connection with gametes and embryos. Since, the judge reasoned, implantation marks the point at which section 58 of the 1861 Act is engaged (see paras 21–22, below), the section 3 prohibition has no application after that point.

18. At first sight, the special status principle supports the case for the early human being regarded as an embryo until it is "born alive", because it is not until that point that it receives protection outside the body as a legal person (see para 36). But the proper interpretation of the word "embryo" must also be compatible with the distinction drawn between an "embryo" and "foetus" elsewhere in the 1990 Act. The Act uses the term "foetus" in two places. The first is section 3ZA, introduced by the 2008 Act, which prohibits the provision of fertility services using "female germ cells taken or derived from an embryo or a foetus". The second is section 37(5), which makes a specific amendment to the Abortion Act 1967 to address the situation where the woman is carrying "more than one foetus". Further, section 37(1) of the 1990 Act replaces section 1(1)(a) of the 1967 Act with one permitting abortion where 'the pregnancy has not exceeded its twenty-fourth week'. Note the use of "the pregnancy" as a term encompassing both embryonic and foetal stages. Thus, the 1990 Act distinguishes between an embryo and a foetus and implies that the transition occurs between the beginning and the 24th week of the pregnancy.

19. As Lord Millett pointed out in the *Bruno Quintavalle* case, the 1990 Act assumes that "the reader knows what an embryo is". The Act similarly assumes that the reader knows when it becomes a "foetus". Those terms do indeed have standard meanings in the relevant field and the 1990 Act imports those meanings. Where fertilisation takes place outside the body, foetal development is by convention taken to begin at the eighth or ninth week after fertilisation. In a standard pregnancy, as here, foetal development is taken to begin at the start of the 10th or 11th week from the last day of the last menstrual period. This is the point at which the early human is generally expected to have a measurable heartbeat, some limb movement and some very basic nascent brain activity.

20. Since B's foetus is in the 12th week of pregnancy and what is proposed is to take place in the 22nd week of pregnancy, Apollo J was correct to conclude that it is not prohibited by section 3 of the 1990 Act. He was, however, incorrect to conclude that it had ceased to be an embryo at the point of implantation in the uterine wall, because section 37 indicates that the entity is not to be regarded as a foetus at the beginning of the pregnancy.

21. Since standard clinical usage provides alternative dates for identifying the point of transition from the embryonic to foetal stage, section 3 is to be interpreted by reference to the special status principle. In my view, that principle is consistent with section 3 being triggered by the earlier of those dates, because an entity that is successfully transferred to an ectogestative device (and therefore alive *outside the body* beyond the specified threshold) would, as discussed in paras 36–45, have the protection bestowed on a "legal person" by virtue of having been "born alive".

Question 2: Does what is proposed involve unlawfully and intentionally attempting to procure a miscarriage, contrary to section 58 of the 1861 Act?

22. Section 58 of the 1861 Act states:

> "Every woman, being with child, who, with intent to procure her own miscarriage, shall unlawfully administer to herself any poison or other noxious thing, or shall unlawfully use any instrument or other means whatsoever with the like intent, and whosoever, with intent to procure the miscarriage of any woman, whether she be or be not with child, shall unlawfully administer to her or cause to be taken by her any poison or other noxious thing, or shall unlawfully use any instrument or other means whatsoever with the like intent, shall be guilty of felony, and being convicted thereof shall be liable … to be kept in penal servitude for life."

23. The term "miscarriage" has been considered by the lower courts twice. *R v Dhingra* (1991), unreported, considered the application of section 58 to the insertion of an intrauterine device. *R (On the Application of Smeaton) v Secretary of State for Health* [2002] EWHC 610 considered the application of section 58 to the sale or use of the morning-after pill. In both cases "miscarriage" was held to relate to expulsion from the womb after implantation. In Smeaton, Munby J discerned four propositions from the case law, at para 350:

"i) the 1861 Act is an 'always speaking' Act;
ii) the word 'miscarriage' is an ordinary English word of flexible meaning which Parliament in 1861 chose to leave undefined;
iii) it should be interpreted as it would be currently understood;
iv) it should be interpreted in the light of the best current scientific and medical knowledge that is available to the court."

Munby J held, at para 351, that the "current meaning" of the word "miscarriage" was "the termination of … a post implantation-pregnancy". The judge added, at para 353, that the word "as a matter of language presupposes some prior carriage" and that was to be understood as more than presence in the body but "attachment to it in a real sense such as occurs only with implantation".

24. This reasoning was followed by Apollo J:

> "I gratefully adopt Munby J's extensive analysis of the meaning of the word 'miscarriage' and the 'four propositions' articulated at para 350 of his judgment. I am unpersuaded that recent developments require any change to Munby J's conclusion, at para 17, that 'the word "miscarriage" today means the termination of an established pregnancy'. In my view, it remains the case that there is 'no substantial dispute as to the current meaning of the word', as per Munby J at para 351.
>
> It follows that the proposed removal of the foetus at 22 weeks for transfer into an ectogestative device will involve the unlawful and intentional procurement of a miscarriage, contrary to section 58 of the 1861 Act."

25. In submissions to this Court, much was made of Munby J's "four propositions" articulated at para 350 of his judgment. We were urged to adopt a more precise interpretation of the word "miscarriage" to give effect to the intention of Parliament that the 1861 Act be "always speaking". Particular reliance was placed upon the

purposes of the Act, as summarised by Munby J in *Smeaton* at para 354: 'two of the purposes of the Act were plainly the protection of women and the protection of the unborn'. It was submitted that the purpose of protecting unborn human life would be frustrated if attempts to ensure continued survival in an ectogestative device are considered to involve the procurement of a miscarriage.

26. I am persuaded that a purpose of section 58 is to protect unborn human life. This conclusion is reinforced by consideration of Parliament's later enactment of the Infant Life (Preservation) Act 1929, the 1967 Act and 1990 Act, whose provisions are directly relevant to the ambit of section 58. In my view, these four Acts are linked by the principle that early human life is to be valued and given some protection. Such a principle explains and justifies the continued criminalisation of abortion where a defence is not available under the 1967 Act, as amended by the 1990 Act. Any ambiguity in section 58 is to be interpreted by reference to this and other principles discerned from these Acts, subject to the limits of legitimate judicial interpretation, which does not permit words to be edited out of legislation. Two interpretative suggestions were made in submissions.

27. The first suggestion was that the word "miscarriage" must now be interpreted as the termination of carriage, rather than the termination of carriage in the maternal body. It was contended that this interpretation enables relocation to another womb or to an ectogestative device to be regarded as transfer, rather than termination, of carriage. I agree with Apollo J's view that this interpretation is inconsistent with the wording of section 58. Section 58 prohibits a woman acting with "intent to procure *her own* miscarriage" and others acting "with intent to procure the miscarriage *of any woman*" (my emphasis). Thus, the relevant carriage is explicitly in the body of the pregnant person. Further, section 5(2) of the 1967 Act, read with section 6, treats procurement of a miscarriage as synonymous with "termination of the pregnancy" and "the procurement of abortion".

28. The second suggestion was that the word "miscarriage" refers to the termination of both carriage in the womb and unborn human life. This interpretation would mean that the *mens rea* of the section 58 offence is not satisfied where the intention is to end carriage in the womb without a concomitant intention to end the life of the foetus. It is common ground that an intention to end foetal life cannot be inferred from what is proposed in this application, because that outcome is neither the purpose nor foreseen as a virtually certain consequence. Apollo J rejected this interpretation of section 58:

> "There are at least three objections to interpreting 'miscarriage' to mean or imply foetal destruction: see Elizabeth Chloe Romanis, 'Artificial Womb Technology and the Choice to Gestate Ex Utero: Is Partial Ectogenesis the Business of the Criminal Law?' (2020) 28(3) *Medical Law Review* 342 at p358. First, the 1861 Act makes no reference to foetal destruction and thereby contrasts with the offence in the Infant Life (Preservation) Act 1939 of 'child destruction'. Secondly, the specific wording of section 58 refers to methods for procuring miscarriage going beyond those that cause damage to the fetus: 'any poison or other noxious thing … *or other means whatsoever*'. Thirdly, section 58 is not concerned with the impact of miscarriage on the foetus: it makes it an offence for anyone to act 'with intent to procure the miscarriage of any woman, whether she be *or be not with child*'. I consider these objections to be persuasive."

29. According to Amel Alghrani and Margaret Brazier, "What is it? Re-positioning the Fetus in the Context of Research?" (2011) 70(1) *Cambridge Law Journal* 51 at p75: "Section 58 envisages a process inevitably designed to kill the fetus". This interpretation is consistent with both the principle of protecting the unborn living human and the 1967 Act's identification of the procurement of a miscarriage as equivalent to "termination of pregnancy" and "the procurement of abortion" in sections 5(2) and 6. It also provides responses to the three objections outlined by Apollo J:

    (1) The 1861 Act makes no reference to foetal destruction because, on this interpretation, it is implicit in the notion of an unlawful act performed with the intent to procure a miscarriage.

    (2) When section 58 prohibits the unlawful use of "any poison or other noxious thing, or … any instrument or other means whatsoever" with the intent to procure a miscarriage, on this interpretation, the words "other means whatsoever" refer to any other potentially foetal-damaging means of termination that do not involve a noxious thing or instrument. This encompasses, for example, the infliction of trauma on the pregnant person's abdomen without using an instrument.

    (3) On this interpretation, section 58 prohibits the intention "to procure the miscarriage of any woman, whether she be or be not with child", because it seeks greater protection for foetuses (from person's other than the woman herself) than would be granted if it were necessary to prove that she was "with child". There are other crimes committed by an intention to bring about an outcome that was not, or could not be, brought about on the facts. The act of intentionally encouraging or assisting suicide is, for example, a crime even if the "act is not capable of encouraging or assisting suicide or attempted suicide": Suicide Act 1961, section 2A(2). Greater protection is offered against a particular outcome – such as foetal death or assisted suicide – by making it unlawful to intend to bring about that outcome by an act that is, unknown to the offender, bound to be unsuccessful.

        For the section 58 offence to be made out against the pregnant woman, she must be "with child". Setting the bar higher for the offence to be made out against the pregnant woman says something about her interests, but does not undermine the claim that one purpose of section 58 is to protect the interests of unborn living humans.

30. It has not escaped my attention that this purposive interpretation of section 58 has implications beyond the termination of carriage in the womb for the purposes of transfer into an ectogestative device. It means that the administration (including self-administration) of substances that are likely to bring about a premature birth is not prohibited by section 58 where the intention is to expel, without harming, the unborn living human.

Question 3: If what is proposed is contrary to the 1861 Act, is a defence available under the 1967 Act?

31. Section 1(1) of the 1967 Act states:

    "Subject to the provisions of this section, a person shall not be guilty of an offence under the law relating to abortion when a pregnancy is terminated by a registered medical practitioner if two registered medical practitioners are of the opinion, formed in good faith–

(a) that the pregnancy has not exceeded its twenty-fourth week and that the continuance of the pregnancy would involve risk, greater than if the pregnancy were terminated, of injury to the physical or mental health of the pregnant woman or any existing children of her family; or
(b) that the termination is necessary to prevent grave permanent injury to the physical or mental health of the pregnant woman; or
(c) that the continuance of the pregnancy would involve risk to the life of the pregnant woman, greater than if the pregnancy were terminated; or
(d) that there is a substantial risk that if the child were born it would suffer from such physical or mental abnormalities as to be seriously handicapped."

32. Section 5(2) adds that "For the purposes of the law relating to abortion, anything done with intent to procure a woman's miscarriage … is unlawfully done unless authorised by section 1 of this Act" and section 6 defines "the law relating to abortion" as including section 58 of the 1861 Act.
33. Having held that what is proposed is contrary to section 58, Apollo J considered whether it would be rendered lawful by section 1 of the 1967 Act. The judge held that it would not, unless the circumstances changed from those envisaged. It was common ground that the circumstances before the Court did not indicate that the termination fell within section 1(1)(b)–(c). In this appeal, it is contended by Counsel for the NHS Trust that *if* what is proposed were rendered unlawful by section 58, it would fall within section 1(1)(a).
34. Most abortions in England and Wales are performed under section 1(1)(a) on the basis that two doctors have certified that the pregnancy is under 24 weeks' gestation and "would involve risk, greater than if the pregnancy were terminated, of injury to the physical or mental health of the pregnant woman". It is common ground that this is satisfied in a standard early pregnancy by the general risks of pregnancy relative to the lower general risks from early medical abortion. Complexities are raised here because the method for terminating carriage involves major surgery with much greater risks than early medical abortion.
35. If B's foetus were to be removed for transfer into an ectogestative device at 22 weeks, then she would need to undergo a mid-term caesarean section. A caesarean is a major operation involving cutting through the abdominal wall and exposing the patient to risks of haemorrhage, infection and organ damage. It generally carries much greater risk of morbidity and mortality than vaginal delivery and that risk is increased if, as is proposed here, the operation takes place mid-gestation.
36. Since I have already concluded that what is proposed is not contrary to section 58 of the 1861 Act, it is not strictly necessary for me to rule on the application of section 1 of the 1967 Act. Nonetheless it is important that Apollo J's declaration on this point be set aside. It requires too much conjecture for any court to specify what two doctors will, in "good faith", judge to be the case in relation to B in ten weeks' time. A court should not, in particular, conclude that no two doctors could, at that point, judge the impact on B's medical health of the continuance of her pregnancy to be greater than the risks posed by a mid-term caesarean section.

The 1967 Act places considerable discretion in the hands of medical practitioners and it is not for the court to narrow that discretion. To do so would go beyond legitimate statutory interpretation because it would undermine another of the Act's purposes: protecting the interests of the pregnant woman.

Question 4: Once successfully transferred to an ectogestative device has a living human foetus been "born alive" and therefore become a legal person?

37. Legal personality is the mechanism by which the law recognises living human beings as possessing certain rights and protections, including standing to bring an action in tort and protection from the law of homicide. It is attained at the point of being "born alive": *Re F (In Utero)* [1988] Fam 122; *C v S* [1988] QB 135; *Burton v Islington Health Authority* [1993] QB 204; *Attorney General's Reference (No 3 of 1994)* [1998] AC 245. This common law threshold has received statutory recognition.
38. Section 1(1) of the Infant Life (Preservation) Act 1929 *(the 1929 Act)* makes it a crime for "any person who, with intent to destroy the life of a child capable of being born alive, by any wilful act [to cause] … a child to die before it has an existence independent of its mother". The meaning of "capable of being born alive" was considered by the Court of Appeal in *C v S* and by the Divisional Court in *Rance v Mid-Downs Health Authority* [1991] 1 QB 587. Lord Donaldson in *C v S*, at p151, held that a foetus was not to be capable of being born alive under the 1929 Act "if incapable of breathing either naturally or with the aid of a ventilator". Brooke J in *Rance*, at p621, held that a foetus was capable of being born alive only when it had the capacity to breathe "through its own lungs alone, without deriving any of its living or power of living by or through any connection with its mother".
39. Section 1(1) of Birth and Deaths Registration Act 1953 *(the 1953 Act)* requires the registration of the "birth of every child born in England and Wales" with different particulars applying to "live-births" and "still-births". Section 41 defines "live-birth" to mean "the birth of a child born alive", and a "still-born child" as one that "has issued forth from its mother" after the 24th week of pregnancy and "which did not at any time after being completely expelled from its mother breathe or show any other signs of life".
40. Apollo J followed the strict wording of Lord Donaldson's decision in *C v S* and held accordingly that "born alive" requires the birth of a human who is alive and breathing "either naturally or with the aid of a ventilator". An early human successfully transferred from the womb to an ectogestative device, Apollo J held, would not "breathe" through its lungs but would instead receive umbilical oxygenation. It follows that it would not become a legal person until the point at which it is transferred to an incubator or otherwise takes its first breath. Consequently, what is proposed does not satisfy the requirements of section 1(1) of the 1929 Act, not only because of the absence of the required intention but also because the foetus would not at that point be "capable of being born alive".
41. Counsel for the Official Solicitor submits that Apollo J's declarations on these points raise significant complications with regard to the legal position of a living early human in an ectogestative device. On Apollo J's view, it is submitted, an early human would be neither an embryo nor a legal person and, for the purposes of birth registration under the 1953 Act, would be neither a "live-birth" nor "still-birth" (because it has not reached the 24th week of pregnancy). If, instead, an early

human is born alive when successfully transferred to an ectogestative device, then its "live-birth" would be registrable under the 1953 Act and the continuance or removal of ectogestative treatment would need to accord with its best interests: *Yates and Gard v Great Ormond Street Hospital* [2017] EWCA Civ 410; *Re E* [2018] EWCA Civ 550.

42. Counsel for the NHS Trust supports Apollo J's declarations with regard to the 1929 Act and the born alive threshold. It was suggested that the law has long since recognised that a foetus is "an organism *sui generis*" until it is born alive: *Attorney General's Reference (No 3 of 1994)* [1998] AC 245 at para 255. The 1956 Act, it was pointed out, does not define "still-birth" as a non-live-birth and recognises that some births are not registrable as live- or still-births: no registration requirement is triggered by a birth with no displayed signs of life before the 24th week of pregnancy. Further, ectogestative technology merely increases the gap between the birth and the first breath, and there is a "live-birth" at the point when both have occurred.

43. The submissions made to this Court are therefore opposed on whether breathing following birth is a necessary or merely a sufficient condition for live-birth/being born alive (with survival in an ectogestative device being equally sufficient). There is no dispute that live-birth requires what section 1(1) of the 1929 Act refers to as "an existence independent of its mother".

44. I note that the 1956 Act's definition of a "still birth" refers to a newborn "which did not at any time after being completely expelled from its mother breathe *or show any other signs of life*" and Brooke J in *Rance*, at p621, expressly stated that he was not considering "the case of life before breathing". Further, in my view, the Court of Appeal in *C v S* cannot be regarded as having set a precedent for the conclusion that breathing is a necessary condition for being born alive. At the time, there was no feasible alternative means of oxygenation following disconnection from the maternal body, so the arguments in that case simply did not address ectogestation.

45. What is significant about "existence independent of its mother" is that it marks a point when the living human no longer resides in the body of a legal person. A crucial reason for the Court of Appeal concluding, in *Re F (In Utero)* [1988] Fam 122, that the unborn foetus lacks the legal personality necessary to make it a ward of court was said, by May LJ at p137, to be that any other conclusion was "bound to create conflict between the existing legal interests of the mother and those of the unborn child and that it is most undesirable that this should occur". To my mind, this expresses the prioritisation principle that underpins the "born alive" rule. Accordingly, a living human foetus (which has a special status) does not have the same status as a pregnant legal person, so it cannot possess legal personality while it resides in the body of a pregnant person. This principle does not apply to a living human in either an ectogestative device or an incubator. It also does not apply if the foetus is temporarily removed from the womb for surgery until it is returned to the womb: cf Elizabeth Chloe Romans, "Challenging the 'Born Alive' Threshold: Fetal Surgery, Artificial Wombs, and the English Approach to Legal Personhood" (2020) 28(1) *Medical Law Review* 93 at pp104–105.

46. It is well established that the law regards all living humans post-birth as legal persons: see eg *In Re J* [1991] Fam 33 (severely brain damaged neonate) and *Airedale NHS Trust v Bland* [1993] AC 789 (very severely brain damaged adult). While Parliament has (in the 1990 Act) legislated for an embryo outside the body,

it has not legislated for a foetus outside the body. Thus, unless and until Parliament determines otherwise, a living human in an ectogestative device must be regarded as a legal person.

Conclusion

47. I would allow this appeal. In my judgment, the removal of B's foetus at 22 weeks' of pregnancy for transfer into the Aed could be lawfully undertaken. What is proposed is not, in my view, contrary to section 3 of the Human Fertilisation and Embryology Act 1990, section 1 of the Infant Life (Preservation) Act 1929 Act or section 58 of the Offence against the Person Act 1861. Further, successful transfer would result in a live-birth, registrable as such under the Birth and Deaths Registration Act 1953.

5

Cybernetic Biohacking

5.1. Introduction

In 2017, Josiah Zayner jabbed himself with a needle in front of a large audience at a biotech conference.[1] He was seeking to be the first person to self-administer CRISPR, the genome-editing technology considered in chapter 3, to give himself bigger muscles. Zayner wants this technology to be widely available for self-administration. As he put it: 'I want to live in a world where people get drunk and instead of giving themselves tattoos, they're like, "I'm drunk, I'm going to CRISPR myself"'. Whatever effect Zayner's experiments had, as he admits, he did not become more muscular.

Self-experimentation has a long history. Barry Marshall famously demonstrated that *Helicobacter pylori* caused stomach ulcers by swallowing the bacteria himself.[2] He, along with Robin Warren, won the Nobel Prize in Physiology in 2015 for this discovery.

The actions of Zayner and Marshall were instances of *biohacking*: experimentation on oneself outside a standard medical or research context. Biohacking can be incredibly risky and, by bypassing clinical research structures, it is usually incapable of generating generalisable knowledge on the efficacy of new therapies.[3] This chapter is concerned with a subcategory of biohacking in which individuals modify their bodies by implanting devices, which I will refer to as cybernetic biohacking. A *cybernetic biohacker* is therefore someone who has a device implanted into themselves, where they develop or modify that device outside a standard clinical or research context.

This chapter first examines current biohacking and cybernetic practices (5.2). It then considers some of the challenges posed by cybernetic biohacking to the interpretation and application of the current law (5.3). The challenges examined pre-empt the scenarios imagined in 5.4, because the purpose of this book is to apply contextual legal idealism to imagined developments in biomedical technology, and biohacking (including cybernetic biohacking) is a method of experimentation, rather than a technology. This chapter's imagined scenarios involve the development and use of a specific type of implantable device, outside of a traditional

[1] See Lee 2017.
[2] See Marshall & Adams 2007.
[3] See eg the discussion in Miller & Brody 2002, 3 and Pattinson 2020, ch 11.

research or commercial environment (5.4). The PGC is then applied to these scenarios (5.5 and 5.6) and the chapter concludes by providing Explanatory Notes to a Bill designed to address the associated legal issues (5.6).

5.2. Biohacking and Cybernetic Devices

'Biohacking' is often described as citizen or do-it-yourself biology (DIYbio). Some of those engaging in such practices do not self-identify as biohackers, whereas others proudly wear the label to align themselves with the computer hacking and free software movement. As indicated above, this chapter is concerned with a subcategory of biomedical experimentation outside a standard medical or research context. My focus is not on broader concerns, sometimes also identified as biohacking, ranging from individuals making health-focused dietary and lifestyle changes[4] to those focused on attaining open access to biological data.[5] Instead, my concern is with biohacking involving the creation and implantation of smart devices, which I refer to as cybernetic biohacking. Recent years have seen a growing movement of cybernetic biohacking with diverse aims, including improvement of the biohacker's health, enhancement of their senses and extension of their other abilities.[6] Before examining the biohacking movement (5.2.2), I will first briefly explore the notion of a cyborg and cybernetic devices (5.2.1). Since my future scenarios will involve cybernetic biohacking of the brain, the third section (5.2.3) will briefly examine extant cybernetic brain technology.

5.2.1. Cybernetic Devices

A wide range of synthetic devices can be worn, attached or integrated into the human body. These include (a) artificial joints and simple prosthetics, such as hip joints and glass eyes, (b) wearable devices, such as external insulin pumps, (c) implanted devices, such as pacemakers and (d) complex prosthetics, such as the 'bionic eye'.[7] So many people now have synthetic replacements and augmentations that, Quigley and Ayihongbe declare, 'Everyday cyborgs are all around us'.[8] The term 'cyborg' was coined by Clynes and Kline[9] and became widely used in

[4] See eg Meisel 2014 and Russlan 2020.

[5] See eg Delfanti 2013, which focuses on three case studies, including the American biologist Craig Venter's open access release of marine microbial genome data and the Italian virologist Ilaria Capua's rebellion against WHO data-sharing policies.

[6] See BBC 2017.

[7] See Quigley & Ayihongbe 2018, 279.

[8] Quigley & Ayihongbe 2018, 276.

[9] Clynes & Kline 1960, 27: 'For the exogenously extended organizational complex functioning as an integrated homeostatic system unconsciously, we propose the term "Cyborg"'.

science fiction to describe human-machine hybrids. It is now a common term for 'a blend of human nature and technology' or even a 'posthuman being'.[10] Haddow and co-authors added the prefix 'everyday' to describe the now commonplace occurrence of persons with integrated automated technology.[11] But the term 'everyday cyborg' has also been used to capture persons with a wider array of integrated materials and technologies: (a)–(d) above.[12]

It seems to me that the language of cybernetics is so readily connected to the human-machine hybrids of science fiction that it is liable to cause confusion if extended to non-integrated wearables. If any wearable or simple prosthesis renders a person a cyborg, then cyborgs have been with us for thousands of years. A mummy in Cairo Museum has a big toe that was amputated and replaced with a prosthesis made from leather and wood.[13] Spectacles and wristwatches are commonplace, but they are not the type of technology readily evoked by the word 'cyborg' and fall outside the focus of this chapter. The future scenarios in 5.4 are more closely associated with the classic human-machine hybrid than what Haddow and co-authors refer to as implantable technologies of the 'carpentry kind', such as hip joints and other simple prosthetics.[14] Thus, without seeking to draw any exclusionary lines between different types of integrated implantables, this chapter's focus is on complex (or 'smart') integrated devices and cybernetic is defined accordingly.

5.2.2. The Biohacking Community

Biological innovations are now happening outside traditional research laboratories in DIYbio labs or 'biohacker spaces'.[15] There are many, including London Biohackspace, Genspace in New York, Biotown in Ottawa and La Paillasse in Paris.[16] They are open spaces providing resources, tools and training to those interested in tinkering with biotechnology. As such, they have the potential to engage people from groups that are underrepresented in traditional academic and commercial laboratories, and whose interests are less likely to attract funding within academia or industry. Biohacker spaces are thereby designed to facilitate what has been called 'inclusive innovation'.[17] They represent one of the many ways in which modern DIYbio differs from biological innovation before the establishment of university and commercial research laboratories, when most participants were gentlemen of independent means or supported by rich aristocrats. Charles Darwin, it has been claimed, 'may have been the original do-it-yourself biologist,

[10] Frias & Javier 2016, 11.
[11] See Haddow et al 2015 and Haddow et al 2016.
[12] See Quigley & Ayihongbe 2018, esp 279.
[13] See Thurston 2007, 114.
[14] See Haddow et al 2016, 212.
[15] See de Beer & Jain 2018.
[16] See biohackspace.org, genspace.org, biotown.ca and lapaillasse.org, respectively.
[17] See eg Schillo & Robinson 2017.

as he didn't work in any institution'.[18] The modern DIYbio movement has, in part, been a response to the domination of biotechnological innovation by universities and corporations, especially 'Big Bio'. According to Delfanti, 'biohacking is laden with anti-institution and anti-bureaucracy claims'.[19] We will return to this biohacking community ethos when considering regulatory options for the development in the imagined future scenarios.

The hardcore biohackers, who seek to implant technology into their bodies and explore options not currently condoned by the medical profession, often refer to themselves as 'grinders'.[20] As indicated above, I use an alternative label, cybernetic biohackers, which is less prone to misinterpretation by those unfamiliar with the relevant practices. They are a relatively small group for the simple reason that few people, even among those who self-identify as biohackers, are willing to have devices implanted into their bodies, other than by healthcare professionals acting in a clinical capacity. Some members of this small group have attracted media attention.

Hundreds of biohackers have now had RFID (radio-frequency identification) microchips implanted into their bodies. Kevin Warwick had an RFID chip implanted into his arm by a surgeon back in 1998.[21] Warwick, then a professor at the University of Reading, became known as 'Captain Cyborg'. The implanted chip was large by modern standards (23mm by 3mm) and worked with transmitters set up in an intelligent building on the university campus. It was removed a week later. Five years later, Amal Graafstra became known for implanting RFID to enable him to open doors with the swipe of his hand.[22] Amal has since worked with others to develop and produce new types of microchip implants and biohacking procedures.

Neil Harbisson is another high-profile cybernetic biohacker.[23] Neil was born with achromatopsia – complete colour-blindness – so could only see shades of grey. He co-developed a wearable device – involving a web camera attached to an antenna, a five-kilogram computer and a pair of headphones – for translated colours into 360 sounds. Over time he refined this device by reducing its bulk and having a chip installed under his skin and an antenna installed directly into his skull. He now experiences colours by bone conduction (the conduction of sound through the bones of the skull). The installation required surgery and Neil found a physician willing to assist, on the condition that his identity remained confidential. Neil can now even identify parts of the electromagnetic spectrum that are invisible to the rest of us, such as infrared and ultraviolet. He has therefore achieved, by mechanical means, one of the traits examined in chapter 3 on genome editing: superhuman vision.

[18] Drew Endy, cited in Delfanti 2013, 119.
[19] Delfanti 2013, 124.
[20] See eg www.transcendyourlimits.com/what-is-biohacking.
[21] See BBC 1998 and Connor 1998.
[22] See his TedX Talk from 17 October 2013: www.youtube.com/watch?v=7DxVWhFLI6E.
[23] See Stix 2016.

Also consider those patients who have banded together to construct DIY systems to better manage their type 1 diabetes.[24] Patients with this lifelong health condition produce little or no insulin. Standard treatment is taxing and time-consuming: self-injection of insulin multiple times per day with the dosage varied in response to blood glucose levels, measured using a finger-prick test.[25] The social media hashtag #WeAreNotWaiting was adopted in 2013 as a rallying call for those wanting to take matters into their own hands.[26] The movement has resulted in the creation of DIY artificial pancreas systems (DIY APS), which use two extant technologies: a continuous glucose sensor and an insulin pump. The sensor is implanted under the skin and continually sends data to a smartphone or other computer. That data is processed using open-source software and instructions are sent to a wearable insulin pump, which delivers insulin throughout the day via a small cannula. The open-source software on which these systems depend has been developed and used outside a regulated clinical or research environment.

5.2.3. The Cybernetic Brain

Recent years have seen significant advances in novel neurotechnologies that involve electrodes interfacing with the nervous system to monitor or modulate neural activity.[27] To date, these devices have been developed and implanted within traditional clinical and research environments. Cybernetic brain technology is briefly examined here because the future scenarios in 5.4 will involve an imagined use of this technology by biohackers.

Deep brain stimulation (DBS) uses electric currents, delivered by electrodes implanted deep in the brain, to alter the functioning of brain cells and neural networks.[28] Brain stimulators have been used to treat movement disorders such as Parkinson's disease, and seem to have a very promising future.[29]

Brain-computer interfaces (BCIs) read and utilise the brain's electrical activity. They directly connect the brain's electrical activity (recorded using electrodes resting on the scalp, resting on the brain or implanted into the brain) to a computer or device. BCIs could enable users to control devices, such as prostheses or wheelchairs, by thinking about movement.

The most invasive neurotechnologies (DBS and brain-invasive BCIs) have greater potential to accurately monitor or modulate brain signals, but they also carry a much greater risk of infection and neural damage. Two of the biggest challenges for the use of electrodes on or in the brain are that their implantation

[24] See Roberts et al 2021.
[25] See Roberts et al 2021, 46.
[26] www.healthline.com/health/diabetesmine/innovation/we-are-not-waiting.
[27] See NCOB 2013 and Goering et al 2021.
[28] See NCOB 2013, xvii.
[29] See Clausen 2010, esp 1152.

requires invasive surgery (with its attendant risks), and implanted electrodes erode quickly. Implantation typically requires part of the skull to be removed to access the brain (craniotomy) and accurate placement of electrodes. Once placed, the intracranial environment is corrosive to the wires used as electrodes. Scientists are currently experimenting with various means of addressing these and other challenges.

Neuralink, a prominent company led by Elon Musk, has been developing BCIs that enable two-way communication between the brain and a phone/computer.[30] The V.0.9 is a coin-shaped device that replaces a small section of the skull and is connected to tiny thread wires that enter the cortex. The implantation is done by a robot and the plan is for the entirety of the surgery to be performed by the robot in under an hour, without bleeding or general anaesthesia. Since the device can both record brain signals and stimulate the brain (read and write), it combines BCI with brain stimulation. Like many modern phones, the V.0.9 is charged inductively by a small pad placed on the device overnight. Initial trials have been on pigs and monkeys. The pig experiments have involved both implantation and, crucially for future upgrades, removal of the V.0.9 device. In April 2021, Neuralink released footage of a macaque monkey playing *Pong*, a table tennis themed video game, by thinking about its moves.[31] The company is working towards its first human trials of the device on people with quadriplegia. Neuralink's long-term aim is to address paralysis, blindness and deafness and (by going deeper into the brain) addiction, anxiety and depression.

A team led by Diego Ghezzi has been experimenting with neural interfaces that can be implanted into a patient's blood vessel (rather than inside the brain) and then break down harmlessly in the body after several weeks or even months.[32] The team provided proof of concept for use of biodegradable materials by implanting polymer-based interfaces into the brains of mice by invasive surgery (craniotomy).[33] They reported that these temporary interfaces were able to monitor brain activity for a few weeks, thereby supporting their view that the use of biodegradable polymers 'opens up new possibilities for transient medical devices'. The team also conducted experiments using a stent-like delivery procedure to target neural tissue from within a blood vessel to avoid the need for a craniotomy.[34] They reported that their device is compatible with 'standard endovascular catheters', and the results to date provide 'a good starting point' for further experimentation in animals.

[30] See the live Neuralink demonstration on three pigs from 29 August 2020 (youtu.be/iOWFXqT5MZ4) and the demonstration of a monkey playing video games through mind control on 11 April 2021 (www.youtube.com/watch?v=ZsOu4FOMD68).

[31] The macaque continued to move the joystick with which it was trained, but that joystick had been disconnected: see Wakefield 2021.

[32] See Fanelli et al 2021 and Feraluto et al 2021.

[33] See Feraluto et al 2021.

[34] See Fanelli et al 2021.

Another team is exploring the possibility of scalable, implantation wireless microsensors (submillimetre-sized chips, known as 'neurograins') to allow greater flexibility in the placement of sensors and stimulators.[35] Innovations in this field are thus continuous and wide-ranging.

5.3. The Law

Many laws are potentially engaged by activities connected with obtaining, creating or implanting an implantable device. The seller of a device or component part is liable in contract law to the purchaser for any breach of an expressed or implied term.[36] The manufacturer is potentially liable to the ultimate consumer for any injury or damage caused by their negligence[37] or defects in their products.[38] My focus here is not, however, on the obligations of sellers and manufacturers in contract or tort law. This chapter is focused on a selection of those laws that potentially hinder or protect the activities of cybernetic biohackers.

The implantation of a device usually requires the assistance of another. It could be provided by healthcare professionals, body-piercers and even those who have no professional qualifications or experience with surgery or implantation. Some high-profile examples were mentioned in 5.2.2. Kevin Warwick had an RFID implanted into his arm by a surgeon, whereas Amal Graafstra's was implanted into his hand by a body-piercer. Neil Harbisson had an antenna implanted into his skull by an anonymous doctor. Patients with DIY APS seek the assistance of health professionals to install a cannula and prescribe component parts.

Someone who treats or experiments on another does not commit a crime merely because they lack medical qualifications or medical supervision. It is, however, a crime to intentionally pretend to be a registered or licensed medical practitioner,[39] and unqualified persons who inflict serious bodily harm cannot rely on the 'medical exception' to criminal assault. The ambit of the criminal law of assault is the first legal issue examined below, because the public policy limitation on consent is a potentially significant constraint on cybernetic biohacking (5.3.1).

The next set of legal issues explored concern the regulation of medical devices (5.3.2). There is a complex system of assessment and registration applying to medical devices, principally concerned with their safety and efficacy. Yet, it will be shown, devices created by biohackers are liable to fall outside that regulatory system.

[35] See Lee et al 2021.
[36] See eg Consumer Rights Act 2015.
[37] *Donoghue v Stevenson* [1932] AC 562.
[38] Consumer Protection Act 1987.
[39] Medical Act 1983, ss 49 and 49A.

The third section (5.3.3) examines the application of the law of property, including intellectual property, because these laws potentially provide mechanisms by which legal control can be asserted over a device or its component parts. The final section (5.3.4) reviews the law applying to computer misuse and data protection. These sections aim to show how implantable devices and biohacking raise legal uncertainties and present challenges to standard legal categories.

5.3.1. Assault and Consent to Bodily Harm

Implanting a device into another person potentially amounts to a crime. The common law distinguishes between a battery (an act that intentionally or recklessly inflicts unlawful force on another person) and an assault (an act that intentionally or recklessly causes another to reasonably apprehend an immediate battery).[40] But 'the term "assault", is now, in both ordinary legal usage and in statutes, regularly used to cover both assault and battery'.[41] There are three types of assault: common assault and battery, assault occasioning actual bodily harm and assault occasioning grievous bodily harm.[42] The common law crime of assault and battery does not require the victim to suffer an injury and carries a maximum sentence of up to six months in jail.[43] Assault occasioning actual bodily harm (ABH) captures 'hurt or injury calculated to interfere with the health or comfort of the [victim]' that is more than transient and trifling.[44] It carries a maximum penalty of five years' imprisonment.[45] Wounding or inflicting grievous bodily harm (GBH) carries a maximum penalty of five years imprisonment[46] or, if GBH is caused intentionally, up to life imprisonment.[47] A wound requires the whole of the skin to be broken (not merely the outer layer)[48] and GBH captures really serious bodily harm.[49]

Unlike common assault and battery, the more serious crimes of assault can still be committed *even if the victim consents*. As Lord Lane CJ put the point in *Attorney-General's Reference (No 6 of 1980)*, 'it is not in the public interest that

[40] *Collins v Wilcock* [1984] 3 All ER 374, 377–378 (Goff LJ).
[41] CLRC 1980, para 158, as quoted in Law Commission 1992, para 9.1.
[42] See *R v Brown* [1994] 1 AC 212, 230.
[43] Criminal Justice Act 1988, s 39. Additional or alternatively, it imposes a level 5 (unlimited) fine: www.sentencingcouncil.org.uk/explanatory-material/magistrates-court/item/fines-and-financial-orders/approach-to-the-assessment-of-fines-2/9-maximum-fines.
[44] *R v Donovan* [1934] 2 KB 498, 509.
[45] Offences against the Person Act 1861, s 47.
[46] Offences against the Person Act 1861, s 20. The defendant must intend or be reckless about causing *some* harm (not necessarily GBH): *R v Savage* [1992] 1 AC 699.
[47] Offences against the Person Act 1861, s 18.
[48] *C (A Minor) v Eisenhower* [1984] QB 331, 339.
[49] *DPP v Smith* [1961] AC 290, 334. The harm need not be physical, so a serious psychiatric injury can amount to GBH: *R v Ireland and Burstow* [1997] UKHL 34.

people should try to cause or should cause each other actual bodily harm for no good reason'.[50] Thus, consent is no defence where, for example, a man beats a girl of 17 for sexual gratification, where injuries are inflicted during a fist fight on a public street or where injuries are inflicted during sadomasochistic homosexual activities.[51] In contrast, no assault is committed where consensual bodily harm is inflicted for a 'good reason', which includes 'proper medical treatment' or bodily harm inflicted 'in accordance with good medical practice'.[52] A 'medical exception' thereby 'takes most medical treatment outside … criminal law regulation' of serious assault.[53]

Not every act performed by a medical practitioner is *ipso facto* 'proper medical treatment'. Criminal assault is still committed where a surgeon cuts off a man's fingers to assist his dishonest insurance claim, circumcises a female for religious reasons, removes both of a healthy patient's kidneys for transplantation into others, or reconstructs the hymen.[54] Such activities are regarded as contrary to public policy, which is an appeal to the values of society or the medical profession at a particular time. The result is legal categorisation of social harm that evolves with the underlying (minimally refined) cultural morality. Consider, for example, the evolution of public policy on contraceptive sterilisation. In *Bravery v Bravery*, Denning LJ expressed the obiter view that non-therapeutic vasectomy was unlawful because it was performed 'so as to enable a man to have the pleasure of sexual intercourse, without shouldering the responsibilities attaching to it' and was therefore 'plainly injurious to the public interest'.[55] In the course of the 1960s, contraceptive sterilisation for consenting patients became accepted as lawful without the need for formal legal intervention.[56] In the 1980s, the House of Lords went further by holding that contraceptive sterilisation could be lawfully performed in the best interests of those who are unable to consent.[57]

Lewis has identified three types of public policy justifications for the application of the medical exception to consensual bodily harm.[58] These are those that are 'patient-focused' (which look to the doctor's intention to treat or otherwise benefit the patient), 'public-focused' (which point to a wider lawful reason or

[50] [1981] QB 715, 719.

[51] *R v Donovan* [1934] 2 KB 498; *AG's Reference (No 6 of 1980)* [1981] QB 715; *R v Brown* [1994] 1 AC 212; respectively.

[52] Lord Mustill in *Airedale NHS Trust v Bland* [1993] AC 789, 891 and *R v Brown* [1994] 1 AC 212, 258–259, respectively. See also the other speeches in *Brown:* 231 (Lord Templeman), 245 (Lord Jauncey) and 276 (Lord Slynn).

[53] Lewis 2012, 356. See also Fovargue & Mullock 2016, 1.

[54] See *State v Bass* (1961) 255 NC 42, SE2d 580; Female Genital Mutilation Act 2003; Law Commission 1995, para 8.31; Health and Care Act 2022, ss 147–158.

[55] *Bravery v Bravery* [1954] 1 WLR 1169, 1180. These comments were not supported by the other two members of the Court on the grounds that they were obiter: 1175.

[56] See Lewis 2011.

[57] *Re B* [1988] AC 199 (child) and *Re F* [1990] 2 AC 1 (adult). The House of Lords in *Re B* emphasised that no issues of public policy arose beyond the paramountcy of the child's welfare: [1988] AC 199, esp 203 and 212.

[58] See Lewis 2012.

public interest) and 'professionally focused' (which build on the standards of the medical profession). This categorisation provides explanatory assistance. All three types of public policy justifications identified by Lewis could be expected to support doctors administering standard medical treatment. Conversely, consensual bodily harm is not lawful if a doctor seeks to act contrary to the patient's health interests and there is little support from the medical profession or wider societal interests. Grey cases arise where these three justificatory strategies are liable to produce inconsistent or unclear responses to a particular procedure. For this reason, delineating proper from improper medical practice presents greater difficulty where the activity is not expected to be uncontroversially beneficial to the patient or, since the courts draw upon cultural morality, where attitudes within the medical profession or society are in a state of transition. Lewis makes the further point that ambiguity about the lawfulness of a new and controversial procedure could be understood as creating a 'cooling-off' period that facilitates dialogue within the medical profession, between the medical and legal profession, and between the medical profession and society more generally.[59]

In other contexts, the courts have identified legitimate medical practice by reference to the standard of a responsible body of medical opinion. This is the standard of care from clinical negligence, commonly referred to as the *Bolam* test.[60] It has been used as a measure of the best interests of patients who lack capacity to consent[61] and interpreted broadly to support the conclusion that experimental treatment could be in such a patient's best interests.[62] This standard will undoubtedly inform judicial consideration of whether a new or controversial procedure is consistent with the medical exception.[63] The case law displays repeated deference to professional medical judgment in the context of surgical interventions.[64] This deference is such that professionally supported cosmetic procedures are widely considered to fall within the medical exception even where their therapeutic rationale is tenuous. The Law Commission was 'unable to identify any English case in which the lawfulness of cosmetic surgery carried out by consent has been called into question', despite it not being 'possible to identify a therapeutic benefit in every case'.[65] The private sector readily provides cosmetic surgery in response to an

[59] See Lewis 2012, esp 375–376.

[60] *Bolam v Friern Hospital Management Committee* [1957] 1 WLR 582, as refined in *Bolitho v City and Hackney HA* [1998] AC 232.

[61] See eg *Re F* [1990] 2 AC 1, 73 (sterilisation of an incapacitated patient) and *Airedale NHS Trust v Bland* [1993] AC 789 (withdrawal of treatment from a patient in a permanent vegetative state).

[62] *Simms v Simms* [2002] EWHC 2734 (Fam), esp [51] and *B NHS Trust v J* [2006] EWHC 3152 (Fam).

[63] See Pattinson 2014, esp 130 (latest edition: Pattinson 2020, esp 132–133) and Brazier & Fovargue 2017, 21.

[64] See eg *Corbett v Corbett* [1971] P 83, 98–99 on the lawfulness of transgender surgery performed to protect the patient's mental health or, more recently, *R v BM* [2018] EWCA Crim 560 on the unlawfulness of body modification procedures unsupported by professional medical opinion (discussed below).

[65] Law Commission 1995, para 8.30.

individual's request for physical alteration in circumstances where the NHS would not consider it required to improve or prevent harm to their physical or mental health.[66] Baker has gone so far as to argue that undue deference to the medical professional has medicalised 'unnecessary harmful nontherapeutic surgery', such as non-therapeutic breast augmentation and labiaplasties.[67] It is therefore clear that the medical exception is regarded as satisfied by the mere 'participation and acceptance of the medical profession'.[68] Borderline cases for the application of the medical exception only potentially arise when a procedure is regarded as problematic by the medical profession itself, such as is the case for surgical amputation of a healthy limb to treat amputee identity disorder/body integrity identity disorder.[69]

Surgery on the female genitalia provides an interesting example of the impact of the participation and acceptance of the medical profession. Such surgery is prohibited by section 1 of the Female Genital Mutilation Act 2003, unless it is performed by a medical practitioner or midwife either in connection with childbirth or because it is 'necessary for her physical or mental health'. But, in practice, what is 'necessary' for mental health is interpreted very loosely. The Explanatory Notes to the Act state that it includes 'cosmetic surgery resulting from the *distress* caused by a *perception* of abnormality'.[70] Further, Chambers observes, it is commonplace for the adverts of commercial providers to be silent about mental health, not saying anything about operating only on patients with a mental health problem.[71]

Unfortunately, virtually all judicial consideration of the public policy limitation has been in non-medical cases, where discussion of the medical exception has been obiter. Many of the leading cases have involved sexual activity, problematic consent or both. *R v Brown*, considered earlier, was a case involving sadomasochistic homosexual activities.[72] Some of the dicta highlight instances of questionable consent. According to Lord Templeman,

> The evidence disclosed that drink and drugs were employed to obtain consent and increase enthusiasm … In one case a victim was branded twice on the thigh and there was some doubt as to whether he consented to or protested against the second branding.[73]

The was even some suggestion of grooming behaviour – one of the recipients of harm had been befriended by a defendant in a cafe 'when the boy was 15 years old' (at a time when the age of consent for sexual intercourse between men was 21).[74] Further, some of the dicta were redolent of a moral conservatism

[66] See Griffiths & Mullock 2017, esp 109.
[67] Baker adds that it is 'difficult to see' how such surgery can be reconciled with the common law authorities: Baker 2014, 611.
[68] See Griffiths & Mullock 2017, 108.
[69] See Bayne & Levy 2005; Elliott 2009; Pattinson 2020, 131–133.
[70] www.legislation.gov.uk/ukpga/2003/31/notes, para 15 (emphasis added).
[71] Chambers 2019, 74.
[72] [1994] 1 AC 212.
[73] [1994] 1 AC 212, 236.
[74] Lord Lane CJ, as quoted by Lord Templeman: [1994] 1 AC 212, 236.

opposed to homosexuality. Lord Lowry dismissed homosexual sadomasochism as 'physical cruelty' that 'can scarcely be regarded as a "manly diversion"'.[75] This can be contrasted with dicta in *Wilson*, where the Court of Appeal permitted a husband who had branded his wife's buttocks to rely on the defence of consent to the infliction of actual bodily harm.[76] Wilson had inflicted injuries that had led to a skin infection, requiring his wife to seek medical treatment. Yet, this buttock branding was considered equivalent to 'tattooing', whereas the activities in *Brown* (for which no medical treatment was required) were characterised as 'sado-masochism of the grossest kind, involving inter alia, physical torture'.[77] According to the Court of Appeal,

> Consensual activity between husband and wife, in the privacy of the matrimonial home, is not, in our judgment, normally a proper matter for criminal investigation, let alone criminal prosecution.[78]

It is difficult to avoid the conclusion that the Court of Appeal's reasoning reflects conservative judicial moral intuitions on the nature of the sexual relationship. The result was that the branding of a wife's buttocks was placed in the same category as tattooing and piercing, infant male circumcision, cosmetic surgery, boxing and other contact sports, rather than in the same category as sadomasochistic homosexual activities, bare fist fighting and female circumcision/genital mutilation.

Neither *Brown* nor *Wilson* concerned the implantation of a device at the request of a biohacker. Reliance upon the medical exception would require the implanter to be a medical professional acting for a recognised clinical purpose. I will return to the application of the medical exception in 5.6.2, after discussing the regulation of medical devices (5.3.2) and outlining imagined future scenarios (5.4). An implanter who is not a non-healthcare professional would need to rely on another exception. *Brown* recognised only one potentially analogous category: the exception for tattooing and piercing.

The Court of Appeal followed *Brown* in *R v BM*.[79] *BM* involved an appeal by a registered tattooist and piercer, Brendan McCarthy, for carrying out 'body modification' procedures without anaesthetic. He had been charged with three counts of wounding with intent to inflict GBH[80] on the basis that he had removed one customer's ear, removed another customer's nipple and split a third customer's tongue into a reptilian fork. The Court of Appeal contrasted the defendant's actions with those of someone with 'medical qualifications which equip him to carry out these surgical procedures' who acts for 'medical reasons'.[81] Lord Burnett LCJ noted that the public policy reasons for protecting the public extend 'beyond

[75] [1994] 1 AC 212, 255.
[76] *R v Wilson* [1997] QB 47.
[77] [1997] QB 47, 50.
[78] [1997] QB 47, 50.
[79] [2018] EWCA Crim 560.
[80] Offences against the Person Act 1861, s 18.
[81] *R v BM* [2018] EWCA Crim 560, esp [8], [17] and [35].

the risks of infection, bungled or poor surgery or an inability to deal with immediate complications' and encompassed the lack of 'mental health assessment'.[82] Accordingly, his Lordship declared, 'There are good reasons why reputable practitioners will not remove parts of the body simply when asked by a patient'.[83] Thus, the Court of Appeal ruled, the consent of the defendant's customers could not provide him with a defence. The defendant then pleaded guilty and was sentenced to concurrent terms of 40 months' imprisonment.[84] This decision, with its emphasis on the legal distance between body modification and proper medical practice, sends a cautionary message to a tattooist-piercer who is considering implanting a device into a customer.

Brendan McCarthy was an experienced tattooist and piercer, which are activities regulated by statute.[85] Legislation gives local authorities the power to impose a registration requirement on business premises and practitioners of acupuncture, tattooing, electrolysis, semi-permanent skin colouring and cosmetic piercing.[86] The Act's offences do not apply where these activities are carried out by or under the supervision of a registered medical practitioner.[87] Their primary purpose is to enable local authorities to maintain standards of safety and hygiene, and thereby increase health protection and reduce the risk of transmission of blood-borne viruses.[88]

Until *BM*, it could be surmised that 'tattooing' and 'ear-piercing' were merely used by their Lordships in *Brown* as examples of lawful wounding, and at least some types of body modification fell into a wider category of legitimate bodily adornment.[89] Body-piercing (rather than merely ear-piercing) had, for example, been recognised at first instance as lawful when performed for 'decorative or cosmetic purposes', rather than for sexual gratification.[90] The Court of Appeal in *BM*, however, refused to countenance a wider exception. Lord Burnett listed 'tattooing', 'piercing' and 'perhaps … those with a religious hue, including ritual male circumcision' as activities that it would be 'unreasonable for the common law to criminalise'.[91] His Lordship had earlier noted that the registration scheme applying to tattooing and piercing did not apply to 'body modification', which he said was a term encompassing 'each of the procedures in issue in this case (and many more)'.[92] Indeed, the closest regulated activity is 'cosmetic piercing', but

[82] [2018] EWCA Crim 560, [43].
[83] [2018] EWCA Crim 560, [43].
[84] *R v McCarthy (Brendan)* [2019] EWCA Crim 2202.
[85] The Local Government Miscellaneous Act 1982, as amended by the Local Government Act 2003.
[86] The 1982 Act, ss 14–16, as amended. The London Local Authority Act 1991 applies to local authorities in London.
[87] 1982 Act, ss 14(8) and 15(8).
[88] See DH 2004, paras 2 and 4.
[89] See Pegg 2019, 585.
[90] *Oversby*, unreported, cited in Law Commission 1995, para 9.7. Mr Oversby was a leading professional piercer and one of the defendants in the trial that ultimately reached the House of Lords in *Brown*. After the judge's ruling, he pleaded guilty and received a suspended sentence.
[91] [2018] EWCA Crim 560, [40].
[92] [2018] EWCA Crim 560, [7].

piercing suggests a procedure in which a hole is made through part of the body[93] and McCarthy had been slicing and cutting off body parts. Surgical biohacking similarly involves something other than putting holes through body parts for decorative or cosmetic purposes; it involves inserting implants below the skin or even deeper into the body. Lord Burnett's conclusion that body modification is contrary to public policy unless it falls within an existing exception would, on the face of it, criminalise the activities of a tattooist-piercer who implants a device into a biohacker.

In sum, the public policy limitation on consensually inflicted serious assault presents problems of both justification and application. Judicial justifications have appealed to a wide set of considerations, including the health interests of the person who is consenting, the interests of society and the views of the medical profession. All three types of considerations appear in the reasoning of the Court of Appeal in *BM*, but they potentially pull in different directions. Judicial applications have:

(a) drawn distinctions between very similar activities (compare *Brown* and *Wilson*);
(b) often concerned situations in which there were apparent deficiencies in the process for obtaining consent (eg *Brown*);
(c) given greater weight to some subcultures over others (compare the lawfulness of ritual male circumcision of children with the unlawfulness of consensual non-medical tissue removal performed on adults in *BM*);[94] and
(d) left the boundaries of the public policy limitation unclear.

As the Court of Appeal recognised in *BM*, the result is a set of 'cases [that] do not lend themselves to a coherent statement of underlying principle'.[95] Crucially for current purposes, the case law seems to criminalise the type of surgical assistance needed by cybernetic biohackers, when provided by those who are not medical professionals. Some ambiguity remains because *BM* was not directly concerned with implantations, and some types of implantations could be considered more like body-piercing than splitting or removing of body parts. Medical professionals providing surgical assistance would fall outside the medical exception if they were not regarded as acting for a medical purpose by their peers. I will return to these issues in 5.6.2, when applying the law of assault to this chapter's future scenarios.

[93] See Pegg 2019, 595.
[94] There are many cases on ritual male circumcision (see eg *Re J* [2000] 1 FLR 571 and *Re B (Children) (Care Proceedings)* [2015] EWFC 3, esp [59]–[62]) and it is generally regarded as lawful even if performed by non-medically qualified practitioners. Lord Burnett in *BM* gave ritual male circumcision, when performed on infants with parental consent, as an example of a lawful procedure outside the medical exception.
[95] [2018] EWCA Crim 560, [24].

5.3.2. The Regulation of Medical Devices

Medical devices are subject to a specific regulatory framework. Up to the end of the Brexit transition period, the United Kingdom gave effect to EU law. The UK Medical Devices Regulations (SI 2002/618) had implemented three EU Directives.[96] The EU has replaced these Directives with two new Regulations, but these had not taken effect at the time of the United Kingdom's exit.[97] The United Kingdom therefore retained a localised version of the previous EU medical devices regulatory system.[98] This section will examine this system and its limits, to discern where it potentially connects with cybernetic biohacking.

The EU system requires medical devices to undergo a conformity assessment before they are placed on the EU market. The onus of the conformity assessment – which involves ensuring and declaring that a medical device conforms to the 'essential requirements' on safety and performance – is placed on the manufacturer.[99] However, in many cases it is subject to approval by a private technical organisation, known as a notified body. The conformity assessment will often require the device to have been clinically tested to verify that it performs as intended by the manufacturer and to identify any undesirable side-effects.[100] Devices passing the assessment receive a 'CE Mark' and can then be placed on the EU market.

In the United Kingdom, the Medicines and Healthcare products Regulatory Agency (MHRA) is responsible for regulating the UK medical devices market under the 2002 Regulations. Various post-Brexit amendments have been made to the 2002 Regulations.[101] The organisations designated by the MHRA to conduct conformity assessments are now referred to as UK approved bodies (ie these replace notified bodies).[102] Devices passing the assessment in Great Britain receive a 'UKCA mark' (which replaces the CE Mark, except in Northern Ireland).[103] Placing a medical device on the market requires both a UKCA mark *and* the manufacturer (or their authorised representative) to register with the MHRA.[104]

[96] Council Directive 90/385/EEC on Active Implantable Medical Devices (1990); Council Directive 93/42/EEC on Medical Devices (1993); Directive 98/79/EC of the European Parliament and of the Council on in vitro Diagnostic Medical Devices.

[97] These are Regulation (EU) 2017/745 (Medical Device Regulations – MDR) and Regulation (EU) 2017/746 (*In Vitro* Diagnostic Regulations – IVDR). The MDR came into full effect in May 2021 and the IVDR in May 2022.

[98] See Dobson 2021, 179.

[99] The essential requirements were specified in Annex I of the three medical device directives. In the EU, these have been superseded by the general safety and performance requirements of the two new EU Medical Device Regulations.

[100] See MHRA 2021b.

[101] See eg the Medical Devices (Amendment) (EU Exit) Regulations 2020/1478, which replaced many EU-specific references with UK-specific references. See also the Medicines and Medical Devices Act 2021, discussed below.

[102] See MHRA 2020d.

[103] There is a transitional period until 2023. See MHRA 2020c.

[104] See MHRA 2021a.

The 2002 Regulations apply to three types of medical device: general medical devices, active implantable medical devices and *in vitro* diagnostic medical devices.[105] These are defined in regulation 2(1). A medical device is any apparatus, appliance, material, software or other article, whether used alone or in combination, intended by the manufacturer to be *used by human beings for a medical purpose*. The other two are specific types of medical devices. An active implantable medical device is a powered medical device that is fully or partially implanted and intended to remain implanted. An *in vitro* diagnostic device is a reagent, reagent product, calibrator, control material, kit, instrument, apparatus, equipment or system intended for use outside the body to examine specimens from the human body. These wide definitions capture all devices used for clinical purposes: contact lenses and other non-powered implants are medical devices, powered implants are active implantable medical devices, and kits for testing blood and tissues are *in vitro* diagnostic devices.

The obligations placed on 'manufacturers' are triggered by 'placing on the market' or 'putting into service'. These terms are also defined in regulation 2(1). Manufacturers are essentially those persons responsible for the design, manufacture, packaging, assembly or various other tasks *before the device is placed on the market under their own name*. 'Placing on the market' means the 'first making available' of a new or fully refurbished device with a view to distribution or use on the UK market. 'Putting into service' means making an active implantable device available to a medical practitioner for implantation or, for other medical devices, the first making available to a final user.

The 2002 Regulations provide for three exemptions to the obligations usually imposed on manufacturers who place on the market or put into service a medical device.[106] The first concerns *exceptional use* of a non-UKCA marked device on what the MHRA refers to as 'humanitarian grounds'.[107] This enables a manufacturer to apply for authorisation from the MHRA to supply a non-compliant medical device where the application is supported by the patient's doctor, there is no alternative compliant device and no comparably effective alternative treatment. The second applies to *custom-made devices* that have been manufactured in accordance with an appropriate written prescription and intended for the sole use of a particular patient and not mass-produced.[108] The third applies to devices *intended for clinical investigation*.[109] Each exemption has its own stringent conditions and requires the support or even instigation of a qualified medical practitioner.

It is not surprising that complexities arise when the provisions of the 2002 Regulations are applied to cybernetic biohacking, because those provisions are

[105] See Parts II (general medical devices), III (active implanted medical devices) and IV (*in vitro* diagnostics medical devices) of the 2002 Regulations.

[106] Regs 12 (general medical devices), 26 (active implanted medical devices) and 39 (*in vitro* diagnostic medical devices).

[107] See MHRA 2020b.

[108] See MHRA 2020c.

[109] See MHRA 2021c.

directed to the use of medical devices in a standard clinical or research context. When biohackers create a new wearable or implantable device (either from scratch or by modifying an existing medical device), it is likely to fall outside the 2002 Regulations. Sometimes it will fall outside the definition of a medical device because it is not 'intended by the manufacturer to be used for human beings' for one of the medical purposes specified in regulation 2(1), such as diagnosis, prevention, monitoring, treatment or alleviation of disease or injury. In other cases, there are difficulties even identifying a manufacturer or otherwise engaging the provisions of the 2002 regulations.

Consider the DIY APS discussed in 5.2.2. These systems have three components: open-source software run on a smartphone or small computer, a glucose sensor to continuously provide glucose readings and an insulin pump to deliver insulin. The insulin pumps and continuous glucose monitors used in such devices are themselves regulated medical devices – they have been commercially produced, marketed and conformity-assessed. The software provides the DIY/biohacking component. As these are DIY systems, they have not received regulatory approval.[110] The biohacking community responsible for the design of these systems acts collectively and does not seek to put the DIY APS on the market in the name of an identifiable legal person. It is therefore doubtful that anyone working on the project could properly be identified as the 'manufacturer' for the purposes of the 2002 Regulations[111] and, in any case, the software component is currently hosted on servers operating outside both the EU and the United Kingdom.[112]

The principal post-Brexit legislation in this area is the Medicines and Medical Devices Act 2021. Its most significant impact is likely to be prospective in that it grants extensive regulation-making powers to the Secretary of State. The Secretary of State may amend the 2002 Regulations to provide for the manufacture, marketing and supply of medical devices (section 16) and address associated regulatory issues (section 17). When making regulations, the Secretary of State is required to have regard not only to the safety and availability of medical devices but also to the likelihood of the United Kingdom being seen as a 'favourable place' in which to research, develop, manufacture and supply medical devices (section 15). Notice the continued focus on the availability and safety of *products* within the *market*. Where a medical device has been integrated into a person, Quigley and Downey argue, the UK regulatory approach continues to pay insufficient attention to the 'patient, end-user, integrated person'.[113] Further, the 2021 Act continues to pay little regard to the activities of biohackers.

[110] An APS system, not created by biohackers, is to be rolled out by the NHS in England: see Gregory 2022.

[111] See Downey & Quigley 2021.

[112] See Roberts et al 2021, 9.

[113] Quigley & Downey 2022, 289. They add that the Act's regulation-making powers enable potentially radical changes to be made to the extant legislation '*without* being subject to the same parliamentary scrutiny that exists for primary legislation or that was in place within the EU regime': Quigley & Downey 2022, 288.

In practice, even where DIY systems lead to new commercial systems that gain the relevant medical device regulatory approvals, biohackers might continue to prefer the unregulated DIY versions, because they are often easier to obtain or provide greater functionality – as has been reported with commercial APS.[114] Nonetheless, cybernetic biohackers need (or would benefit from) the assistance of healthcare professionals to implant devices or obtain some components. With regard to DIY APS, Roberts and others have argued that the General Medical Council's guidance does not proscribe doctors from recommending such devices or prescribing component parts, as it could be clinically appropriate for them to do so.[115] Dickson and others have argued that, applying standard legal principles, clinicians are unlikely to be negligent for discussing or even recommending DIY APS with patients, where clinically appropriate.[116] These conclusions are plausible because there are now many reports on the use of these systems, which would not be the case, at least initially, for a future biohacker-created device.[117]

5.3.3. Property and Intellectual Property

Before integration into the body, implantable objects and devices are unequivocally regarded as goods/chattels and the law has well-established rules for transferring and protecting chattels as items of personal property.[118] Once implanted, however, potential uncertainties arise from the law's distinction between persons and property. Additional complexities arise from the intellectual property rights (IPRs) that can attach to implantable objects and devices. Cybernetic biohacking therefore operates in legal waters that are potentially murky.

The ownership of a device implanted into a patient by an NHS hospital was addressed by a circular issued by the then Department of Health and Social Security in 1983:

> On implantation an implant becomes the property of the person in whom it has been implanted and it remains his or her property even if it is subsequently removed. Following the patient's death it forms part of his or her estate unless there is any specific provision to the contrary.[119]

This view has been endorsed by later documents.[120] There is, however, no legislation or case law on this precise issue.

It has long been a maxim of the common law that there is no property in a dead body or its parts, unless different attributes are later acquired by the application

[114] See Dickson et al 2021.
[115] See Roberts et al 2021.
[116] See Dickson et al 2021.
[117] The clinical appropriateness of recommending a DIY system becomes less plausible as alternative, approved systems are rolled out. See Gregory 2022 for recent developments in England.
[118] See Quigley & Ayihongbe 2018, 287.
[119] DHSS 1983, [3].
[120] See eg MHRA 2011.

of skill, such as when it has been preserved for exhibition.[121] It has also been held that living individuals do not have property in their attached body parts, at least for the purposes of possession in the criminal law, on the basis that they 'cannot possess something which is not separate and distinct' from themselves.[122] In contrast, it has been held that where sperm is removed for the sole purpose of using it for the benefit of the person in whose body it was generated, that individual has ownership over the sperm for the purposes of maintaining an action in negligence.[123] The courts have yet to directly address ownership of an implant within or removed from a person's body.

The 1983 guidance recommended that medical consent forms include an acknowledgement that supply/implantation of an implant is 'subject to the condition that if it is subsequently removed for examination or replacement the ownership will vest in the health authority on behalf of whom it is removed'.[124] More recently, guidance from the Resuscitation Council, British Cardiovascular Society and National Council for Palliative Care has recommended that 'in situations where the person's prior agreement has not been obtained, given the legal ambiguities, it is advisable to proceed as if the patient has ownership of the device'.[125] In practice, ownership disputes of this type are unlikely, particularly where a cybernetic biohacker has something they have bought or designed implanted into their body.

Biohackers who modify existing devices could violate the IPRs attached to those devices. The hardware components of an implanted device are potentially protected by patents, design rights and trade marks, and any software is potentially subject to copyright.[126] The sale of devices and other goods does not usually transfer (assign) the originator's IPRs to the purchaser, though the relevant rights are capable of being assigned, licensed or mortgaged.[127] The purchaser of a device and the person into whom it is implanted will usually only acquire a licence and thereby be subject to licensing terms and conditions.[128] It can, however, be difficult to fully articulate what a restrictive licence may restrict.

Consider patent law. A person who obtains a patented product would usually be able to repair or make some modifications, but the patent holder can prevent them from making the patented product or making modifications amounting to the creation of a new product. The practical difficulty is that determining whether a particular activity involves 'making' a product that contravenes the patent

[121] See *R v Kelly* [1999] QB 621, 631, following *Doodeward v Spence* (1908) 6 CLR 406 and *Dobson v North Tyneside HA* [1997] 1 WLR 596, 601–601. The 'no property' maxim itself has dubious origins: see Matthews 1983.

[122] *R v Bentham* [2005] UKHL 18, [8] (Lord Bingham with whom the other Lords agreed).

[123] *Yearworth v North Bristol NHS Trust* [2009] EWCA Civ 37, [44].

[124] DHSS 1983, [6].

[125] Resuscitation Council et al 2015, 7.14.

[126] See Quigley & Ayihongbe 2018, 299.

[127] Patents Act 1977, s 30; Copyright, Designs and Patents Act 1988, s 90; Trade Marks Act 1994, s 24.

[128] See Quigley & Ayihongbe 2018, 301.

depends on the 'legal and factual context'.[129] Repair of a car could include replacing an old engine with a new one, or an old body with a new one,[130] but making the type of functional changes likely to be sought by cybernetic biohackers may well go too far. Much will depend on the nature, effect and general context of those changes.

Complexities are added where changes are made to the software controlling a device. Quigley and Ayihongbe point out that open questions arise as to the limits of installing different software on a device or otherwise modifying the software in a way that potentially infringes copyright.[131] Self-help options generally open to manufacturers of e-devices seeking to prevent contravention of their terms and conditions – such as rendering the device non-functional, withdrawing support, refusing to issue software updates or remotely deactivating the device – can be dangerous and even fatal if applied to an implanted device.[132] To this it could be added that manufacturers of implantable devices must also be careful not to restrict access to their devices in ways that would prevent medical personnel from dealing with a patient's emergency.[133] In practice, it is thus very difficult for manufacturers to enforce their terms and conditions on individuals who seek to self-implant a modified version of their device or modify the device in situ.

In sum, while legal uncertainties arise over ownership and control of implants, these do not seem to present insuperable hurdles for cybernetic biohackers.

5.3.4. Computer Misuse and Data Protection

Cybernetic biohacking potentially engages a vast array of other laws beyond those already addressed. This section will briefly address two areas not hitherto mentioned: the law applying to computer misuse and data protection.

Back in 2007, former United States Vice President Dick Cheney's doctors disabled his pacemaker's wireless capabilities to prevent malicious hackers from attempting his assassination.[134] Under UK law, an attack of this type would involve committing crimes under the Computer Misuse Act 1990 and, if successful, potentially homicide. The 1990 Act criminalises unauthorised access to computer material (ss 1 and 2), unauthorised acts impairing the operation of a computer (section 3), unauthorised acts causing or risking serious damage (section 3ZA) and making, supplying or obtaining articles for use in these offences (section 3A). Although dated, this Act has a wide ambit. It deliberately

[129] *Schutz v Werit* [2013] UKSC 16, esp [26]–[29] and [48]–[52] (on s 60(1)(a) of the Patent Act 1977).
[130] *Coleborn & Sons v Blond* [1951] 1 KB 43, 49–50 (Denning LJ) cited with approval in *Schutz v Werit* [2013] UKSC 16, [51].
[131] See Quigley & Ayihongbe 2018, 301.
[132] See Quigley & Ayihongbe 2018, 301.
[133] See European Commission 2020, 10: 'during an emergency, the medical personnel must be able to access an implanted cardiac device without restrictions'.
[134] See BBC 2013b.

does not define a computer, so there is little doubt that malicious attacks on cybernetic devices would fall within its ambit.[135]

Quigley and Ayihongbe argue that the 1990 Act is focused on objects (computers), rather than subjects (persons), so the prison terms and fines imposed 'are in line with this and not as serious as when harm to persons occurs'.[136] It is the case that the penalty specified for most of the Act's offences (a maximum prison sentence of 12 months or a fine) is far below that applying to serious offences against persons, such as assault, manslaughter or murder. However, the section 3ZA offence, introduced in 2015, carries far more severe maximum penalties. This offence applies to any unauthorised act in relation to a computer that intentionally or recklessly causes (or creates a significant risk of) serious damage. Where that damage is loss of human life or human illness or injury, this offence carries a maximum penalty of life imprisonment.[137] The purpose of this provision was to criminalise computer-based terrorist attacks, but its breadth is such that it would capture anyone who recklessly or intentionally creates a significant risk to another's life or health by hacking an implant. Where a device is hacked by a third party with the intention of improving its functioning, the hacker will lack the requisite intention and it could be very difficult to establish that their actions were reckless. Quigley and Ayihongbe make this point in relation to the crimes of murder and involuntary manslaughter (for which they point out that it would also be very difficult to prove causation)[138] and it would seem to hold in relation to the 1990 Act's section 3ZA offence, which they do not specifically address.

Third parties who gain access to personal data by hacking an implanted device could commit an offence under the Data Protection Act 2018. It is, in particular, an offence under section 170 to knowingly or recklessly obtain or disclose personal data without the consent of the person concerned. Data protection law need not present difficulties for cybernetic biohackers and those who operate with the consent of the person into whom a device is implanted.

In sum, there are fewer gaps with regard to the application of computer misuse and data protection law to cybernetic biohacking than initially appears to be the case.

5.4. Two Future Scenarios

We have seen that biohacking is a method and a movement, rather than a technology. Since this book is focused on developments in biomedical technology, this chapter's future scenarios concern hypothetical developments in do-it-yourself

[135] See Quigley & Ayihongbe 2018, 298.
[136] Quigley & Ayihongbe 2018, 298.
[137] s 3ZA(7).
[138] See Quigley & Ayihongbe 2018, 298–299.

biological augmentation: cybernetic brain biohacking. Two scenarios are envisaged.

Scenario one involves a DIY brain sensor device. It envisages developments in the functionality and sensitivity of external brainwave sensors. A biohacker, Jason, has modified commercially available brainwave sensors that had been designed to rest on the scalp, ie for use in a wearable device.[139] These sensors are about the size of 2 pence coins and Jason has coated them in silicate glass. He arranges for a professional tattooist and piercer, Sebastian Upgrade, to implant them under his scalp.[140] He then asks the tattooist-piercer to fasten a light (LED) device to his head with piercings and subdermal anchors.[141] Jason has designed that device to receive signals from the implanted sensors and he is now able to change its colour with his thoughts. He has become a media star.

In *scenario two*, various developments have culminated in the creation of DIY brain implants. Long-lasting electrodes have been developed that can be implanted into the brain and connected to medical devices that have been built modularly for ease of upgrading. It is further envisaged that a bi-directional implant has been designed to assist those with brain injuries and degenerative brain conditions to create new memories. Both the electrodes and this bi-directional device are regulated medical devices in clinical use. In such a scenario, it is a small step to envisage DIY versions, rather like the way that DIY APS (artificial pancreas systems) have been developed using existing devices (insulin pumps and continuous glucose monitors). In my scenario, cybernetic biohackers have found a way to upgrade the two-way brain-computer interface once it has been implanted. It involves leaving the electrodes in place but replacing part of the modular device and using biohacker-created software to control the operation of the device via a Bluetooth connection to a mobile phone. Over time it could become possible for the electrodes and device to be implanted together, outside a clinical context, by a robot – in 5.2.3 we saw that Neuralink is anticipating a robotic implantation procedure taking place in an hour without general anaesthetic. But for the purposes of this chapter, we need not imagine that this further step has already taken place. It suffices to imagine that the device has been implanted for a particular clinical purpose and patients have found a way to extend the functionality of their implants by biohacking, whereby part of the device is replaced and controlled by new software. This would require surgery to gain access to the device under all skin layers, but not brain surgery as such.

[139] My two biohackers take their names from a soldier of fortune from Greek mythology and his mistress: Jason and Medea. Jason is the biohacker in scenario one and Medea is the biohacker in scenario two.

[140] Alan Oversby, the tattooist-piercer convicted in the trial that ultimately reached the House of Lords in *Brown*, adopted the professional title Mr Sebastian (alluding to the story of St Sebastian, who was shot with arrows).

[141] Subdermal anchors are often used by body-piercers and involve small pieces of titanium jewellery being inserted into the skin with the stem protruding for another piece to be attached: see Public Health England et al 2013, 62.

Medea uses various online resources to create a replacement part for the implant in her brain. She then arranges for Sebastian Upgrade to modify her implant by replacing a component with the one she has provided. Her aim is to increase the functionality of the implanted device to enable her to monitor and trigger specific electric currents and thereby improve her memory. The modification is successful. Medea can now achieve memory feats beyond those available to those with the unmodified device – indeed, beyond those available to those whose brains are uninjured but lack the implanted device. These feats have made her a media star.

It is commonplace for parliamentary attention to be triggered by a scandal or by a conviction eliciting public sympathy. The activities of the defendant in *BM* – Brendan McCarthy, known as Dr Evil – did not elicit sufficient public support to trigger a review of the law.[142] It might be different if the 'victims' are considered by the public to have benefited from the body modification. Both of my scenarios involve apparently beneficial implantations undertaken by a tattooist and piercer, known professionally as Mr Upgrade. It is envisaged that Mr Upgrade is successfully prosecuted for unlawful wounding contrary to section 20 of the Offences against the Person Act 1861, with consent ruled out as a defence in accordance with the law as set out in *Brown* and *BM*. I will defend the plausibility of this legal conclusion in 5.6.2.

5.5. Application of the PGC

The earlier discussion highlighted problems with the justification and application of the public policy limitation on consensual serious assault (3.5.2). This limitation, along with the medical exception to it, has been defended by reference to a wide set of potentially conflicting moral and social considerations. Its application has drawn distinctions between very similar activities. Body modifications (such as tongue splitting or removal of an ear) fall foul of public policy, whereas consent can permit tattooing and piercing, and the medical exception permits a surgeon to perform a wide array of consensual cosmetic procedures.

This section will first draw out the implications of the PGC for consensual body modifications (5.5.1), consider when a request or response may be treated as a valid consent (5.5.2) and then consider the relevance of the implanter's status as a healthcare professional or tattooist-piercer (5.5.3). These considerations will be brought to bear when discussing the hypothetical response of Themis Walpole in the next section (5.6), which will start by briefly addressing the other legal issues raised in this chapter.

[142] A legislative response was recognised as 'unlikely' at the time: see Laird 2018, 850.

5.5.1. Consensual Bodily Modification

The PGC holds that all agents have rights to what they need to act for any and all purposes: the generic rights. These are will-rights, so rights-holders may waive their benefits. It follows that the PGC generally supports consensual activities. The only justifications for prohibiting apparently consensual harm are the inadequacy of the consent process and the violation of the more important generic rights of others.

The two key cases on the public interest limitation contain dicta questioning the adequacy of the process by which consent was obtained. In *Brown*, doubts were expressed about whether those whose buttocks, nipples and genitals were subjected to sadomasochistic attention had provided adequate and continuing indications of their consent. Lord Templeman noted that drink and drugs had been used to encourage participation and one victim had seemed to object to the second branding.[143] In *BM*, Lord Burnett LCJ expressed concern about the potential vulnerability, and absence of mental health assessment, of the recipients of body modification.[144] His Lordship also noted that one customer had consented to ear removal on the assumption that 'the defendant was appropriately qualified to carry it out'.[145] But the judges were not indicating that bodily harm would have been lawfully inflicted if the process for obtaining consent had been robust and the consent unequivocal. The victim's consent was held to afford no defence to a charge of serious assault in those circumstances. Since the PGC cannot support protecting people from the harmful effects of their own free choices, this regulatory approach requires either reform or justification as a suitable mechanism for protecting those who do not consent.

A wound or bodily damage is a prima facie basic generic harm. But is the blanket rejection of consent as a defence the appropriate mechanism for addressing the risk of mistakenly concluding that its infliction is consensual? The blanket rejection of this defence prevents those who do choose to initiate or otherwise consent to another inflicting bodily harm from giving effect to their will. This is no mere liberty. The PGC's recognition of agent-dignity and generic rights implies a 'rule-preclusionary' right to decide for oneself, within the limits of one's decision-making abilities, whether to permit interference with one's bodily integrity.[146] Further, the law's rejection of consensual activities can prevent individuals from obtaining the benefits of those activities. For those who attain sexual satisfaction through sadomasochism or self-expression through body modification, the activity could be expected to produce a net benefit to their generic needs. That is to say that in those circumstances where participation in such practices is

[143] [1994] 1 AC 212, 236.
[144] [2018] EWCA Crim 560, [39].
[145] In the later sentencing appeal: *R v McCarthy (Brendan)* [2019] EWCA Crim 2202, [18].
[146] See Beyleveld & Brownsword 2011, ch 8 (esp 188) and Pattinson 2018, 74–82 (esp 77).

predicted to have positive psychological effects, it can enable the participants to maintain or even advance their ability to achieve their purposes as such, despite the wound or injury. Thus, alternative mechanisms for protecting those who do not consent must first be rejected as inadequate before concluding that a blanket rejection of the defence of consent is appropriate.

In *Brown* and *BM*, the courts were considering a set of events in which there had been few procedural safeguards directed to ensuring that the consent was adequately assessed. The House of Lords in *Brown* were not prepared to consider alternative tools available to the court, such as specifying stringent requirements for establishing the defence. Instead, they considered it settled law that public policy limited the availability of the defence of consent and focused on identifying the level of bodily harm at which public policy operated as a block (with a limited category of exceptions). The Court of Appeal in *BM* considered itself bound by *Brown*. The judicial toolkit is, in any event, more limited than that available to the legislature, because the latter can put ex ante procedural safeguards in place to facilitate and assess the expression of a prospective participant's will.

The courts in *Brown* and *BM* considered the public policy limitation to be required to protect societal values and other members of society. The PGC is opposed to reliance upon social values and the interests of other members of society beyond their generic rights and the implications of those rights. In *BM*, weight was attached to the 'general interest of society in limiting the approbation of the law for significant violence' and the 'risk of unwanted injury, disease or even death' and the imposition of substantial cost on 'society as a whole'.[147] The exceptions to the public policy limitation were, in the view of the Court of Appeal, partly explained by reference to the potential for 'discernible social benefit' or cultural acceptance.[148] These considerations need to be interpreted narrowly to be compatible with the PGC and, once again, less restrictive mechanisms for protecting the rights of others must first be shown to be inadequate.

In sum, the only circumstances where consent is not an answer to the infliction of bodily damage are where (a) the consent process is insufficiently robust or the situation is such that consent cannot be suitably identified, (b) the burdens of discerning consent disproportionately interfere with the exercise of generic rights or (c) the activity or responses to it pose disproportionate danger to the generic rights of others. Prohibitions on consensual bodily interventions can therefore only be justified if a more targeted regulatory response cannot be suitably implemented to address these constraints. With regard to surgical biohacking, the principal issues are the inadequacies of the process for identifying consent and the need to protect others from harm.

[147] [2018] EWCA Crim 560, [39].
[148] [2018] EWCA Crim 560, [40].

5.5.2. Consent and Cybernetic Biohacking

Consent represents the waiving of the burden of an otherwise binding duty. As such its existence is a binary: either the individual in question permits the relevant activity or she does not.[149] Under the PGC, consent is an essential feature of the exercise of the generic rights: the conclusion that an agent has freely chosen to either defend her possession of the generic needs or accept damage to her possession of the generic needs. Since we do not have access to the minds of others, however, determining whether a decision of this type has been made requires interpretation of any signals given by that individual in the context of whatever additional information we have access to about that individual and her context.

While only an agent possesses the attributes required to make choices,[150] the exercise of an agent's will with regard to a specific task or activity requires more than agency as such. It requires the functional exercise of the requisite cognitive abilities, (specific task) competence, along with the freedom and information needed to make that decision.

Understood in this way, *competence* is the judgment that the individual has displayed the cognitive-functional ability to understand the relevant available information and weigh her desires in relation to that information. One complexity is there are degrees of informational understanding and reflection. The available information can be limited (especially for a novel activity or device), and understanding of that information can range from the broad-brush to the detailed: from understanding only the general nature and effects of what is to be done to understanding the detailed nature and possible and probable effects of a wide range of options. Similarly, the process of weighing desires can range from intuitive immediate reaction to considered evaluation.[151]

Judgments on displayed levels of understanding and reflection have implications for the burdens placed on both the signaller and signal interpreter. Imagine Sigmund expresses a preference for Tania to do something to him or something that affects him. Consider Tania treating that signalled preference as determinate of Sigmund's will only if she is fully satisfied that he has expressed his reflective will by weighing the salient available information on the nature and consequences of available options by reference to his overall values and desires. That would impose significant purpose-restricting burdens and could hinder or even prevent Sigmund from exercising his generic rights. Conversely, consider Tania treating Sigmund's signalled preference as determinate of his will even if there is little or no evidence that he has understood or weighed the options. This would impose few burdens

[149] I use 'she' for mere linguistic convenience. An individual who consents need not have a particular gender.

[150] From the perspective of a third party, this means someone who acts like an agent (an agent-behaver): see 2.3.1.

[151] This point has been expressed as a distinction between first- and second-order desires (Dworkin 1988, 15–20), and between 'current desire autonomy' and 'best desire autonomy' (Coggon 2007, 240).

on the process of Sigmund expressing his preference, but would also provide little basis for Tania to conclude that Sigmund's expressed preference coheres with what he wants to achieve in this instance or by reference to his overall values. If acting on Sigmund's preference exposes him to risk of generic harm, he has been treated as accepting a risk to which he might be opposed.

Any enquiry or threshold concerning Sigmund's level of understanding and reflection must be relative to what is capable of being understood at that time about the severity and likelihood of generic harm being caused by a mistaken conclusion as to Sigmund's will. For some purposes, such as acting on Sigmund's choice of beverage where there are no known allergies, no enquiries as to his understanding and reflection are usually required to avoid mistaken non-consensual interference with his generic needs. In contrast, irreversible bodily damage should not be treated as the object of Sigmund's will unless it is properly concluded that he has exercised his reflective will. It follows that concluding that consent has been given to temporary bodily adornments generally requires far fewer precautions than concluding that there is consent to the irreversible removal of healthy body parts.

When and how to access the *voluntariness* of an individual's expressed wishes must be similarly risk-relative. That is to say that the precautions taken by those acting on another's apparent will must be proportionate to the *likelihood* of reaching a mistaken conclusion and the *gravity* (for the agent-behaver's generic needs) of acting on such a mistake. The socio-cultural context is crucial to this judgment because it can place considerable pressures and expectations on the individual, particularly in relation to their external appearance or culturally valued attributes.[152]

How, then, are we to apply precautionary risk-relativity to cybernetic biohacking? Different devices and implantation procedures present different evidential bases for predicting the likelihood and severity of generic harm. The likely effects of implanting a magnetic device or an RFID chip into the hand are now well understood, whereas scenario two in 5.4 involves an experimental modification of brain function with what is likely to be a high probability of irreversible, long-term basic generic harm. Mr Upgrade was in no position to properly conclude that Medea had applied her reflective and suitably informed will to this modification to her implanted device. The assessment process required to support the conclusion that brain-implant upgrades of this type are consensual would be extremely taxing on both the implanter and the biohacker. The biohacker would need to display consideration of her overall values by reference to the principal details of the latest clinical research, including understanding the gaps in the evidence base.

This brings me to the claim that is often made that there cannot be appropriately informed consent at all for an untested procedure with potentially significant unknowns. In another context, it was claimed by the 2003 working party report of the Royal College of Surgeons that the lack of sufficient reliable data on the risks

[152] See eg Chambers 2019 on female genital cosmetic surgery.

of face transplants meant that 'patients will not be able to choose it in an appropriately informed way'.[153] This report went on to claim that since the risks were uncertain and potentially very high,

> obtaining *adequate informed consent* to incurring these physical risks appears impossible. There seems no way of coherently aggregating these risks for the purposes of *informed decision making* in such a way that the duty to respect autonomy overrides the duty to protect patients from unacceptable or unknown levels of potential harm.[154]

The implication was that an early recipient of a face transplant *who had a clear understanding of the available information relevant to her decision*, including information that reliable risk estimates were not available, would not be adequately informed. The rhetorical power of the quoted words is parasitic upon a conceptual conflation, whereby the conditions for an adequate indication of an individual's will are confused with the conditions for the justificatory sufficiency of that will. What is really being contested is not whether a patient could exercise her will in relation to a face transplant, but whether that will would be a morally sufficient justification for proceeding. Similarly, in relation to cybernetic biohacking, the mere existence of many unknowns and certainties does not prevent an individual from exercising her will, *if* she is aware of this lack of knowledge and that it could mean that the harm and likelihood of harm is much greater than she or anyone else predicts. The question is whether the biohacker displays sufficient understanding of known consequences and informational gaps. I will refer to this as the *informed consent concern.*

One difficulty with addressing the informed consent concern is that the biohacker's contribution to the creation or implantation of the device is likely to lead her to assume that she knows more about the likely consequences of implantation than she, or indeed anyone else, could know. I will refer to this as the *contributor bias concern.* This is plausible because hopes and expectations often facilitate misunderstandings. Patient participants in clinical research are, for example, prone to mistakenly assuming that the research aligns with their therapeutic needs.[155] The contributor bias concern could support foreclosing reliance on the biohacker's consent only if a response better tailored to this concern is not available.

5.5.3. The Biohacker, the Implanter and Other Affected Individuals

Whether the implanter is a healthcare practitioner, tattooist-piercer or some other person could be relevant to whether the biohacker has sufficiently evidenced consent and to the assessment of the risk to others.

[153] RCS 2003, 19 and the discussion in Pattinson 2009, 176–177. Cf RCS 2006.
[154] RCS 2003, 19 (my emphasis).
[155] See discussion of the 'therapeutic misconception' in Appelbaum et al 1982, esp 321 and Pattinson 2020, 283 and 387–388.

In *BM*, Lord Burnett LCJ noted that significantly invasive body modification procedures performed by those who are not qualified surgeons carry increased risk of infection and complications from the procedure being bungled or poorly performed.[156] This point is poignant to cybernetic biohacking in that qualifications and experience are likely to be relevant to an implanter's ability to safely perform the implantation procedure. The implanter's skill could thereby be relevant to the biohacker's consent and to the direct and indirect effects on third parties.

The consent issue is whether the biohacker has properly understood the implanter's qualifications and experience. I will refer to this as the *informed-about-qualifications concern*. This concern requires a regulatory process designed to ensure that the biohacker receives adequate informational opportunities, by regulating the provision of information and the process by which the implanter is qualified or registered. It is an instance of the *informed consent concern*, discussed above.

Predictable direct effects on third parties will vary in accordance with the nature of the procedure. Removal of a customer's nipple is not something likely to directly endanger the generic needs of third parties who have not been subjected to this intervention. In contrast, cybernetic brain biohacking of the type in scenario two is likely to give rise to complications, such as brain damage or an improperly connected or malfunctioning implant, that could lead the modified person to later lose control over their motor functions or to act recklessly or aggressively towards others. The modified subject's consent cannot waive the burden of duties owed to third parties. I will refer to this as the *endangering others concern*. A tailored response to this concern would require regulatory distinctions between different types of devices, implanters and implantation procedures.

Since infections and other complications are likely to require medical treatment, another implication of Lord Burnett's comment is that some procedures are likely to increase the burdens placed on the public health system. I will refer to this as the *public resources concern*. This legitimate concern does not automatically require the blanket prohibition of consensual surgical procedures outside the medical exception or even the blanket prohibition of anything more invasive than tattooing or piercing. Consideration must be given to whether legislation could introduce a regulatory response appropriately targeted to the risk to others. There are, for example, many ways to address potential increased costs for the healthcare system, including imposing licensing fees, insurance requirements or extra tax on service providers.

The implanter's skill or expertise could also be relevant to that person's ability to properly assess the biohacker's understanding. I will refer to this as the *implanter-assessment concern*. In *BM*, Lord Burnett placed emphasis on the ability of a doctor to identify when a patient needs to be referred for specialist mental health assessment. According to his Lordship,

> a cosmetic surgeon would be on the look out for potential psychiatric or psychological problems and, if necessary, refer the patient for an assessment. The General Medical

[156] [2018] EWCA Crim 560, [43].

> Council has also introduced rules which require a two week cooling off period before surgery is performed to enable a patient to change his or her mind.[157]

Lord Burnett draws attention not only to the cosmetic surgeon's expected skills but also to the regulatory requirements imposed on the process by which a health-care professional obtains consent. Healthcare professionals are subject to specific regulatory oversight, including professional guidance (supported by disciplinary procedures) and well-established legal norms (supported by the civil and criminal law process).[158] These requirements can address concerns beyond implanter-assessment. The cooling-off period, for example, can decrease the likelihood of a rash decision in which the patient does not consider the procedure by reference to her overall values or have the opportunity to seek the support of friends and loved ones.

A further complication is that some surgical interventions carry a significant risk to the subject's life. While the case for permitting consensual infliction of bodily harm is similar to the case for voluntary termination of life, euthanasia brings additional complexities. The procedure for euthanasia would have to be very carefully designed to protect others, which would include significant measures to minimise the pressure that the lawfulness of euthanasia would be likely to place on the disempowered and those made to feel unwanted. I will refer to this as the *assisted suicide concern.* Themis Walpole would want to legalise euthanasia but not by the backdoor means of legalising a greater range of consensual body modifications. The options for legislation below will therefore exclude attempts to legalise consensual procedures likely to cause death.

In summary, cybernetic biohacking raises many ethical concerns. One set focuses on whether biohackers have adequately evidenced their will, including:

(1) the *informed consent* concern, including the *informed-about-qualifications* concern;
(2) the *contributor bias* concern; and
(3) the *assister-assessment* concern.

These three concerns are overlapping: the contributor bias and assister-assessment concerns present obstacles to addressing the informed consent concern. Another set of concerns relate to how the biohacker's actions affect others:

(4) the *endangering others* concern;
(5) the *public resources* concern; and
(6) the *assisted suicide* concern.

Regulatory attention to these concerns should not assume that the implanter's wishes or interests align with those of the biohacker. Perhaps the implanter is a doctor who deliberately encourages a patient to mistakenly believe that the

[157] [2018] EWCA Crim 560, [13].
[158] See Pattinson 2020, chs 5 and 6.

intervention is likely to deliver benefits, or a tattooist-piercer who is only concerned with the expression of his own artistic skills. I will refer to this as:

(7) the unscrupulous assister concern.

Collectively these will be referred to as the *seven concerns*.

5.6. Hypothetical Bill

As explained in 3.6, UK primary legislation begins as a Bill in either the House of Commons or the House of Lords. This section reviews the areas of law for which the case for legislative reform could be made and then provides a summary of the case to be put before the House of Commons at the Second Reading of a Bill presented by a majority government led by an imaginary prime minister (Themis Walpole). The Second Reading is the first opportunity for Parliament to debate the main principles of a Bill and is usually opened by a government minister, who sets out the case for the Bill and explains its provisions.

5.6.1. Legislative Reform

In 5.3, I outlined many areas where the law is uncertain or otherwise problematic. It might be thought that my attempt to envisage legislative reform in accordance with contextual legal idealism will lead me to make the case for putting a Bill before Parliament directed towards addressing every issue identified earlier in this chapter. As Mark Twain is reputed to have said: if you have a hammer, everything looks like a nail. However, the preface 'contextual' refers to the need for sensitivity to societal and situational context in the application of legal theory. Legislation is a blunt instrument. Some of the legal issues examined do not require a legislative response.

The discussion of the system for regulating medical devices concluded that biohacking is likely to involve the creation or use of devices that fall outside that system (5.3.2). That system regulates the availability and safety of specific types of products placed on the market and cybernetic biohacking does not generally involve the creation of products for the healthcare system or market. Where biohacking practices later lead to the marketing of a medical device, it will then be captured by this regulatory framework. DIY APS have, for example, led to regulatory approval for commercially developed devices. The medical device regulatory framework's inapplicability to the activities of cybernetic biohackers is only a problematic lacuna if other legal mechanisms provide insufficient means of preventing or otherwise addressing non-consensual generic harms.

There are uncertainties as to the ownership of some types of implanted and removed devices, but ownership disputes of this type are unlikely to arise in practice (5.3.3). If such disputes arise, the common law is equipped to deal with them. I have elsewhere made the case for ownership of excised bodily materials by the person from whose body they were derived, which would have implications for excised implants.[159]

Legal uncertainties and practical questions also arise with regard to the application of intellectual property law (5.3.3). The manufacturer of a device would have difficulties enforcing their intellectual property rights against a biohacker, because most individuals are not worth suing and many self-help remedies (such as using software to stop the implanted device from working) could cause significant harm. Legal enforcement is more feasible against professionals assisting biohackers to modify the devices contrary to the IP holder's terms and conditions. I do not, however, propose to consider IP law further here. While IP law has the potential to both protect and undermine generic rights, reforms are difficult in light of the complex global system (supported by significant financial interests and international treaties) in which it operates.

Other legal mechanisms apply to harms potentially inflicted on others. Where someone hacks a cybernetic device implanted into another for malicious purposes, or without consent, their activities would be likely to fall within the Computer Misuse Act 1990 and the data protection legislation (5.3.4). The principal remaining legal issue concerns the role of criminal assault (5.3.1), to which I now return.

5.6.2. The Future Scenarios and the Law of Assault

The future scenarios outlined in 5.4 provide the context for the proposed Bill. It is imagined that there have been developments in cybernetic brain biohacking, and the assistance provided by a professional tattooist-piercer has led to his conviction. Mr Upgrade has implanted two devices: a DIY brain sensor device for Jason (scenario one) and a DIY brain implant modification for Medea (scenario two). The question this presents to Themis Walpole's government is whether it should allow such convictions to continue or seek to reform the criminal law of assault.

The moral evaluation in 5.5 does not support the blanket rejection of consensual bodily implantations nor restricting all consensual implantations to qualified surgeons or medical practitioners, *if more targeted regulatory responses are available.* I have highlighted seven concerns for particular attention: the informed consent, contributor bias, assister-assessment, endangering others, public resources, assisted suicide and unscrupulous assister concern. This section will consider the application of the current criminal law of assault to my imagined scenarios and the next section will consider some alternative regulatory responses.

As explained in 5.3.1, someone who implants a device into a biohacker cannot rely on that person's consent to a charge of assault, unless the implantation falls

[159] See Pattinson 2011 and Pattinson 2018, 168–172.

within one of the exceptions to the public policy limitation. Two categories of exception require further consideration: the medical exception and the piercing exception.

The *medical exception* applies to medical professionals acting in accordance with 'good medical practice'. There is a paucity of case law on what this means. Legislation sometimes provides steer by prohibiting or permissively regulating an activity. The medical device regime has a role to play and, where no biohacking is involved, its implications are usually straightforward. Implantation of a UKCA marked medical device in accordance with the manufacturer's instructions is clearly compatible with good clinical practice. There are three grounds for manufacturers to supply a non-conforming medical device within the regulations: MHRA-approved exceptional use, custom-made devices provided in accordance with a written prescription to a specific patient and use in an approved clinical trial.[160] All three of these grounds could enable a doctor to obtain a non-conforming device for implantation in accordance with good clinical practice.

Cybernetic biohacking involves the implantation of a device where that device or its implantation falls outside a standard clinical or research context. A biohacker might ask a healthcare profession to (a) supply or implant a conforming medical device for 'off-label' use (ie not within the manufacturer's instructions) or (b) implant a non-conforming device that is not covered by one of the three grounds in the 2002 Regulations.

The MHRA warns doctors that if they use a device off-label, they do so at their own risk and this could lead to dangers including adverse reactions, inadequate sterilisation, insufficient device strength, integrity or durability, or misuse due to adequate training for the device.[161] Nonetheless, off-label use – situation (a) – could potentially conform to good medical practice. A doctor could, for example, have an appropriate clinical rationale for advising on or even recommending a patient's use of DIY APS.[162] These systems involve use of two conforming medical devices (an implanted continuous glucose monitor and a wearable insulin pump) with the DIY/biohacking component being the open-source software installed on a phone or other computer to process data from the continuous glucose monitor and control the insulin pump. DIY APS are therefore systems that have been created outside a clinical or research environment that use component parts that fall within situation (a). The safety and performance of the DIY APS software (and therefore the device for which it is a component) has not been assured and confirmed as required for a UKCA mark, nor has it been supplied by a registered manufacturer within the terms of the medical device regulations. Since the implanted component has

[160] See MHRA 2020a (exceptional use of non-UKCA marked devices), 2020b (custom-made non-UKCA marked devices) and 2021a (clinical investigations of non-UKCA marked devices).

[161] See MHRA 2014.

[162] See Roberts et al 2021 and the discussion in 5.3.2.

been conformity-assessed, however, the act of implanting should not give rise to additional risks of the type listed by the MHRA for off-label use of medical devices, such as adverse reactions, inadequate sterilisation and so forth. Also, since these systems have been in use for some time, doctors should be able to suitably assess the benefits and type of risks presented by use of this software and advise their patients accordingly. Thus, doctors implanting components for use in DIY APS could plausibly invoke the medical exception. Whether this is the case for other off-label implantations of conforming medical devices would turn on the specifics of what is proposed in terms of the evidence that implanting the device is likely to benefit the patient.

In contrast, it is highly unlikely that situation (b) – a doctor implanting a non-conforming device that is not covered by any of the three grounds in the 2002 Regulations – would be acting in accordance with good clinical or research practice. This could involve using a device that has not been manufactured for implantation or even a device that the biohacker had modified or created themselves. The risks to the patient could be very serious and the doctor might not even be able to properly assess those risks. In my imagined future, if Jason and Medea's devices were implanted by a doctor, rather than a tattooist-piercer as envisaged, the implantation would almost inevitably fall outside the medical exception. The problem is that their creation of those devices has made it difficult for the doctor to be sure that they are suitably safe. These devices could be insufficiently sterile and might corrode or disintegrate inside the body. Even if Jason and Medea fully understand and accept those risks (ie the informed consent concern is addressed), implanting these devices does not seem to track their clinical needs. Implanting Medea's DIY brain implant is the furthest away from good clinical practice, because there is no therapeutic need to modify her existing implant and there is good reason to suspect that it might malfunction and cause serious harm. That harm could be to others if the malfunction were to cause a sudden loss of function or control (engaging the endangering others concern).

There is some ambiguity about the application of the public policy limitation to body-piercers who implant objects and devices into their customers. The Court of Appeal in *BM* rejected all body modification except tattooing and piercing, but the case was not directly concerned with implantations. Some types of implantations could be considered more like body-piercing than splitting or removing of body parts. Lord Burnett considered the body modifications before the court to be contrary to public policy because they went far beyond piercing and presented increased risks from infection, bungled or poor surgery, an inability to deal with immediate complications and lack of mental health assessment (which are relevant to the informed consent, assister-assessment, endangering others and public resources concerns). It is plausible that a future court might consider the consensual subdermal implantation of objects that do not extend outside the skin by a licensed tattooist-piercer to be lawful; though this is far from certain, and it would pose difficulties since the licensing regime does not strictly apply to any insertion not amounting to a piercing. In any case, Lord Burnett's concerns suggest that it would be unlawful for a tattooist-piercer to implant into another a medical device, a customer-provided implant or anything that could potentially interfere with physiological functions. From this analysis, the prosecutions envisaged in the future scenario seem to be highly plausible. Mr Upgrade almost certainly commits assault in scenario two and very likely does so in scenario one by implanting the subdermal sensors.

In sum, the public policy limitation operates as a considerable hurdle to the implantation of a device into a biohacker. The medical exception only supports doctors who act in accordance with professionally accepted treatment or research practices. As things currently stand, it is very unlikely that a professionally supported clinical rationale could be provided for implanting a device created by the biohacker into whom it is to be implanted. A tattooist-piercer who assists a cybernetic biohacker could not rely on the tattooist-piercing exception, because any implantation would either be clearly outside that exception or within its grey area. The law of assault thereby rejects some activities that could (if new procedures were implemented) be identified as consensual and as posing few risks to others.

5.6.3. Legislative Reform of the Public Policy Limitation and the Medical Exception

Many issues are raised by the current law of assault. *Brown* trespasses deeply and arbitrarily into consensual sexual practices. Ritual male circumcision on infants stands out as an instance of non-medical tissue removal where the subject's consent is not obtainable. The medical exception unduly defers to professional value judgments on the acceptability of the intervention. These issues go beyond this chapter's focus.[163] This section will consider two suggestions for reform of the public policy limitation: the Law Commission's proposal to raise the trigger threshold and the case for removal of the public policy limitation. It will then consider the case for reform of the medical exception. It will be argued that legislative proposals like these would not provide appropriate or sufficient responses to cybernetic biohacking.

In its 1995 Consultation Paper on consent in the criminal law, the Law Commission proposed raising the level of injury triggering the public policy limitation, from wounding or causing actual bodily harm to 'serious disabling injury'.[164] Consent would only provide a defence to injuries above this threshold if they fell within the established category-exceptions, including the medical exception, which would be put on a statutory footing.[165] Body decoration injuries

[163] Wider issues will be left to other works. See eg Ó Néill 2018, ch 6, on ritual male circumcision.
[164] See Law Commission 1995, esp paras 4.47 and 9.22.
[165] See Law Commission 1995, paras 8.50–8.51.

below that threshold, the Law Commission suggested, could be subject to 'effective statutory controls' to ensure that they 'are properly and hygienically carried out by licensed practitioners in appropriately licensed premises'.[166]

The Law Commission's proposed definition of 'serious disabling injury' is a modified version of the definition advanced by Williams for a different purpose, requiring:

> loss of a bodily member or organ or permanent bodily injury or permanent functional impairment, or serious or permanent disfigurement, or severe and prolonged pain, or serious impairment of mental health, or prolonged unconsciousness.[167]

Two of the three body modifications procedures in *BM* involved 'loss of a bodily member'. Pegg avers that tongue splitting might fall outside this definition, because it does not involve loss of a body part and, she submits, it does not result in 'serious or permanent disfigurement'.[168] It was performed without anaesthetic, but perhaps it could be argued that the resultant pain was not severe *and* prolonged. In any case, the quoted words above only form part (b) of the Law Commission's definition of serious disabling injury. Part (a) requires that the injury 'causes serious distress'. The body modifications procedures in *BM* did not appear to cause any distress beyond the pain of the procedure itself. This is to be expected, given that the customers had consented. Alldridge argues that a 'natural reading' of the part (a) requirement would take gender reassignment, cosmetic surgery, organ donation and other consensual medical procedures outside the scope of the criminal law, thereby apparently removing the need for a medical exception.[169] Such an interpretation would mean that the Law Commission's proposed system would permit consensual implantations that risked but do not happen to cause serious distress, including the implantation envisaged in scenario two. That would leave the process by which a biohacker's consent is identified and the risks to third parties insufficiently addressed.

The Law Commission's proposal was to retain the law's three-level structure of rule, exception and exception to the exception.[170] That is:

(1) the consent of the victim is a defence to all crimes with victims (*rule*);
(2) *except* where the level of harm is such as to require removal of the defence of consent in the public interest (*exception*); and
(3) *except* if the activity is one for which the public interest requires the defence of consent to be available, despite the harm being above this level (*exception to the exception*).

The content of the level 2 and 3 exceptions is meant to track the public interest. Under *Brown*, the level 2 exception is set at 'actual bodily harm' and the level 3

[166] Law Commission 1995, para 9.22.
[167] Law Commission 1995, para 4.51, citing Williams 1990, 1229.
[168] See Pegg 2019, 597.
[169] See Alldridge 1996, 136.
[170] See Alldridge 1996, esp 134–135.

exception comprises a handful of categories, including the medical exception and tattooing/piercing. Under the Law Commission's proposals, the level 2 exception is set at 'serious disabling injury' and the level 3 exception comprises the same category-based exceptions.[171]

As an alternative, Alldridge proposes a two-level structure of *rule* and *exception*.[172] That is:

(1) the consent of the victim is a defence to all crimes with victims (*rule*);
(2) *except* where (a) the victim is killed or (b) actual bodily harm is foreseen and/or caused in pursuance of a sexual encounter (*exception*).

This proposal removes the need for a 'quantitative approach', specifying the level of injury/harm above which consent cannot generally be a defence.[173] Alldridge provides for an exception to the availability of consent as a defence where the victim is killed, on the assumption that consensual killing will remain illegal. A further exception is made for certain types of sexual encounters on the assumption that the conclusion in *Brown* on its facts continues to hold.[174] He points out that other crimes would continue to apply. Consensual fights are, for example, illegal as affrays.[175] Other crimes could similarly address the Law Commission's concerns about surgery being carried out for eugenic purposes or to assist someone to make a dishonest claim against an insurance company.[176] Someone who, for example, seeks to defraud an insurance company potentially commits many inchoate offences of dishonesty.[177]

Alldridge's proposal adopts a simple structure. It also removes the need for the medical exception with regard to consensual bodily interventions, which I have argued unduly defers to the value judgments of the medical profession. Further, since the PGC's concern will be with the consent process and protecting third parties, it is important that other crimes remain. It is, for example, significant that consensual fights could be prosecuted as affrays, because unregulated fights are likely to take place in circumstances where any apparent consent is alcohol-fuelled or otherwise defective and third parties are placed at risk of injury.

Alldridge's proposal could not, however, be implemented without considerable elaboration on the exceptions, alternative crimes and structures for identifying and assessing consent. The required elaborations would need to go far beyond this chapter's focus on cybernetic biohacking. Consideration of Alldridge's exception

[171] The Law Commission accepts that the 'public interest' is an 'elusive criterion' (1995, para 15.4) and suggests that things become clearer if 'particular fact-situations' are evaluated individually by reference for the merits for and against criminalisation (1995, C.111).

[172] See Alldridge 1996, esp 135.

[173] See Law Commission 1995, C.5. The Law Commission itself recognised that there is 'a powerful prima facie case against slavishly adopting a quantitative approach': 1995, C.15.

[174] For criticism of *Brown* see Bibbings & Alldridge 1993.

[175] See Alldridge 1996, 135 (n 37).

[176] See Law Commission 1995, para 8.52, citing Dukeminier 1970.

[177] See Alldridge 1996, 142.

for sexual encounters would, for example, require detailed analysis of the gendered and cultural complexities of sexual encounters.[178]

A second reason why it is not appropriate for this chapter to seek to undertake this elaboration concerns the inadequacies of arm-chair legal theorising. Significant regulatory reforms need to be trialled before being adopted and require extensive public engagement. Extensive reform of the type proposed by Alldridge would be likely to have many unanticipated consequences and engage a disparate array of interests.

This chapter's Explanatory Notes will therefore not present a Bill that seeks to remove the public policy limitation or reform its harm threshold. Giving proper recognition to the rights of biohackers to modify and take risks with their bodies (including with the assistance of others) does, however, require clarification and liberalisation of the law. Since any proposed reforms will need to address the seven concerns, they are unlikely to fully satisfy the biohacking community whose ethos is opposed to restrictive institutional structures (5.2.2). Concerns about driving cybernetic biohacking further underground are countered by the fact that what is proposed increases the range of activities that are legal.

At first sight, the medical exception is too restrictive because the PGC does not require that a doctor's assistance address the therapeutic needs of the biohacker, or that the proposed procedure be part of an approved clinical trial, or even require that it have the support of the medical profession. Yet, legislative reform of this feature of the criminal law is not proposed here for three reasons. First, reforming the ambit of the medical exception would have consequences beyond cybernetic biohacking and therefore beyond this chapter's analysis. Secondly, the current criminal law offers some protection to cybernetic biohackers from unscrupulous doctors who act with insufficient regard for identifying their will or protecting third parties. Thirdly, the medical exception does not seem to prohibit conduct when protective mechanisms are in place, at least where those mechanisms are considered sufficient by the medical profession. Many cosmetic surgical procedures are, for example, considered lawful even where there is no clear therapeutic rationale.[179] This means that a process could be created to enable doctors to provide more extensive assistance to cybernetic biohackers, by ensuring that the biohacker is sufficiently informed and protected from unscrupulous doctors, within the medical exception as it currently operates. Themis could therefore seek the support of the medical profession to trial a system whereby the knowable effects of novel types of implants would be reviewed by a panel to ensure that any biohacker is properly advised and ensure that the biohacker's consent is assessed

[178] The conclusion of such an analysis is likely to be the need for carefully crafted consent rules, rather than preventing reliance on consent.

[179] See the discussion in 5.3.1. I am not arguing that the procedures applying to cosmetic surgery are sufficient to ensure that the patient has properly consented, only noting that the law regards it sufficient for the medical exception to be triggered that a doctor acts in accordance with accepted medical practice.

by an independent doctor. The principal limitation is that such a process would be resource-intensive and cybernetic biohacking is a tiny subculture. Since there would be no need for any such trial to be put on a statutory footing, this response is not considered in the Explanatory Notes below.

5.6.4. The Proposed Bill

The legislative intervention proposed below involves modification and supplementation of the registration system applying to piercing and tattooing. The purpose of the Bill is to provide for a process to support the identification of a subject's will and protect others when a non-healthcare professional implants a device. I offer the Explanatory Notes as no more than a suggestion of the type of legislative reform that could be advanced by Themis. There is no single appropriate regulatory response, and any proposal of this type would need to be trialled and subject to public consultation. This section will consider two options (Models I and II). The Explanatory Notes will outline a Bill for Model II.

Model I involves a slight modification of the current registration system to explicitly add a narrow category of subdermal implantations. Permitted implants would be restricted to sterile objects, magnets and microchips, sourced from recognised suppliers. Implantations like those in scenarios one and two would not be encompassed.

The technology for implantable microchips has advanced considerably since Kevin Warwick and Amal Graafstra had RFID transponders implanted into their bodies (5.2.2).[180] RFID transponders used for this purpose are now typically about the size of a grain of rice and encased in silicate glass. The implantation process usually involves injection of the microchip into the skin just above the thumb, using a syringe similar to that used for giving vaccinations. It poses the same types of physical risks as current practices in relation to tattooing and implanting dermal anchors (whereby small pieces of titanium jewellery are inserted into the skin with the stem protruding for another piece to be attached).[181] The manufacturers of implantable microchips would be liable for any defects under the existing law. Data protection law already regulates others access and use of personal data, and customers could be warned about others potentially illicitly accessing data about them from an implanted microchip.

If supplemented by a new procedure to facilitate cybernetic biohackers being assisted by health professionals (such as that suggested in the previous section), Model I should be sufficient to address the rights of biohackers, while addressing the seven concerns. Its modifications to the tattooing-piercing licensing system should be relatively straightforward to implement.

[180] See OpenMind BBAV 2021 and Latham 2022.
[181] On the existing practices see Public Health England et al 2013, esp 62.

The Explanatory Notes below present more ambitious reforms. Model II illustrates the type of steps that Themis would need to consider if she were to seek to permit non-healthcare professionals to provide greater assistance to cybernetic biohackers. It would permit a wider array of implantations, potentially including the assistance provided in scenario one. Model II avoids the need to define a device by capturing the implantation of any non-biological object or device. Biological implantations are not included because that could undermine the regulatory systems applying to transplantation and assisted reproduction (governed by the Human Tissue Act 2004 and the Human Fertilisation and Embryology Act 1990, respectively), where expert skills are required to minimise the risks to third parties. To keep within the remit of this chapter, the proposed Bill will involve no changes to the regulation of tattooing or cosmetic piercing.[182] Its starting point is to reject the defence of consent where the new statutory system is not followed.

In response to the endangering others concern, the proposal seeks to prevent tattooists-piercers from relying on consent for processes and types of devices that are likely to harm third parties. This includes those likely to interfere with the functioning of the brain or the ability to drive a vehicle or otherwise operate machinery. It would therefore not permit scenario two. Model II's response to the public resource concern relies on accreditation and registration. Registration fees could be used to offset any likely increase in costs to the healthcare system. In response to the informed consent concern, contributor bias and assister-assessment concerns, the proposal requires implanters who wish to rely on consent to be qualified, registered and comply with various conditions addressed at identifying and assessing the subject's will. This will include a compulsory cooling-off period. In response to the assisted suicide concern, nothing in the proposed Bill changes the law of homicide, and consent does not permit activities likely to cause death. These responses require a mechanism to identify the information the subject needs to understand and the risks to third parties and public health.

Neither model modifies the law applying to the administration of pain relief. Anaesthetics are medicinal products and many features of their distribution and administration are restricted to appropriately qualified healthcare professionals. This is a defensible regulatory response, given the need for anaesthetic access and application to accord with a procedure addressing the informed consent, endangering others and public resources concerns. Recipients of implantations into the skin will generally be able to obtain local anaesthetic creams, gels and sprays from a pharmacist, though the most effective of these will require a prescription.[183]

[182] There is a powerful case for additional national level regulation for tattooing and body piercing, particularly for irreversible procedures with long-term social consequences, such as eye and face tattooing. According to Public Health England et al 2013, 38: 'The absence of tattoo and body piercing accredited training and competencies is an area that needs to be addressed nationally.'

[183] On topical anaesthetics (ie anaesthetic creams, ointments, eye drops, gels or sprays that temporarily reduce sensation in the area to which they are applied), see See Kumar et al 2015 and www.salonexpert.co.uk/post/topical-anaesthetic-and-the-law.

These products would not be sufficient for deeper implantations, such as implanting the antenna into Neil Harbisson's skull (5.2.2). Without anaesthetic the pain is likely to be overwhelming, impeding the recipient's ability to think or control their movements and significantly increasing the likelihood that involuntary movement or a rushed procedure will require emergency medical attention. Thus, if the seven concerns are to be addressed, a healthcare professional would need to be involved with deeper implantation procedures, so both models are limited to subdermal implantations.

Extending subdermal implants beyond commercially sourced objects and microchips (as per Model I) requires a process to assess the attributes and consequences and provide for suitable information to be available to the recipient of the implant. Model II proposes the establishment of a committee to assess different types of implants and procedures and issue guidance, including model information sheets. In practice, I would expect this committee to operate within the UK Health Security Agency (UKHSA). UKHSA replaced Public Health England in April 2021 as the body responsible for public health protection. Public Health England was the lead of four bodies responsible for national guidance on tattooing and body-piercing.[184]

The Explanatory Notes below draw on existing Explanatory Notes, such as those on the Local Government Act 2003. Provisions of that Act amended the Local Government (Miscellaneous Provisions) Act 1982 to provide for the regulation of cosmetic piercing and semi-permanent skin colouring.

[184] See Public Health England et al 2013.

5.6.5. Explanatory Notes to the Bill

NON-MEDICAL IMPLANTATION BILL

EXPLANATORY NOTES

What these notes do

These Explanatory Notes relate to the Non-Medical Implantation Bill as introduced in the House of Commons on 1 August 2022 (Bill 2).

- These Explanatory Notes have been prepared by the Department of Health and Social Care in order to assist the reader of the Bill and to help inform debate on it. They do not form part of the Bill and have not been endorsed by Parliament.
- These Explanatory Notes explain what each part of the Bill will mean in practice; provide background information on the development of policy; and provide additional information on how the Bill will affect existing legislation in this area.
- These Explanatory Notes might be read alongside the Bill. They are not, and are not meant to be, a comprehensive description of the Bill.

Overview of the Bill

1 The Bill amends the law applying to businesses providing tattooing, piercing and acupuncture services in England and Wales. It amends the Local Government (Miscellaneous Provisions) Act 1982 and the London Local Authorities Act 1991, and the application of the Offences against the Person Act 1861. The Bill also sets up a body to maintain registers and issue guidance on non-medical implantation.

2 The following terms are used throughout the Explanatory Notes:

The 1861 Act	Offences against the Person Act 1861
The 1982 Act	Local Government (Miscellaneous Provisions) Act 1982, as amended
The 1991 Act	London Local Authorities Act 1991

3 To assist the reader of the Bill, the Department of Health and Social Care has produced an illustrative consolidated text of the 1982 and 1991 Acts, as amended. This shows the effect of the amendments made by the Bill. The text has no official status. The final form of the amended Acts will be available after enactment of this Bill in accordance with the *Policy on Public Availability of Acts of Parliament.*

Policy and legal background

4 This Bill fulfils the Government's commitment to ensuring that the law of England and Wales provides for a process by which a person who is not a registered medical practitioner may implant objects or devices below the skin of a person who provides a valid consent.

5 Under the 1982 Act, as amended, local authorities are responsible for regulating and monitoring businesses offering cosmetic piercing, permanent tattooing, semi-permanent skin colouring, electrolysis and acupuncture. This legislation requires the registration (licensing) of practitioners and premises. It also provides powers for local authorities to make byelaws relating to the cleanliness and hygiene of premises, practitioners and equipment. London local authorities have such powers under the 1991 Act. The powers granted to local authorities under the 1982 and 1991 Acts do not apply where the activities are carried out by or under

the supervision of a registered medical practitioner. Nor do these powers apply to body modification or other invasive procedures beyond those listed above.

6 There is no statutory age of consent for cosmetic piercing of the ears or body. Cosmetic piercing of a minor is lawful where a valid consent is given. Body-piercing for sexual gratification is unlawful. Children under the age of 16 are not able to provide a valid consent to a piercing that would be regarded as indecent assault. A statutory minimum age of consent for tattooing (18 years of age) is specified in the Tattooing of Minors Act 1969.

7 The government has sought views and information in accordance with the *Policy on Public Engagement and Consultation.* This process supports the government's view that wider reforms are required to the role of consent in the criminal law. Detailed proposals can be found in the consultation document entitled *The Future of Consent in the Criminal Law.* Interim proposals were presented in the consultation document entitled *The Future of Consensual Body Modification and Implants.* The Government took account of the views and information provided by the public when publishing the White Paper: *Review of the Law on Consensual Non-Medical Implants.*

8 There were two key proposals in the White Paper. The first key proposal was to broaden the remit of the tattooing, piercing and acupuncture registration system to cover the consensual subdermal implantation of objects and devices. The second key proposal was to provide for the defence of consent for offences against the person involving wounding and intentional infliction of bodily harm, where a practitioner complies with registration and other requirements. This Bill implements the proposals in the White Paper.

Commentary on provisions of Bill

PART 1: PRELIMINARY

Clause 1: The preamble

9 Clause 1 provides a preamble to the Bill comprising a set of principles to explain and justify its provisions:

- The Bill seeks to regulate non-medical implantations: implantation of non-biological objects and devices below the skin surface, when not cosmetic piercing nor undertaken by or under the supervision of an appropriately qualified healthcare practitioner.
- The only justification for non-medical implantation is the consent of the person into whom the object or device is to be implanted.
- The consent of the person into whom an object or device is to be implanted does not justify inflicting harm on third parties.
- The Bill seeks to put into place a procedure to support the identification of a valid consent to non-medical implantation and protect third parties from harm.
- The person giving consent must have been provided with information about the qualifications of the person implanting the object or device and the relevant known consequences of the implantation.
- This Bill provides for regulatory structures to support the application of these principles. It empowers local authorities to regulate practitioners, premises and equipment. It also establishes the Non-Medical Implantation Committee to issue guidance and maintain registers of manufacturers and their products.

- This Bill does not alter the law applying to cosmetic piercing or the temporary placement of a needle under the skin, such as for the purposes of acupuncture or tattooing.
- The Bill does not provide any defence to a charge of manslaughter or murder.

PART 2: REGISTRATION OF PERSONS AND PREMISES WITH LOCAL AUTHORITIES

Clause 2: Registration for non-medical implantation

10 Clause 2 inserts a new section 15A into the 1982 Act and amends section 4 of the 1991 Act. These amendments empower local authorities in England and Wales to require persons carrying on the business of implanting objects and devices below the surface of the skin to register themselves and their premises and to observe byelaws on hygiene and cleanliness. This clause does not apply to "excluded procedures", defined as the temporary placement of a needle into the skin (unless that needle is used to insert an object or device), cosmetic piercing, implantation or transplantation of biological material, and implantations undertaken by or under the supervision of a registered medical practitioner, dentist or nurse.

11 This clause brings non-medical subdermal implantation within the registration framework that applies to acupuncture, tattooing, semi-permanent skin colouring, cosmetic piercing and electrolysis.

Clause 3: Conditions for person registration

12 Clause 3 requires a local authority exercising power under clause 2 (registration for non-medical implantation) to be satisfied that any person registered is qualified. Relevant qualifications and qualification renewal periods are those specified on a register maintained by the Non-Medical Implantation Committee (see paragraphs 13 and 14).

PART 3: NON-MEDICAL IMPLANTATION COMMITTEE

Clause 4: The Committee

13 Clause 4 establishes the Non-Medical Implantation Committee (hereafter the Committee). It also gives effect to Schedule 1, which deals with the membership of the Committee.

Clause 5: Qualifications register

14 Clause 5 provides for the Committee to administer a register of qualifications in relation to subdermal implantation of non-medical implants. The Committee may specify a renewal period for any registered qualification. Relevant qualifications and renewal periods are those reasonably considered by the Committee to relate to the implanter's ability to perform, understand and advise on subdermal implantation, including identifying and minimising risks to third parties.

Clause 6: Registered manufacturers and non-medical implants

15 Clause 6 gives effect to Schedule 2, which sets out the powers and duties of the Committee in relation to the registration of manufacturers and non-medical implants. Registered non-medical implants provided by registered manufacturers are referred to in this Bill as "registered NMIs". Before registering a non-medical implant for subdermal implantation, the Commission must be satisfied that the information provided by the manufacturer about that implant is sufficient to

ensure that a practitioner registered with a local authority is able to implant and advise customers on its implantation and predictable effects.

Clause 7: Guidance

16 Clause 7 requires the Committee to issue written guidance for those registered to perform subdermal implantations with a local authority exercising power under clause 2 ("registered implanters"). This guidance should address the matters specified in Schedule 3.

17 These matters include subdermal implantation techniques for which suitable qualifications are available, the information that is to be provided to the person into whose body the implantation is to be made (the "client") and the steps registered implanters should take to support a reasonable belief that the procedure is a compliant procedure (on which see paragraphs 23–27).

Clause 8: Report

18 Clause 8 requires the Committee to produce a report when requested by the Secretary of State and otherwise annually. Any such report is to be made publicly available online.

19 The annual report should address the matters specified in Schedule 4, which relate to the activities in connection to registered and non-medical implants and the operation of the Guidance.

PART 3: MANUFACTURERS OF REGISTERED IMPLANTS

Clause 9: Registration obligation on manufacturers

20 Clause 8 requires manufacturers to register with the Committee (see paragraph 13) before supplying non-medical implants to implanters other than healthcare professionals.

PART 4: COMPLIANT PROCEDURES

Clause 10: Offences against the Person Act 1861

21 Clause 10 states that consent is not a defence to an offence under sections 18, 20 or 47 of the 1861 Act where a person intentionally cuts or penetrates another's skin for the purpose of implanting an object or device, unless it is an excluded or compliant procedure. Nothing in this clause alters the law applying to excluded procedures, which are those listed in clause 2 (see paragraphs 10 and 11).

22 This clause provides for consent to be a defence for compliant procedures. A "compliant procedure" is defined as a subdermal implantation performed by a registered implanter on registered premises (see paragraphs 10 and 11), where the implanter reasonably believes that the conditions in clauses 10–14 are satisfied (see paragraphs 21–26).

Clause 11: Consent and age requirement

23 Clause 11 provides that the person into whose body the subdermal implant is to be implanted (the "client") must be at least 18 years old and have provided their voluntary consent to the implantation.

Clause 12: Written specifications

24 Clause 12 provides that the client must have been provided with the written materials specified in Schedule 5. These relate to the implantation procedure,

the manufacturer's information sheets with regard to registered NMIs (on which see paragraph 15) and the Committee's guidance on client-provided implants (on which see paragraph 17).

Clause 13: Understanding of written materials

25 Clause 13 provides that the client believes and understands the written specifications.

Clause 14: Cooling off periods

26 Clause 14 provides for cooling off periods between the time at which the registered implanter provides the written specifications (see paragraph 24) to the client and the implantation procedure. Where the implantation relates to a registered NMIs implant, the cooling off period must be no less than 1 day and no more than 28 days. Where the implantation relates to an implant provided by the client, the cooling off period must be no less than 14 days and no more than 28 days.

Clause 15: Risk to third parties

27 Clause 15 requires the implantation not be into vascular tissues other than the skin and the implant not be one that could interfere with the functioning of the brain or the ability to operate machinery. Where the implant is provided by the client, the client must have provided a written specification of its components to the registered implanter.

PART 5: MISCELLANEOUS PROVISIONS

Clause 16: Criminal offences

28 Clause 16 provides for criminal penalties in relation to intentionally or negligently making a false statement in any of the written specifications required by this Bill.

Schedule 6: Transitional provisions

29 The clauses above should be read in conjunction with Schedule 6 which contains transitional provisions.

6

Cryonic Reanimation

6.1. Introduction

In late 2016, the mother of a terminally ill 14-year-old girl applied to the Family Division of the High Court for an order to obtain sole responsibility for making post-mortem decisions with regard to the disposal of her daughter's body.[1] What made this case unusual was that the girl, JS, wanted to have her body cryopreserved. She had her mother's support and her maternal grandparents had raised the necessary funds. Jackson J focused on JS's best interests and wishes as she approached the end of her life. He granted the application. JS therefore died with the expectation that her body would be frozen and hoping that she would one day be brought back to life.

Jackson J added a disturbing postscript to his judgment about what occurred on the day of JS's death. Her mother was said to have 'been preoccupied with the post-mortem arrangements at the expense of being fully available to JS' and the volunteers undertaking the preservation process were said to have been 'under-equipped and disorganised'.[2] A judge making a best interests determination on similar facts would be likely to have regard to this postscript and consider the likely impact of a loving parent being engaged with the cryonic preservation process on the day of the child's death.[3]

This chapter will first examine the current state of cryonic science and practice (6.2), before considering the challenges presented by cryonics to the interpretation and application of the law. Cryonic preservation raises many legal issues (6.3) and additional complexities will arise in the unlikely event that it delivers on its promise of reanimation (6.4). The future scenario will imagine a giant leap toward cryonic reanimation becoming a reality (6.5). The PGC will then be applied to that future scenario (6.6) and it will give rise to an imagined case before the UK Supreme Court (6.7). This case will explicate the rights and status of a reanimated cryonically preserved human – a future JS brought back to life after three years of cryopreservation. The legal questions addressed will therefore be very different to those raised in *Re JS*.

[1] *Re JS (Disposal of Body)* [2016] EWHC 2859 (Fam).
[2] [2016] EWHC 2859, [68].
[3] Cf Huxtable 2017, 490 (n 97): 'if a case akin to JS's were to arise in this jurisdiction, it is difficult to see how the same principles could not apply to same effect'.

6.2. Cryonic Science and Practice

The focus of this chapter belongs more to the realm of science fiction than the others in this book. Many hundreds of individuals have been frozen shortly after death, but none appear to have any realistic hope of future reanimation. This section will first address existing practices for cryopreservation of the body after death (6.2.1), before considering the cryopreservation of living tissue (6.2.2).

6.2.1. Cryopreservation of the Human Body

James Bedford is the only individual frozen before 1974 whose body is still preserved today.[4] Bedford was frozen in January 1967, a few hours after his death from kidney cancer that had spread to his lungs. The story is told in a book dictated by Bob Nelson, a TV repairer who became obsessed with cryonics.[5] Nelson was involved in the freezing of Bedford's body and later became President of the Cryonics Society of California. The method of preservation was crude by modern standards: Bedford's body was injected with dimethyl sulfoxide and other preserving chemicals, frozen with dry ice and then transferred to a liquid nitrogen environment.[6] His body was stored in various places, including a garage. Its current home is Alcor Life Extension Foundation.[7] Alcor, founded in 1972 and located in Arizona, claims to be the world leader in cryonics. Fifty years later, as of August 2022, it has 193 stored bodies.[8] Alcor's optimism for future reanimation is conveyed by the inclusion of the words 'Life Extension' in its full name. Those suspecting a financial motivation might be surprised to discover that, like most cryonic organisations, it operates on a non-profit basis.

The body of the 14-year-old JS is being stored by another US cryonics company: the Cryonics Institute in Clinton Township, Michigan.[9] The Cryonics Institute reports 217 stored bodies.[10] JS is designated number 143. Nelson, the man involved in the freezing of Bedford, has a place secured at the institute.[11] At least three other organisations provide cryonic storage. KrioRus, founded in 2003 and based near Moscow, has 85 bodies in storage, as of August 2022.[12] In September 2021, police were asked to stop a lorry removing containers with

[4] See Perry 1992.
[5] See Nelson & Stanley 1968. Bedford is given the pseudonym Harold Greene in this book. Bob Nelson published a follow-up memoir: see Nelson et al 2014.
[6] See Nelson & Stanley 1968, 59, 70–71 and 136–156 (Appendix).
[7] See Starr 2017.
[8] See www.alcor.org.
[9] See Beal 2017.
[10] www.cryonics.org/ci-landing/patient-details.
[11] See Nelson et al 2014, ch 19.
[12] kriorus.ru/en.

frozen bodies from KrioRus.[13] A former CEO of the company was accused of stealing the bodies by her ex-husband, who is also a former CEO. Both now own separate cryonics businesses and are involved in a battle over the bodies stored by KrioRus. It is, alas 'unclear what kind of damage the bodies might have sustained during the back-and-forth'. News reports do not mention any legal actions being brought by the families of those whose bodies are stored. What is perhaps surprising is that the bodies stored by KrioRus have increased from the 81 stored at the time of the alleged theft.

Oregon Cryonics (founded in 2005) and Cryonics Germany (founded in 2015) store only the brain.[14] During the Covid pandemic, a heightened awareness of mortality seems to have increased interest in the services of cryonic storage organisations.[15] Despite this, the actual numbers of additional bodies and brains cryopreserved decreased from previous highs of around a dozen a year. Covid-19 precautions limited the availability of medical-grade antifreeze solutions and rendered it more difficult to process and transport frozen bodies.

There are also several organisations offering cryonic resources or services other than cryonic storage. Trans Time in San Leandro, California was set up to 'help people bridge the technological gap that exists between the medical technology as it exists today and the medical technology that will exist in the future'.[16] Cryonics UK, the operating name of the charitable Human Organ Preservation Research Trust, was set up in 1991 to assist those in the United Kingdom who seek access to cryonic services.[17] They help to prepare and ship deceased bodies to the storage facilities provided by Alcor, the Cryonics Institute and KrioRus. Their services are provided by volunteers at a cost of around £28,000 for 'emergency assistance'. Cryonics UK reportedly arranged the preservation of JS's body in preparation for its transportation to the United States.[18] Recall the disturbing postscript from Jackson J, reporting the hospital's concern that the cryonic organisation's volunteers were 'under-equipped and disorganised, resulting in pressure being placed on the hospital to allow procedures that had not been agreed'.[19] The handling of the preservation process was said to have 'caused real concern to the medical and mortuary staff'. Following media interest in the case, and indicating the controversial nature of cryonic services, a member of the public made a complaint about Cryonics UK to the Charity Commission. It was removed from the charity register, but later reinstated on appeal.[20]

[13] See Pashaeva 2021.
[14] oregoncryo.com and cryonics-germany.org/en. The cryopreservation and thawing of whole brains is discussed below (6.2.2).
[15] See Wilson 2021.
[16] www.transtime.com.
[17] cryonics-uk.org.
[18] See Fernandez et al 2016.
[19] [2016] EWHC 2859, [68].
[20] *Hipkiss v The Charity Commission for England and Wales* [2018] 8 WLUK 229, esp [9] and [126].

Storage providers – such as the Cryonics Institute where JS's body is now stored – have their own fee structures. JS's body was reportedly stored at a cost of £37,000.[21] Most of that money was used to purchase stocks and bonds with the interest being used to pay for the ongoing costs of storage. Whole body preservation typically requires an annual membership fee while alive, plus a lump sum charged at the time of storage. Alcor typically charges $210,000 (including emergency assistance and shipping), Cryonics Institute $35,000 and KrioRus $36,000.[22] These are large sums and providers generally recommend that those who intend to use their services take out life insurance to cover these costs when they die.

The websites of the cryonic storage organisations outline procedures to prepare a body for storage as soon as possible following clinical death. The first step involves bringing about initial cool-down and transport to the cryonics company. The body is to be cooled in an ice water bath or body bag and specific substances injected and circulated through the body to prevent the blood clotting and the organs deteriorating. The specific substances used vary: Alcor refers to 'protective medications' and 'an organ preservation solution', whereas the Cryonics Institute refers to 'the anticoagulant, Heparin'. The second step involves replacing the patient's blood and body water with cryoprotectants to prevent ice formation. This step is known as perfusion. The third step involves steadily cooling the body to an ultra-low temperature (−196°C) and transferring it to a long-term storage unit. Bodies are usually stored in an inverted position to limit damage to the brain if there is a leak.[23] The three biggest cryonic storage organisations also store cryopreserved pets.

The cryopreserved body is referred to by these organisations as 'the patient', which is a word intentionally loaded with expectation of future reanimation. The current state of medical science, explicated in the next section, is such that the 'frozen corpse' would be a more accurate label. Others refer to the frozen corpse by a label coined 40 years ago: a 'cryon'.[24]

6.2.2. Cryopreservation and Reanimation of Living Tissue

The revival of a cryopreserved body has yet to be shown to be feasible. It has, however, been possible to freeze and revive some tissues.

Gametes and early-stage embryos are regularly cryopreserved. The first successful pregnancy using frozen-thawed human sperm was reported in 1953[25] and live births have been reported from sperm that has been frozen for more than

[21] See Beal 2017.
[22] Figures from cryonics-uk.org/faq.html.
[23] See Brahmabhatt 2021.
[24] See Smith 1983, 119–120 (see n 2).
[25] See Sherman & Bunge 1953.

two decades.[26] Frozen-thawed embryos have been successfully used since the early 1980s and the first pregnancy after human oocyte cryopreservation (egg freezing) was reported a couple of years later.[27] Figures published by the Human Fertilisation and Embryology Authority show that egg freezing increased tenfold from 2009 to 2019 (from 230 to nearly 2,400 cycles) and frozen embryo transfers increased by nearly threefold in the same 10-year period (from 9,796 to 28,317 cycles).[28]

The cryopreservation of gametes and early-stage embryos can now be achieved using a fast-freezing process known as vitrification. Vitrification causes less cryodamage than slow freezing and significantly increases survival rates.[29] The term literally means turn into glass and refers to the transformation of cells into a glass-like state.[30] The process involves removing and replacing water molecules with higher levels of a preserving solution (usually comprising a mix of permeable and non-permeable cryoprotectants), before rapid freezing in liquid nitrogen. Cryoprotectants can induce cellular damage, but, unlike slow freezing, vitrification can prevent ice crystal formation both inside and outside cells.[31] Repeat vitrification does not appear to reduce the viability of gametes and embryos – it is now commonplace for a vitrified egg to be used to create an embryo that is then vitrified and thawed before use.[32]

Some other tissues have been cryopreserved and successfully revived for use. Ovarian tissue cryopreservation has been used to preserve the fertility of patients before treatment for cancer and some other conditions, and is increasingly being considered as a way of postponing pregnancy and menopause in healthy women.[33] The first pregnancy from cryopreserved ovarian tissue was reported in 2004.[34] Over 130 babies had been born by 2017 after part of the ovary was removed, slow frozen in liquid nitrogen and later thawed and transplanted after treatment.[35] Several centres worldwide are now experimenting with vitrification and some live births have been reported following use of this procedure.[36] The success of vitrification is influenced by the volume of the sample.[37] The smaller the sample, the lower the probability of ice crystal formation and damage from the cryoprotectants. That is because larger samples do not cool uniformly, and require a lengthier cooling process and higher concentrations of cryoprotectants (which become increasingly toxic with higher temperatures and prolonged exposure).

[26] See BBC 2004.
[27] See, in particular, Zeilmaker et al 1984 and Chen 1986, respectively.
[28] See HFEA 2021. I have also used the HFEA's separately tabulated data, a link to which can be found at this source.
[29] See Nagy et al 2020.
[30] See Mukaida & Oka 2012, 800 and Nagy et al 2020, 242.
[31] See Nagy et al 2020, 241–242.
[32] See Nagy et al 2020, 243.
[33] See Donnez & Dolmans 2017 and Leonel et al 2019.
[34] See Donnez et al 2004.
[35] See Donnez & Domans 2017, 1661.
[36] See Kawamura et al 2013 and Suzuki et al 2015.
[37] See Leonel et al 2019, 176.

In humans, cryopreservation beyond reproductive cells has been restricted to blood and blood cells[38] and samples or slices of specific tissue. Whole human organs are proving to be much more resistant to successful reanimation after cryopreservation. The only reported success has been in another species: a rabbit kidney has survived vitrification and subsequent transplantation.[39] There have been other more marginal successes with animal brains. Some early experiments with isolated cat brains did show bioelectric discharges after revival[40] and there have been more recent experiments involving the thawing of cryopreserved rabbit and pig brains.[41]

The future revival of a cryopreserved body is, however, a distant and perhaps unattainable endeavour. Cryobiologist Arthur Rowe is widely quoted as declaring that 'believing cryonics could reanimate somebody who has been frozen is like believing you can turn a hamburger into a cow'.[42]

Alcor expresses hope that 'nanotechnologies and other future medical technologies' will bring appropriate methods for repairing biological structures at a molecular level to 'recover any cryopreserved person where the structures encoding memory and personality remain inferable'.[43] The Cryonics Institute expresses hope that future technological developments will enable the repair of damage due to ageing, disease and cryonic suspension, and the 'revival of people in a healthy and youthful state'.[44] KrioRus present a graphic in which they express the hope that future technology will enable a 'new body' to be built into which a revived and repaired brain would be transplanted from a cryopreserved body.[45] None of these methods are anywhere near worked out or approaching delivery.

Optimistic predictions of future scientific developments are clearly considered sufficient by those who make arrangements with cryonic storage providers. Several theorists have argued that the extremely low probability of future revival should be considered by reference to the alternatives to cryonic preservation. David Shaw suggests that we consider a modified version of Pascal's Wager, according to which the possible benefits of believing in God outweigh what you will lose if you do not believe in God.[46] Shaw argues that someone who takes a bet on cryonic preservation risks losing 'a bit of money' without being able to regret it and potentially gains a longer life and perhaps immortality.[47] He reasons that the 'Cryonic Wager' provides a prudential rationale for cryonic preservation and withstands the

[38] eg human umbilical cord blood responds well to vitrification: see Djuwantono et al 2011.
[39] See Fahy et al 2009. See also research on vitrification of rabbit kidney precursors: Marco-Jiménez et al 2015.
[40] See eg Suda et al 1966 and 1974.
[41] See McIntyre & Fahy 2015.
[42] Quoted in eg Conway 2016, 53 (n 206) and Wilson 2021.
[43] www.alcor.org/what-is-cryonics.
[44] www.cryonics.org/about-us/faqs.
[45] kriorus.ru/sites/kriorus/files/angl_1200.jpg.
[46] See Shaw 2009 and Pascal 1670 (as translated: Krailsheimer 1966, 151).
[47] Shaw 2009, 520.

standard arguments against Pascal's Wager. But Shaw's calculation is incomplete: being revived only equates to winning the wager if the revived life is worth living. A longer life of unremitting suffering, perhaps due to irreparable nerve damage or even the actions of an evil reviver, is unlikely to be considered preferable to non-revival. More recently, Francesca Minerva says that cryonics 'is a bit like buying a rather expensive lottery ticket knowing that the chances of winning are extremely small, but that the prize would be exceptionally valuable'.[48] But buying a lottery ticket risks no more than the purchase price. Minerva's analogy makes no reference to the chance of an outcome that is worse than death: the extremely small chance of a prize includes a prize that is worse than no prize at all.

6.3. Complexities Arising before the Point of Reanimation

Potential legal issues arise in the period leading up to death (only some of which were addressed in *Re JS*), at the moment of death, during freezing, transportation and storage, and at and beyond the point of reanimation. In the United Kingdom, there are no current laws specifically targeted at cryonics. This section will address the issues arising up to the point of reanimation and the next will address the issues that would arise in the very unlikely event that a cryopreserved body is reanimated.

6.3.1. Certifying and Bringing about Death

There is no statutory definition of death. The few cases addressing the determination of death have deferred to clinical practice. In *Re A*, a young boy who satisfied the clinical criteria for brain-stem death was declared to be dead, by Johnson J in the Family Division, 'for all legal, as well as medical, purposes'.[49] Satisfaction of clinical criteria for brain-stem death has been held to be sufficient for legal purposes in obiter statements in the House of Lords and in subsequent first instance decisions.[50] The latest professional guidance is a Code of Practice issued by the Academy of Medical Royal Colleges in October 2008, which states:

> Death entails the irreversible loss of those essential characteristics which are necessary to the existence of a living human person and, thus, the definition of death should be regarded as the irreversible loss of the capacity for consciousness, combined with irreversible loss of the capacity to breathe.[51]

[48] Minerva 2021, 239.
[49] *Re A* [1992] 3 Med LR 303, 305.
[50] See *Airedale NHS Trust v Bland* [1993] AC 789, 856, 863, and 878; *Re A (A Child)* [2015] EWHC 443; *Manchester University NHS Foundation Trust v Namiq* [2020] EWHC 5 (Fam).
[51] AMRC 2008, 11.

This Code identifies death as the 'irreversible cessation of brain-stem function'. It goes on to advise that, where death is determined by brain-stem testing, it should be done by at least two experienced doctors who have no clinical conflict of interest and are not members of the transplant team.[52] In my view, this is a single restriction: determinations of death are not to be at the hands of the transplant team to avoid a clinical conflict of interest. It follows that the doctors determining death should not be members of the cryopreservation team. In the United Kingdom, the cryopreservation team typically comprise volunteers without medical qualifications, as was the case for JS.

The realisation of cryonic reanimation threatens to cause difficulties for the clinical certification of death in a similar way to how the arrival of ventilators required a means to certify death without requiring certification of irreversible cardiopulmonary failure. The difficulties presented would turn on what is involved in the process of reanimation. If biomedical developments enable future reactivation of the brain stem, then it becomes more difficult to certify irreversible cessation of brain-stem function. Difficulties certifying death would not be insurmountable, but technological developments could require reconsideration of what death involves. Certification of human death already differs from certification of death for other living entities: brain-stem death criteria could not be applied to plants and are not in practice applied to animals.[53] Supporters of cryonics typically advance a criterion of death premised on the idea that an individual's existence only ends when the information stored in the brain is irretrievably lost: the information-theoretic account of death.[54] A concomitant account of personal identity attached to memory retention is then required to determine what degree of displayed recollection is required for that individual to be considered the same individual by others.[55] The information-theoretic account could also be applied to non-human animals, and the three big organisations store cryopreserved pets.

The discussion so far might suggest that the advent of cryonic reanimation would create pressures to move the clinical and legal identification of death to a later point. But the pressures could also go the other way, at least while death remains a legal precondition for cryopreservation of a human body. Pre-mortem suspension could avoid the need to repair damage to the body beyond that caused by cryopreservation itself. Gametes and tissues are, after all, cryopreserved for later reanimation while alive. As the law currently stands, however, cryopreserving a body before legal death or bringing about death to assist with cryopreservation would involve several very serious crimes. Murder, punishable

[52] AMRC 2008, 19. See *Barts Health NHS Trust v Dance* [2022] EWCA Civ 935, [37], where the Court of Appeal strongly cautioned judges against declaring death on a basis outside the Code where none of the medical witnesses has themselves made a diagnosis of death.

[53] See Singer 1994, 21–22.

[54] See Moen 2015, 677; Minerva & Sandberg 2017, 527–528; Minerva 2021, 236.

[55] For further discussion of personal identity see Pattinson 2017.

by up to life imprisonment, involves causing another's death by an act or by an omission constituting a breach of duty, where the intention is to kill or cause serious bodily harm. Intention can be inferred from foresight of death or serious bodily harm as virtually certain.[56] The lesser offence of assisted suicide, punishable by up to 14 years' imprisonment, is committed where a person intentionally encourages or assists the suicide or attempted suicide of another.[57] These crimes are committed by ending another's life or assisting them to end their own life, even if what is done is with their consent for the purpose of facilitating their cryopreservation and even if they are already dying.

Pre-mortem cryopreservation has been considered by the Californian courts. Thomas Donaldson was concerned that his brain cancer would destroy too much of his brain before killing him, so sought a declaration that he had a constitutional right to be cryopreserved before his legal death and to be assisted by others to achieve this.[58] He argued in the alternative that he had the right to be assisted to end his own life by a lethal dose of drugs. He lost at first instance and on appeal. Gilbert J, in the Court of Appeal, held that there was no constitutional right to assisted death and it was constitutionally prohibited by a criminal law statute. In the judgment of June 1992, it was stated that physicians had 'predicted his probable death by August 1993, five years from initial diagnosis'.[59] That proved to be wildly pessimistic: he died in 2006 and his body is now cryopreserved at the Alcor Life Extension Foundation.[60] Clinical predictions of life expectancy are often little more than best guesses[61] and such imprecision can render preparations for cryopreservation difficult.

Were voluntary euthanasia to be permitted (as it is in some jurisdictions), the case against bringing about an earlier death to facilitate cryonic preservation would be more difficult to maintain. Minerva and Sandberg have gone further by arguing that 'cryothanasia … achieves the positive goal of euthanasia (ending suffering) without its negative instrumental side-effects (permanent cessation of life)'.[62] They respond to those who object that 'cryothanasia uses up resources that could otherwise have been used for other people's treatment' by pointing out that it would be likely to shorten end-of-life care and the costs of cryopreservation and storage do not currently fall on the state.[63] This provides only a partial response to justice/equity objections, because considerable future resources would be required to attempt reanimation and, if the attempt is successful,

[56] See eg *R v Woollin* [1999] 1 AC 82.

[57] Suicide Act 1961, s 2(1).

[58] *Donaldson v Van de Kamp*, 4 Cal Rptr 2d 59 (Cal Ct App 1992). See also Pommer 1993.

[59] 4 Cal Rptr 2d 59, 61.

[60] See Schwartz 2017. Commentators do not seem to mention the discrepancy between what was predicted at the time of the hearing and what occurred.

[61] eg the scientist Stephen Hawking was 21 when told that he had only two years to live, but lived until he was 76: see Sample 2018.

[62] Minerva & Sandberg 2017, 528.

[63] Minerva & Sandberg 2017, 532.

the reanimated individual would require financial support for their extended life. Further, if the technology delivers its full potential, a reanimated individual could attain advantages available to no others by virtue of an exceptionally extended healthy lifespan. I will return to justice concerns in 6.6.1.

6.3.2. Preservation and Storage of Human Bodies

Strict burial laws can hinder cryonic suspension. A French court required the burial of two frozen bodies, one of which had been stored in the basement of a chateau for 18 years, on the basis that the Civil Code 'only envisages the burial or cremation of deceased persons within a time limit of six days after death'.[64] The son of the frozen couple had intended to appeal the decision, until the freezer in which they were stored broke down and they started to thaw.[65] French law does not prohibit frozen bodies being shipped to other countries for storage.

The Canadian Province of British Columbia has legislation explicitly prohibiting selling or arranging cryonic services where these services are provided 'on the expectation of the resuscitation of human remains at a future time'.[66] This seemed to have a chilling effect (pun intended) on cryonic activities in the province. A change occurred in 2018, when the provincial government settled a constitutional challenge by clarifying that it was 'not intending to investigate and prosecute responsible cryonics practices in the province'.[67]

The case with which this chapter began, *Re RJ*, demonstrates that cryonic suspension is not unlawful in this jurisdiction. The current law applying to the disposal and storage of humans is not, however, specifically targeted at cryonic preservation and storage. The Human Tissue Act 2004 has no application, so there is no regulatory body overseeing the associated procedures.

Many individuals have views on what should happen to their bodies after their death. Many want to be cremated, some want to be buried and a tiny minority want to be cryopreserved. In England and Wales, individuals have no legal right to determine what happens *post mortem*.[68] This follows from the long-established maxim of the common law that there is no property in a dead body or its parts.[69] Lawful rights over disposal of a corpse vest in the executor under the deceased's will[70] or in the highest-ranked next-of-kin when administering the estate of an

[64] Quoted in Daley 2002.
[65] See Chrisafis 2006.
[66] Cremation, Interment and Funeral Services Act 2004, s 14. This prohibition had appeared in the previous legislation, albeit worded slightly differently: Cemetery and Funeral Services Act 1996, s 57.
[67] Macintosh & Wong 2018, 8.
[68] *Re JS* [2016] EWHC 2859, [48].
[69] Despite the dubious origins of this maxim (see Matthews 1983), it has been confirmed by the Court of Appeal: *Dobson v North Tyneside Health Authority* [1997] 1 WLR 596 and *R v Kelly* [1999] QB 621.
[70] *Grandison v Nembhard* [1989] 4 BMLR 140.

intestate.[71] The executor or administrator has the final say: the wishes of other family members and the deceased are no more than factors for them to take into account.[72]

Irrespective of the wishes of the deceased, executor or administrator, a coroner may take temporary possession of a body to investigate the cause of death using a post-mortem examination.[73] No consent is required. Where this does not occur, a hospital may seek to carry out a post-mortem examination for medical purposes. This requires 'appropriate consent'.[74] Any post-mortem examination would very likely render the body unfit for cryopreservation.

In the absence of cryonic storage facilities in the United Kingdom, frozen bodies are transported to facilities overseas (see 6.2.1). Regulations require that if the person in possession of the body intends to transport a dead body out of England, they must first notify the coroner and provide the certificate of death.[75] The body cannot be removed from the country until four days have passed from notification of the coroner.

In extreme circumstances, those delaying burial or cremation could be charged with a common law offence. *R v Hunter*, a decision of the Court of Appeal from 1973, seems to be the first example of a prosecution of this type since the nineteenth century.[76] The defendants had strangled a girl in a field during 'horseplay' and then hidden her body under paving stones. The Court of Appeal dismissed the appeal from the conviction for conspiracy to prevent lawful burial, notwithstanding that prevention of burial was not the defendants' object when they hid the body. Cairns LJ declared that an offence occurs if a 'decent burial' or cremation is prevented 'without lawful excuse'.[77] There have been many subsequent successful convictions.[78] In one case, a husband who killed, chopped up and froze his wife was sentenced more severely for preventing her lawful burial than for her manslaughter.[79] This crime, however, poses few difficulties for the cryonic preservation of bodies, at least where there has been no obstruction of the coroner or the administration of justice. It is concerned with the *unlawful disposal* of a corpse,[80] and cryopreservation has been judicially recognised as a lawful means of disposing of a corpse.[81]

[71] Administration of Estates Act 1925, s 46.
[72] See Conway 2018, 137.
[73] Coroners and Justice Act 2009, ss 14–15.
[74] The Human Tissue Act 2004, s 1(2) and Sch 1, Pt 1.
[75] The Removal of Bodies Regulations 1954/448, regs 4–6.
[76] [1974] QB 95. See Jones & Quigley 2016.
[77] [1974] QB 95, 98.
[78] See eg *R v Swindell* (1981) 3 Cr App R (S) 255; *R v Parry* (1986) 8 Cr App R (S) 470; *R v Peddler* [2000] 2 Cr App R (S) 36. Jones and Quigley (2016) convincingly argue that there is little need for this crime, given that more suitable alternative crimes exist to capture serious wrongs.
[79] *Attorney General's Reference (No 90 of 2005)* [2006] EWCA Crim 270.
[80] See Jones & Quigley 2016, 362.
[81] See *Re JS* [2016] EWHC 2859, [19] and *Hipkiss v Charity Commission for England and Wales* [2018] 8 WLUK 229, [120].

6.3.3. Damage to a Frozen Corpse

Damage to a corpse during the process of preservation or when in storage raises many legal complexities. The application of criminal damage and various torts is limited by the long-established maxim of the common law that there is no property in a dead body or its parts.[82] An exception to this maxim applies if the corpse or body part has 'acquired different attributes by virtue of the application of skill, such as dissection or preservation techniques, for exhibition or teaching purposes'.[83] This exception is not as straightforward as first appears. The brain preserved in paraffin for autopsy in *Dobson* did not thereby become property, but the conviction for theft of two men who took body parts from the Royal College of Surgeons was upheld in *Kelly*. I have argued elsewhere that these decisions are reconcilable if property is understood to be acquired by the application of work and skill *with an appropriate intention*.[84] That is to say that the legal status of the dead body and its parts is not altered by preservation unless there is an intention to assert ownership. In *Dobson* the preservation had been to comply with the Coroners Rules without the intention of retaining it for any other purpose,[85] whereas in *Kelly* the preservation had been for the purpose of exhibition and teaching. Where this exception to the no property maxim applies, it only grants property rights to the preserver. It would therefore not seem to assist a case against the person who performs the preservation process.

Another exception to the no property maxim was recognised in *Yearworth*.[86] This was a case in which the Court of Appeal held that men whose sperm had been negligently allowed to thaw had an ownership interest in the damaged sperm sufficient to support an action in negligence. Ownership of the sperm was held to vest in the men because it had been generated and ejaculated by their bodies alone, and the 'sole object of the ejaculation of the sperm was that, in certain events, it might later be used for their benefit'.[87] The preservation of a frozen corpse for improbable future reanimation is, however, very different from the preservation of the sperm of a living person for their future reproductive use. The sperm-producers were living claimants with a clear loss, which would not be the case for the frozen corpse. But this case does indicate that the law in this area is still developing.[88]

[82] This maxim was confirmed by the Court of Appeal in *Dobson v North Tyneside Health Authority* [1997] 1 WLR 596 and *R v Kelly* [1999] QB 621.
[83] *R v Kelly* [1999] QB 621, 631; following *Doodeward v Spence* (1908) 6 CLR 406 and *Dobson v North Tyneside HA* [1997] 1 WLR 596, 601–601.
[84] See Pattinson 2011, 404.
[85] [1997] 1 WLR 596, 602.
[86] *Yearworth v North Bristol NHS Trust* [2009] EWCA Civ 37.
[87] [2009] EWCA Civ 37, [45].
[88] See Pattinson 2017 for an argument that the work-skill exception is reconcilable with *Yearworth* and both are applications of the same underlying principle.

Relatives who have contracted with a cryonic storage organisation could have an action for breach of contract. Such actions would usually be brought in the jurisdiction of the cryonic organisation and would turn on the terms of the relevant contract. The Cryonics Society of California and Cryonics Internment (both now defunct) were successfully sued when deliveries of liquid nitrogen lapsed and bodies in their care thawed.[89] It is reported that relatives received a jury award of $928,594 for breach of contract and civil fraud. The case was settled on appeal.[90] It led Bob Nelson, the TV repairer who became President of the Cryonics Society of California, to change his name and disappear from the public eye for two decades.

In this jurisdiction, a further legal option is suggested by a case decided in the Leeds County Court.[91] In *Brennan*, surviving family members brought a claim under the Human Rights Act 1998 against a hospital and a council. They argued that the defendants' failure to freeze the body of a deceased family member constituted an unjustified interference with their article 8 rights to private and family life. Instead of freezing the corpse, the defendant public bodies had kept it refrigerated for over a year, so that it had decomposed to such an extent as to render it unfit for viewing before burial. The applicants succeeded and were awarded damages under the 1998 Act. The judge was clear that his conclusion rested on the rights of the surviving family, as 'a dead body itself has no article 8 rights'.[92] This first instance decision is not strictly a precedent, but it does indicate that the Convention right to private and family life of surviving relatives has a potentially wide impact on the activities of public bodies in possession of a corpse. Public bodies are not, however, currently involved in the cryonic preservation and storage of bodies for the purpose of enabling future reanimation.

6.4. Complexities Arising from the Point of Reanimation

Since cryonic reanimation might never be achieved, it is hardly surprising that its legal consequences have yet to receive judicial or legislative attention. This section will consider the legal rights and status of a reanimated person (6.4.1), their legal age (6.4.2) and the possibility of legal actions for damage or harm inflicted prior to reanimation (6.4.3).

[89] See *Halpert v Nelson*, No 161229 (Cal LA County Super Ct 1981) and Time 1981.

[90] See Nelson 2014, ch 16.

[91] *Brennan v City of Bradford Metropolitan District Council and Leeds Teaching Hospitals NHS Trust* [2021] 1 WLUK 429.

[92] [2021] 1 WLUK 429, [80]. Cf Davey & Mead 2022.

6.4.1. The Reanimated Person and Connections

Cryonic reanimation envisages the reanimation of a body that has been legally declared dead. It evokes many legal questions. Would the reanimated individual be considered the continuation of the previous legal person, or a new legal person? Could the reanimated individual reclaim previously owned assets that had been inherited by others on death? If the reanimated individual had been married to someone who remained alive, could that marriage be reinstated? Similar questions have already been considered by courts and legislatures where a person has been mistakenly declared dead after going missing, only to reappear years later. In several cases, individuals have faked their deaths, or attempted to do so, for fraudulent purposes, which has led to their conviction for various crimes.[93]

Under the Presumption of Death Act 2013, missing persons can be declared dead by the High Court, where thought to be dead or not been known to be alive for at least seven years.[94] A declaration of presumed death determines the missing person's date and time of death, unless later varied or revoked by a variation order.[95] A variation order does not revive a marriage or civil partnership that was ended by a declaration of presumed death. Nor does it affect any property interest acquired as a result of a declaration of presumed death, though the court is empowered to make such further orders as it considers reasonable.[96] This Act provides a useful template for a suitable legal response to a reanimated frozen body. It provides for mechanisms for continued legal personality and the balancing of competing interests. By way of contrast, consider the Ohio case in which it was held that a US man declared dead after disappearing nearly three decades earlier remained 'legally dead', even though he appeared in good health before the court.[97] The judge found that Ohio legislation provided that a judicial decree stating that a person is presumed dead could only be set aside within three years of being issued. If cryonic reanimation technology were to deliver its full promise, provisions similar to those in the Presumption of Death Act 2013 would prevent potential injustices stemming from rules that completely sever the legal link with the previous legal person.

The Presumption of Death Act also contains provisions addressing insurance, to limit negative financial consequences to others from a variation order. A court may direct a trustee of a trust affected by a declaration of presumed death to take out an insurance policy in respect of any claim that could arise as a result of a variation order.[98] Further, an insurer may require a person receiving a pay-out under an insurance policy as a result of a declaration of presumed death to take out an

[93] See eg *DPP v Stonehouse* [1978] AC 55 and *R v Darwin* [2009] EWCA Crim 860, esp [2].
[94] s 1. This applies only to England and Wales.
[95] ss 3 and 5.
[96] ss 6 and 7.
[97] See BBC 2013a.
[98] s 13.

insurance policy in respect of any claim the insurer might make if a variation order is issued.[99] Provisions of this type are an appropriate way of countering potential unfairness from the application of a variation order. Similar provisions, with the necessary changes made, could be adopted if cryonic reanimation technology were to become feasible.

In the period between a person going missing and being declared presumed dead, the legal estate of that person remained in legal limbo. The Guardianship (Missing Persons Act) 2017 rectified that by enabling a guardian to be appointed to administer a missing person's property and financial affairs for up to four years.[100] Guardianship powers of this type would not be needed for a frozen body unless and until short-term cryonic freezing (perhaps for the purposes of space travel) becomes a reality.

It might be thought that one way in which a person may, in contemplation of their post-mortem cryonic preservation, provide for their future self would be to set up a trust for which their future self would be the beneficiary. A long-standing limitation on leaving money for future persons is the 'rule against perpetuities', which restricts the creation of future interests in private property that would vest or take effect a long time in the future. Under current legislation, the perpetuity period (ie the time limit) is now 125 years.[101] This rule does not affect the operation of the so-called 'wait and see rule', which prevents the engagement of the rule against perpetuities unless and until it becomes clear that the estate or interest will not vest within the perpetuity period.[102] Extending the perpetuity period so that individuals could benefit their future selves, which would require legislation, would not be a straightforward response to cryonic reanimation given the advantages that super-longevity would already bestow. Issues of distributive justice will be discussed in 6.6.1.

6.4.2. Legal Age

Legal age is ordinarily a straightforward calculation from the date of birth. In England and Wales, a child's parents are required to register the birth of a child within 42 days.[103] In the case of an abandoned child who is thought to have been born in England and Wales but for whom the date of birth is unknown, the child's date of birth may be registered as the most likely date.[104] Where a birth certificate is not available, passport policy recognises that discretion may be exercised when acting on documentation produced as near as possible to the date of birth.[105]

[99] s 14.
[100] See, in particular, ss 1, 2 and 7(2) of the 2017 Act.
[101] Perpetuity and Accumulations Act 2009, s 5(1).
[102] s 7(6).
[103] Births and Deaths Registration Act 1953, s 2.
[104] s 3A.
[105] See HM Passport Office 2019.

In short, legal age is to be determined by reference to the known or most likely date of birth. In the absence of any legislation or court decision to the contrary, the default assumption following the reanimation of a deceased individual would be that their legal age remains determined by the time elapsed since birth. This could mean that there is little connection between the individual's development or appearance and their legal age. A reanimated individual could have been born a matter of moments or many decades before their legal death, and that individual could have spent an extensive period in a frozen state, perhaps even hundreds of years. For most legal questions, it matters more whether reanimation continues legal personhood or triggers the creation of a new legal person. The future scenario outlined in 6.5, however, is one in which legal age is of significance for the law as it currently stands.

6.4.3. Suing for Damage Inflicted Prior to Reanimation

A question not addressed when considering damage to the suspended corpse in 6.3.3 was whether an action could vest with the reanimated individual. It might be thought that an analogy could be drawn with prenatal injury actions brought in the name of a child born alive with disabilities as a result of negligently inflicted injuries in the womb.[106] These legal rights and protections, considered in 4.3.5, are said to 'crystallise' at the point of being 'born alive', before which the claimant was not a legal person. There are points of disanalogy. While a late-term fetus *in utero* is not a legal person, it is recognised as a living human worthy of some legal protection. As Judge LJ put the point in *St George's Healthcare*: 'Whatever else it may be a 36-week foetus is not nothing: if viable it is not lifeless and it is certainly human'.[107] Also, crucially for the operation of standard negligence principles, it is reasonably foreseeable that a healthy late-term fetus will be born alive. Extremely improbable technological leaps would be required for reanimation to become reasonably foreseeable for a frozen human body.

If giant leaps in cryonic reanimation technology were to occur, granting the reanimated person rights to sue for damage inflicted when frozen would need to be supplemented by further protections for the frozen body prior to reanimation. The prospect of reanimation triggering legal liability would not only be a disincentive for attempting reanimation, it would be an incentive for destroying a body once it has been damaged. Laws protecting the fetus *in utero* are far more robust than laws protecting frozen bodies. In the absence of legislative intervention, a court applying modified law as integrity should be wary of recognising a reanimated individual's standing to sue for pre-reanimation damage. This is therefore an issue in which an approach within contextual legal idealism could be very different, depending on whether it is addressed by the courts or the legislature.

[106] Congenital Disabilities (Civil Liability) Act 1976 and *Burton v Islington HA* [1993] QB 204.
[107] [1999] Fam 26, 45.

6.5. A Future Scenario

My scenario envisages a 15-year-old girl being frozen and reanimated three years later. I will call her Chione, after the goddess of snow in Greek mythology, which conveniently gives her the same initial letter as cryon.[108] The required developments in cryonic freezing and reanimation technology are far more extensive than the future biomedical developments imagined in the other chapters. Chapter 3 imagined plausible refinements to current genome-editing technology, chapter 4 imagined extension of ectogestation technology currently being developed using lamb fetuses and chapter 5 imagined the development of current nascent brain sensor and implant technology (albeit including an entirely imagined application to memory creation abilities). This chapter's future scenario is not a plausible extension of existing biomedical science. Fortunately, a detailed scientific backstory is not required since the purpose of my future scenario is to enable exploration of tensions and gaps in the existing law. Nonetheless, to reduce the imagined scientific leaps, Chione is envisaged as having been frozen prior to her death. As we have seen, this would be criminal even if undertaken on an adult with her unequivocal consent: where the freezing process is the cause of legal death, a preserver with appropriate knowledge would satisfy the requirements of murder.

For the purposes of this scenario, it is imagined that an evil doctor (with the help of various collaborators) deliberately misdiagnoses a fatal condition and then later improperly certifies Chione's death. He has the unwitting support of her parents, who are prominent advocates of cryopreservation. Her body is then frozen, using improved cryopreservation techniques, and stored until the doctor's abominable actions are discovered just over two years later. During the cryopreservation period, her body displays no living processes, and she is clinically and legally considered dead. It is further imagined that there have now been significant leaps in the reanimation of animals that have been frozen when alive. Chione's parents are able to use these leaps to persuade a group of scientists and healthcare professionals to attempt her reanimation.[109] Her body had been in cryonic storage for three years at the point of reanimation and they were concerned that longer storage would reduce the already extremely low chances of reanimation. This (admittedly implausible) scenario means that Chione's reanimation would only require repair of the damage caused by her cryopreservation, rather than treatment for the effects of ageing, a major underlying health condition and a cause of death unrelated to the cryopreservation process.

Science would still have to have taken giant leaps forward. Not only is revival from cryopreservation currently not possible, current cryopreservation processes also cause extensive damage from ice crystal formation (especially in tissues

[108] Chione is pronounced 'Hee aw nee'.
[109] This would not strictly require a court declaration, because Chione would be legally dead.

that do not successfully vitrify), oxygen deprivation, cryoprotectant toxicity and thermal stress.[110] It is not imagined that Chione has been revived without complications: her liver and kidneys have been damaged. Less plausibly, Chione is envisaged as suffering from little or no brain damage. The court case with which this chapter concludes is triggered by Chione's refusal of the organ transplants required to sustain her life, contrary to the views of the medical team and her parents. The case will therefore focus on her legal age and whether, if she remains a child, her refusal is legally effective.

6.6. Application of the PGC

Discussion of the application of the PGC in this section will focus on two issues: distributive justice and the weight to be attached to the will of the reanimated individual.

6.6.1. Distributive Justice (Equitable Access and Opportunities)

My future scenario differs from those typically imagined in science fiction and by proponents of cryonics. Chione did not consent to cryonic suspension while alive to facilitate long distance space travel, as in some science fiction. Nor does she have much in common with the damaged lifeless bodies currently stored by the three big cryonic storage organisations. The brevity of the storage period means that she does not wake up in a technologically alien world in which all those for whom she cared are dead. Perhaps most strikingly, the freezing of Chione's body did not grant her advantages denied to others. Chione was deceived and almost fatally endangered by her premature cryonic preservation.

For most envisaged futures involving cryonic reanimation, the most pressing ethical issues concern distributive justice. Any criteria for access to medical and societal resources must recognise the equal status of all agent-behavers as rights-bearers. The extension of healthy lifespan is something to which all have equal claim. Continued life is the most basic generic need. Yet, cryonic preservation currently depends on the ability to pay, which means that the opportunity for extended longevity from cryonic reanimation is restricted to a small subsection of the population. For now the likelihood of future reanimation is extremely low and the likelihood of the resultant extended life being without purpose-destructive suffering even lower, so cryonic preservation must give way to other

[110] There have been incremental steps towards suspended animation, with reports of the cooling of a patient to 10 to 15°C to prolong the time available for surgery: see Thomson 2019.

uses for public funds more likely to address basic generic needs. If healthy cryonic reanimation becomes feasible, its benefit to recipient individuals would be immense. Completely random allocation does not seem to be a feasible allocative mechanism in the light of extant societal and global forces. Even if it were, receipt of such a benefit would still perpetuate significant social divisions and distinctions between recipients and other agent-behavers.

If super-longevity, by cryonic reanimation or other means, could not be provided to everyone, it ought not to be provided to anyone.[111] Maximising bodily existence for only some could not even be an aspiration without discrimination between agents at the point where all human agents are most fundamentally equal. Unfortunately, giving effect to the principle that super longevity ought to be available to everyone or no one, would require economic, social and regulatory structures beyond those that seem to be currently feasible. Those with resources frequently prevent or bypass regulatory restrictions, aided by globalisation. If, as I fear, opportunities to benefit from developments towards super-longevity will not be distributed fairly, we must hope that cryonic science will fail to achieve its most ambitious aims. In any case, Chione's situation involves only a small step towards the realisation of cryonic reanimation associated with super-longevity.

Once cryonic reanimation has occurred, access to preservation and reanimation opportunities become historical issues for the reanimated individual. The distributive justice issues raised by Chione's current situation centre on the demands she is making on healthcare resources as someone in need of urgent life-sustaining care. These are no different from those made by others suffering from multiple organ failure.

Even if individual responsibility were a relevant factor for the allocation of human organs and other scarce healthcare resources, Chione is in no way responsible for her predicament. That is not to suggest that individual responsibility is an appropriate allocative criterion. Context and opportunities are so vastly different for individuals that attempts to assess individual responsibility seem to be bound to misfire by giving undue credit or discredit for things beyond the control of the relevant individual. Here, I merely seek to indicate that this issue does not arise in my future scenario.

The focus of my scenario is also not on the acquisition and allocation of available organs. Chione's *life-sustaining need* for an organ transplant satisfies the first principle of any PGC-compatible system for the allocation of scarce human organs. If this chapter were about organ transplantation as such, I would want to revisit the United Kingdom's empowerment of the will of deceased potential organ providers over the needs of potential recipients of life-saving organs and the prohibition of financial incentives to organ providers in the Human Tissue Act 2004, but those issues are not of direct concern to cryonic reanimation.[112]

[111] For an earlier defence of this principle, though not directly referring to cryonic reanimation, see Beyleveld & Pattinson 2004.

[112] See further Pattinson 2003; 2008; 2020, chs 12 and 13.

6.6.2. The Age and Decisions of the Reanimated Individual

On its face, the application of the PGC to my future scenario does not require consideration of Chione's identity over time or her age.

Chione's *identity over time* arises if we ask whether the person prior to cryopreservation (living-Chione) remains the same individual during cryonic storage (frozen-Chione) and after reanimation (reanimated-Chione).[113] Different accounts of personal identity support divergent conclusions on whether living-Chione and reanimated-Chione remain the same person. On the psychological account of personal identity, which requires psychological continuity with one's past self, they do.[114] On any account that requires uninterrupted persistence as a living entity, they do not.[115] If they are different people, then it is difficult to support the obligations and decisions of living-Chione binding reanimated-Chione. In my scenario, however, living-Chione did not make decisions that were intended to apply during the cryopreservation of her body or after her reanimation.

Reanimated-Chione's *age* arises if specific rights or liberties are legitimately triggered by attainment of a specific age. Chione was born 18 years ago, the reanimation occurred just over four months ago and no ageing or other developmental processes took place during cryopreservation. Calculating different periods could lead us to conclude that reanimated-Chione is 18 years, 15 years or only four months old. At first, it seems that her age is not relevant. Chione is not, for example, set to inherit at the age of 18. Different legal rights in this and other jurisdictions are, however, triggered by the attainment of specific ages. Those under 18 cannot, for example, legally purchase alcohol or vote in UK parliamentary elections.[116] In my scenario, the relevant legal right is the right to refuse medical treatment, which the case law indicates cannot be exercised by a child against the consent of the court or even a parent.[117]

In some circumstances, age-specific legal rights are plausible outcomes of indirect applications of the PGC. We change as we age, so age thresholds can track species-level expectations of displayed cognitive or physical attributes. This means that age could be used as a rule of thumb or an automatic trigger for rights associated with those attributes. The age threshold would need to be appropriately associated with the relevant attributes and the legal consequences of reaching that age suitably selected and assessed. The weight of any legal presumption that an

[113] See eg Huxtable 2018, 485–487.

[114] See Locke 1690 and Parfit 1984, 204–209 and the discussion in Pattinson 2017.

[115] See Huxtable 2018, 486–487.

[116] Licensing Act 2003, s 146(1) and Representation of the People Act 1983, s 1(1), respectively.

[117] See eg *Re W* [1993] Fam 64 and *An NHS Foundation Hospital v P* [2014] EWHC 1650. In *Re D* [2019] UKSC 42, [26], Baroness Hale noted that: 'Whether the consent of a parent remains effective even if a child, with capacity, has refused consent is a more controversial question (which fortunately does not arise in this case).'

individual possesses the relevant attributes associated with attaining a specific age must be proportionate to the consequences of a mistaken attribution and the difficulties of individualised assessment.

Where the relevant attribute is decision-making ability, age could only be used as a *conclusive* indicator of developmental characteristics in very limited circumstances. One situation is where a very young age is simply incompatible, given the features of species development, with decision-making ability on the relevant issue. No newborn human, for example, displays the ability to make any decisions. Other situations would be where age is highly suggestive of possession of the relevant decision-making abilities, and the consequences of a mistake are trivial or more direct assessment is too burdensome relative to the rights affected. In most situations, age may provide no more than a presumptive starting point.

In my future scenario, Chione needs a life-sustaining combined liver-kidney transplant. The transplant involves major surgery and post-operative interventions, which involve basic generic harm. But it is expected to improve the quality and duration of Chione's life, thereby protecting even more important basic generic needs. If, however, Chione's refusal properly represents her will, then it must be determinate. That's because her generic rights are will-rights, and the interests of her parents and others in her survival have less weight than her engaged right to bodily integrity.[118]

I argued in 5.5.2 that the exercise of an agent's will where it involves acceptance or rejection of generic harm requires more than agency as such. It requires the exercise of the cognitive-functional abilities to make that type of decision (competence), along with the freedom and information needed to make that decision. The precautions taken by those acting on another's apparent will must be proportionate to the likelihood of reaching a mistaken conclusion and the gravity (for the agent-behaver's generic needs) of acting on such a mistake. Since acting on Chione's refusal is likely to shorten her life, it would be appropriate for others to start from a presumption that she lacks the requisite cognitive-functional abilities and require that her refusal be demonstrated to represent the exercise of her reflective will. Her reflective will is the product of her weighing the salient available information on the nature and consequences of available options. What is salient is to be determined by reference to her generic needs and her overall values and desires, because those are the values to be weighed in the exercise of her generic rights.

In determining whether Chione's refusal properly represents her will, the key issue in my future scenario is thus whether she is competent to apply her reflective will to that decision. There is no magical age at which all humans suddenly become competent to make decisions of this type. Chione's developmental features place her in the same category as a 15-year-old, because the evidence suggests that her brain neither developed nor deteriorated during cryopreservation.

[118] See Pattinson 2018, 74–82 (esp 77).

6.7. Hypothetical Case

Below I present a judgment of Lady Athena in relation to a hypothetical case triggered by the future scenario outlined in 6.5. This is a judgment of the UK Supreme Court to enable presentation of differing plausible judicial responses at three judicial levels. The judges in the lower courts are, like Chione and Athena, given names from Greek mythology. The judge at first instance is given the same name used in chapter 4: Apollo J. The lead judge in the Court of Appeal is referred to as Hercules LJ, which is the name used by Ronald Dworkin for the judge he imagines reasoning in accordance with his theory of law as integrity.[119] A judge applying modified law as integrity would seek to interpret the law to best align its requirements to those of the PGC, which is the approach taken by Lady Athena.

The judgment on the next page adopts the style of recent Supreme Court judgments.

[119] See Dworkin 1986, discussed in 2.4.1.

6.7.1. Re C (Supreme Court)

Lady Athena PSC

Introduction

1. The facts of this appeal are unique and, above all, tragic. C was a healthy 15-year-old girl who was frozen ("cryonically preserved") despite being neither dead nor dying at the time. Dr X and his collaborators deceptively convinced C, her parents and other healthcare professionals that C had a terminal condition. He used this as a pretext to make arrangements with C and her parents for her post-mortem cryopreservation. With his collaborators he then faked her death. C was therefore sedated, rather than dead, at the time of her cryopreservation.
2. These deceitful and unlawful actions were not discovered until C's body had been in cryonic storage for over two years. By this time Dr X had himself died. I will not here comment further on his actions, which are the subject of an ongoing investigation.
3. Due in no small part to the efforts of her loving parents, a clinical team was persuaded to attempt to revive ("reanimate") C. The probability of success was considered extremely low. Despite some recent successes with other animals, no human had been revived after cryonic preservation. C spent three years in a cryonic state, during which time her body displayed no life signs, but she is now very much alive. She has, alas, suffered damage to her extremities and such damage to her liver and kidneys that her continued life will at some soon require multiple organ transplantation. These facts were uncontested before this and the courts below.
4. C refuses to consent to transplantation. She simply does not want to extend her life in this way. It has become clear that C had supported the cryopreservation of her body only because she had wanted to give some comfort to her parents and thought it extremely unlikely to result in her reanimation.
5. The NHS Trust, with the full support of C's parents, made an application to the Family Division of the High Court. The Trust applied for an order incorporating a declaration that it was lawful and in C's best interests for her to undergo a combined liver and kidney transplant operation. Apollo J held that X was only 15 years old in law and her refusal was not determinate as to her best interests. The judge granted the requested order. The Court of Appeal reversed that order. Hercules LJ, giving the judgment of that court, held that C was legally 18 years old and, as such, had "the right to refuse life-sustaining treatment for any or no reason at all, because she does not lack capacity at this time". In this appeal to the Supreme Court, the Trust argues for reinstatement of the order issued by Apollo J.
6. This appeal has been expedited. At the time of the hearing before this court, C had been reanimated for just over four months.

Consent and refusal of life-sustaining treatment

7. The law applying to consent and refusal of medical treatment differs according to whether the patient is a child or an adult. A core difference between the decisions of the courts below is that Apollo J considered C to be a 15-year-old child and the Court of Appeal considered her to be an 18-year-old adult.

8. Adults are presumed to be able to make legally effective decisions on whether to permit medical treatment. An adult who has not been shown to be unable to make a decision may provide a valid consent. Since to treat such an adult without their consent is to commit both a tort and a crime, they are also entitled to refuse treatment, even if it is life-sustaining: *Airedale NHS Trust v Bland* [1993] AC 789, especially at pp 857 and 864, and *Re B* [2002] EWHC 429.
9. The Mental Capacity Act 2005 provides for the lawfulness of treating those who are "unable to make a decision" for themselves in relation to the matter (section 2(1)). Such a person is said to "lack capacity". The 2005 Act only applies to those who are at least 16 years old and lack capacity or are reasonably believed to lack capacity (section 2(5)). In accordance with standard legislative practice, the 2005 Act refers to an individual using the singular male pronoun (he/him).
10. Section 1 sets out five underlying principles. Three concern the process for determining whether the person in question ("P") lacks capacity. The first principle is the presumption that P has capacity unless it is established otherwise (s 1(2)). The second principle is that P is not to be treated as lacking capacity unless "all practicable steps" have been taken to help P to make a decision without success (s 1(3). The third principle is that P is not to be treated as lacking capacity merely because "he makes an unwise decision" (s 1(4)). The criteria for determining incapacity are set out in sections 2–3.
11. Section 2(1) provides that "a person lacks capacity in relation to a matter if at the material time he is unable to make a decision for himself in relation to the matter because of an impairment of, or a disturbance in the functioning of, the mind or brain". As Lord Stephens noted in *A Local Authority v JB* [2021] UKSC 52, at paras 66, 67 and 78, applying this section requires us to ask two questions. The first question is whether P is "unable to make a decision for himself in relation to the matter". The second question is whether that inability is "because of" an impairment or disturbance in the mind or brain.
12. Section 3 sets out what Lord Stephens refers to as the "statutory descriptions and explanations which support the core provision in section 2(1)" (para 65). P is unable to make a decision for himself in relation to the matter (section 2(1)) if he is unable to understand the relevant information, retain that information, use or weigh that information, or communicate his decision (section 3(1)).
13. Sections 1 to 3 thus make it clear that P is to be treated as lacking capacity only when reasonably believed to lack the cognitive-functional ability to make that decision at that time (decision-specific competence). P's lack of competence therefore provides the explanation and justification for exercising the 2005 Act's powers in relation to P.
14. The law treats children differently from adults in several ways. While the 2005 Act applies to children who are 16 or 17, it does not capture all decision-making powers over such children and it is silent on younger children. It has long been recognised, by both the common law and statute, that consent to the medical treatment of a child can be given by the court and by the child's parents. Parental authority to consent on behalf of their children is now encapsulated in the concept of "parental responsibility" in section 3(1) of the Children Act 1989. The capacity of competent children to make decisions for themselves is more complex.

15. A child's consent is partly dealt with by legislation. Section 1 of the Family Law Reform Act 1969 reduced the age for majority from 21 to 18. Section 8(1) states:

> "The consent of a minor who has attained the age of sixteen years to any surgical, medical or dental treatment which, in the absence of consent, would constitute a trespass to his person, shall be as effective as it would be if he were of full age; and where a minor has by virtue of this section given an effective consent to any treatment it shall not be necessary to obtain any consent for it from his parent or guardian."

This states that the "consent" of a 16 or 17-year-old to "any surgical, medical or dental treatment … shall be as effective as" that of an adult. Since an adult who has not been shown to be able to make decision under the capacity test in the 2005 Act is able to give an effective consent, it follows that this is also the case for a child of the specified age.

16. Section 8(1) does not apply to a child below the age of 16. The consent of such a child was considered by the House of Lords in *Gillick v West Norfolk and Wisbech Area Health Authority* [1986] AC 112. *Gillick* was a challenge to Department of Health and Social Security guidance to health authorities, which advised that in exceptional circumstances a doctor may prescribe contraception to a girl under 16 without her parents' knowledge or consent. The challenge to this guidance failed at first instance. It succeeded in the Court of Appeal on several grounds, including that a girl under 16 cannot give a legally valid consent to contraceptive treatment. The majority of the House of Lords (Lord Fraser, Lord Scarman and Lord Bridge of Harwich; Lord Brandon of Oakbrook and Lord Templeman dissenting) allowed the appeal.

17. The majority in *Gillick* held that the capacity (legal power) to consent to medical treatment was possessed by a child under 16 who is capable of understanding what is proposed. According to Lord Fraser, at p 169:

> "Provided the patient, whether a boy or a girl, is *capable of understanding what is proposed*, and of expressing his or her own wishes, I see no good reason for holding that he or she lacks the capacity to express them validly and effectively and to authorise the medical man to make the examination or give the treatment which he advises." (Emphasis added.)

Lord Scarman declared, at p 188:

> "I would hold that as a matter of law the parental right to determine whether or not their minor child below the age of 16 will have medical treatment terminates if and when the child achieves a *sufficient understanding and intelligence to enable him or her to understand fully what is proposed*." (Emphasis added.)

Lord Bridge agreed with both.

18. It was clear that their Lordships considered the required abilities to relate to the complexity of what is proposed. Lord Fraser, at p 169, specifically indicated that a child of 15 could ordinarily be expected to display the ability to consent to the examination of trivial injuries or even the setting of a broken arm. His Lordship went on to hold that some would also be able to give a valid consent to contraceptive advice or treatment.

19. The principle explaining and justifying the decision in *Gillick* was embedded in the common law. The decision of the House of Lords in *R v D* [1984] AC 778 had considered the ingredients of the common law offence of kidnapping in relation to children under 14 and concluded that it encompassed taking away a child by force or fraud without that child's consent or another lawful excuse. Lord Brandon of Oakbrook (with whom the other Lordships agreed) reasoned at p 806:

> "I see no good reason why, in relation to the kidnapping of a child, it should not in all cases be the absence of the child's consent which is material, whatever its age may be. In the case of a very young child, it would not have the understanding or the intelligence to give its consent, so that absence of consent would be a necessary inference from its age. In the case of an older child, however, it must, I think, be a question of fact for a jury whether the child concerned has *sufficient understanding and intelligence to give its consent*; if, but only if, the jury considers that a child has these qualities, it must then go on to consider whether it has been proved that the child did not give its consent." (Emphasis added.)

20. In *Gillick*, at p 188, Lord Scarman explained *R v D* thus:

> "The House must, in my view, be understood as having in that case accepted that, save where statute otherwise provides, a minor's capacity to make his or her own decision depends upon the minor having *sufficient understanding and intelligence to make the decision* and is not to be determined by reference to any judicially fixed age limit." (Emphasis added)

21. The principle that the capacity of a child under 16 depends on possession of "sufficient understanding and intelligence to make the decision" thus underpins both *R v D* and *Gillick*. I contend that this is simply another way of stating that the capacity of a child under 16 is to be determined by possession of the cognitive-functional ability (competence) to make that decision.
22. Against this view, Counsel for the NHS Trust submits that interpreting *Gillick* and the 2005 Act as applications of the principle that capacity tracks competence would require the two tests to be identical. It was further submitted that such a view would be contrary to the case law on the application of the *Gillick* test and to the intention of Parliament in restricting the 1969 and 2005 Acts to those who are age 16 or above.
23. Let me first address the burden of proof. The 2005 Act places the burden of proof upon those who deny that P is able to make a decision (see para 8). Section 8(1) of the 1969 Act has the same effect with regard to the consent of a 16 to 17-year-old to medical treatment (see para 13). In contrast, *Gillick* did not alter the burden of proof. It follows that there is no presumption of capacity where the relevant provisions of the 1969 and 2005 Acts do not apply. That is to say that there is no presumption that either a child under 16 is able to make treatment decisions or that a 16 or 17-year-old child is able to refuse medical treatment. This conclusion does not, however, imply rejection of the principle that capacity tracks competence. Rather, it implies that there is a second principle in operation to the effect that competence may be presumed in the specified circumstances. The age-related presumptions in the 1969 and 2005 Acts represent starting points adopted by Parliament to balance the burdens of competence-assessment and the

risk of making a mistake as to an individual's competence in the light of generally expected developmental abilities. On this interpretation, Parliament is to be understood as selecting attainment of the ages of 16 and 18 as triggering evidential presumptions about competence. An individual is presumed competent to consent to medical treatment upon attaining the age of 16 and presumed competent to refuse medical treatment upon attaining the age of 18.

24. Further, the principle that capacity tracks competence does not imply that the criteria for assessing an individual's competence cannot vary in accordance with the risk of a mistaken conclusion. Defensible differences between the *Gillick* criteria and those in sections 2–3 of the 2005 Act could be justified by the adoption of a slightly more cautious approach taken before concluding that the relevant child is competent than would be the case for an adult.
25. Lord Scarman in *Gillick* stated that parental decision-making "yields" to the child's rights and "terminates" when a child satisfies the *Gillick* test (at pp184–185). Subsequent to *Gillick*, however, the lower courts have drawn a distinction between capacity to consent and capacity to refuse medical treatment that goes beyond Lord Scarman's conclusions and the statutorily provided evidential presumptions. The status of this case law is central to this appeal. It was accepted by both courts below that if C is 15 years old, then the case for overriding her refusal in her best interests is a powerful one.

The capacity of a child to refuse life-sustaining treatment

26. The implications of *Gillick* for refusals of treatment were considered by two decisions of the Court of Appeal in the early 1990s.
27. In *Re R* [1991] 4 All ER 177, the Court of Appeal held that while the 15-year-old girl with a fluctuating mental state failed to satisfy the *Gillick* test, even if she had satisfied the test, the court's wardship powers could be used to override her refusal. Lord Donaldson added that parental consent could also override the refusal of a child who satisfied the *Gillick* test (at pp 183 and 187). These conclusions were criticised by many academics at the time. Gillian Douglas described it as a "retreat from *Gillick*" ((1992) 55 *MLR* 569) and Ian Kennedy argued that the judgment drove "a coach and horses through *Gillick*" (in chapter 3 of Clare Dyer, ed, *Doctors Patients and the Law*, Oxford: Blackwell, 1992).
28. A year later, in *Re W* [1993] Fam 64, the Court of Appeal affirmed Thorpe J's view that the refusal of a 16-year-old girl who had "sufficient understanding to make an informed decision" could be overruled using the court's inherent jurisdiction (at p 76). The Court of Appeal held that section 8(1) of the Family Law Reform Act 1969 (on which see para 13) only applied to consent, as opposed to refusal of medical treatment. In the Court's view, consent from the court or someone with parental responsibility could override the refusal of a competent child. A refusal would be a "very important consideration", increasing in importance with the child's age and maturity, but it would not be determinate (at pp 84 and 88). Balcombe and Nolan LJJ suggested that the power to override a competent child's refusal was limited to situations where the treatment is necessary to prevent death or serious permanent harm (at pp 88 and 94, respectively). Nolan LJ limited this power to the courts where the refusal to be overridden was of major surgery or procedures such as abortion (at p 94).

29. Before continuing, let me address the Court of Appeal's interpretation of the 1969 Act. Section 8(1) requires a 16- or 17-year-old's "consent" to medical treatment to be "as effective as" that of an adult. Section 8(3) states:

> "Nothing in this section shall be construed as making ineffective any consent which would have been effective if this section had not been enacted."

Lord Donaldson considered subsection (3) to support his reading of subsection (1). His Lordship reasoned that that it "preserves the common law as it existed immediately before the Act which undoubtedly gave parents an effective power of consent for all children up to the age of 21, the then existing age of consent" (at p 77). Balcombe LJ expressly agreed, adding that Lord Scarman did not intend to suggest otherwise and, if he did, then his view was "inconsistent with the express words" of subsection (3) (at p 88).

30. Subsection (3) undoubtedly preserves the effectiveness of any consent at common law. The issue is therefore whether, at common law, parental or judicial consent can override the refusal of a competent child. The 1969 Act is silent upon this issue. With respect to Lord Donaldson and Balcombe LJ, the common law position should not be regarded as having ossified in 1969. I argued above that the principle that explains and justifies *Gillick* is that capacity tracks competence. Along with the principle that the legal presumption is to be determined by whether the person in question is aged 16 or 18, this principle explains section 8(1) of the 1969 Act and the 2005 Act. It follows that, unless an overriding legal principle applies, a person who is properly judged to be competent (against the appropriate presumption and criteria) can have capacity to refuse medical treatment.
31. Both Lord Donaldson and Balcombe LJ stated that "it is a feature of anorexia nervosa that it is capable of destroying the ability to make an informed choice": [1993] Fam 64 at pp 81 and 84. This is an expression of doubt about whether W was competent. Where such doubts exist, particular caution is required before concluding that the presumption of incompetence has been rebutted.
32. In many subsequent cases the lower courts have overridden refusals, despite explicitly concluding that the child in question had the cognitive-functional ability to make decisions of that type.
33. In *An NHS Foundation Hospital v P* [2014] EWHC 165, Baker J authorised life-saving treatment contrary to the refusal of a 17-year-old girl who, he held, satisfied the capacity test in the 2005 Act. The judge expressly stated that he was "not satisfied that she lacks capacity to make decisions concerning her medical treatment" (at para 9). Nonetheless, following *Re W*, the judge exercised the court's inherent jurisdiction to "override the child's wishes in her best interests and give its consent to her treatment" (at para 12).
34. In *University Hospitals Plymouth NHS Trust v B* [2019] EWHC 1670 (Fam), MacDonald J overrode the refusal of intravenous infusions for diabetes by a 16-year-old girl. B was said, at para 9, to be aware of the implications of her refusal and simply wished to die. The judge, following *Re W*, stated at para 18 that

> "the law is clear that the court is not mandated to accept the wishes and feelings of a competent child where to honour those wishes and feelings would result in manifest, and even fatal, harm to that child".

35. In *An NHS Trust v CX* [2019] EWHC 3033 (Fam), Roberts J overrode the refusal of blood products by a 14-year-old boy for the treatment of lymphatic cancer.

The judge emphasised that CX was "plainly an intelligent child" who had confirmed the strength of his religious beliefs by becoming a baptised Jehovah's Witness (at para 10) and concluded that he was "*Gillick* competent to make the decision as to whether or not to undergo the proposed treatment" (at para 22). Following *Re W*, she nonetheless overrode CX's refusal on the basis that it was "undoubtedly in his best interests to undergo the treatment which has been planned for him" (at para 26).

36. *An NHS Trust v X* [2021] 4 WLR 11 was another case concerned with the refusal of a blood transfusion by a child with strongly held religious beliefs as a Jehovah's Witness. Sir James Munby overrode that refusal of a girl of almost 16 who was considered to satisfy the *Gillick* test and be "mature and wise beyond her years" (para 4). The judge contrasted the *Gillick* test with that in the 2005 Act. The 2005 Act was said to be focused on the existence of "some impairment or disturbance of mental functioning" (citing Butler-Sloss LJ in *Re MB (Caesarean Section)* [1997] 2 FLR 426 at p437 and s 2(1) of the 2005 Act). Whereas, the *Gillick* test was said to be "tied to the normal development over time of the typical child and teenager" (para 73). Sir James concluded that they are "both historically and conceptually quite distinct" (para 75). With respect, this analysis conflates the historical origins of the law with the principle that explains and justifies that law. As indicated earlier, two principles (capacity tracks competence and the legal presumption depend on whether the person in question is under 16 or refusing treatment) explain and justify the existing law.

37. Sir James Munby then considered whether the European Convention of Human Rights, as given circumscribed domestic effect by the Human Rights Act 1998, requires revision to the approach in *Re W*. The judge extensively considered various articles of the Convention: articles 2 (the right to life), 3 (the prohibition of human or degrading treatment), 5 (the right to liberty and security), 8 (the right to respect for private and family life), 9 (the right to freedom of thought, conscience and religion), and 14 (the prohibition of discrimination in the exercise of one's Convention rights). He concluded at para 157 that there is nothing in the jurisprudence to throw doubt upon the validity of *Re W*. I do not intend here to review that analysis other than to point out that the Convention jurisprudence similarly does not require parents or the court to be able to override the refusals of competent children in circumstances where they have no such powers in relation to adults.

38. In *E v Northern Care Alliance NHS Foundation Trust* [2021] EWCA Civ 1888, the Court of Appeal considered a conjoined appeal from orders from judges in the Family Division declaring it lawful to administer blood contrary to the wishes of competent minors. E was a girl of 16 years eight months and F was a boy aged 17 years five months. Each was considered by their doctors to satisfy the *Gillick* test, had made their decisions independently and had the support of their parents.

39. Sir Andrew McFarlane P gave the judgment of the court. The President considered the Court of Appeal in *Re W* to have "asserted the primacy of the welfare principle, while emphasising the importance of the decision of a capacitous young person" (at para 57). The President went on to declare that:

> "In our view, this approach remains good law. It survives the Human Rights Act 1998 and the Mental Capacity Act 2005, and it has not been overtaken by subsequent decisions, by the passage of time, or by the evolution of societal values."

40. While these cases span a period of over three decades, they do not bind this court. Counsel for the NHS Trust submitted that even if *Re W* involved a misstep insofar as it indicated that a parent's consent could override the refusal of a competent minor, the court's powers are unlimited.

The inherent jurisdiction and the Children Act 1989

41. Counsel for the NHS Trust submitted that the court's inherent jurisdiction enables protection of the vulnerable, even if they would otherwise have capacity under *Gillick* or the 2005 Act. Nolan LJ in *Re W* therefore correctly identified "the unlimited nature of the court's inherent jurisdiction over minors" (at p 91).
42. When exercised on behalf of a child, the court's powers serve that child's welfare, which section 1(1) of the Children Act 1989 requires to be "the court's paramount consideration". When the court is considering whether to make, vary or discharge an order under section 8 (child arrangement and other orders in respect to children), it is to have particular regard to circumstances listed in section 1(3). The first of these is "the ascertainable wishes and feelings of the child concerned (in the light of his age and understanding)"(s 1(3)(a)). Counsel for the Trust submits that this demonstrates that the child's wishes are no more than an important factor for the court to take into account when exercising its statutory or inherent jurisdiction.
43. With respect, the application of this interpretation of the 1989 Act to treatment decisions made by a competent child would be inconsistent with section 1 of the 1969 Act (on which see para 13), unless the valid consent of a competent adult could also be overridden by the court in the relevant circumstances. Counsel made three submissions in response.
44. First, insofar as the 1969 Act limited the court's powers in relation to the consent of a competent child, it was impliedly repealed by the Children Act 1989. I disagree. The 1989 Act expressly removed section 7 of the 1969 Act (which gave the High Court power to place a ward of court in the care, or under the supervision, of a local authority in care). In my view, if Parliament had intended to modify section 1 of the 1989 Act, it should and would have done so explicitly.
45. Secondly, it was submitted that the court's inherent jurisdiction over vulnerable adults may, in extreme circumstances, be used to override the treatment decisions of a competent adult.
46. The application of the inherent jurisdiction to vulnerable adults was recognised by the Court of Appeal in *Re L* [2012] EWCA Civ 253. In this case, the inherent jurisdiction was used to protect an elderly couple from the abusive and controlling behaviour of their son. It was accepted that the couple did not lack capacity within the meaning of the 2005 Act, because neither "was incapable, by reason of any impairment of or disturbance in the functioning of the mind or brain, of managing their own affairs" (at para 9). The Court of Appeal held that the inherent jurisdiction was available to protect adults who have "borderline capacity" under the 2005 Act and therefore fall outside the statutory scheme, but are nonetheless unable to make a decision by reason of "constraint, coercion, undue influence or other vitiating factor" (at paras 10 and 31–32).
47. The inherent jurisdiction has subsequently been used to authorise the administration of nutrition and hydration and medical treatment to vulnerable adults: see, for example, *A NHS Trust v A* [2013] EWHC 2442; *Great Western Hospitals NHS*

Foundation Trust v AA [2014] EWHC 132 (Fam) and *A Local Health Board v AB* [2015] EWCOP 31. (In these cases, the concerned adults were regarded as lacking capacity under the test in the 2005 Act.)

48. Counsel for C invited this court to overrule or narrowly construe *Re L*. According to the late Barbara Hewson, *Re L* "is wrong and represents an example of impermissible judicial law-making" and is of such constitutional importance that it ought to have gone to the Supreme Court ((2013) *Public Law* 459, at pp 451 and 469, respectively). While this is not an appropriate case for this court to hear full argument on the application of the inherent jurisdiction to adults, I do not accept Hewson's claim that *Re L* created "quasi-wardship of competent adults" (p 458). In my view, the decision was concerned with a category of *incompetent* adult, namely, those who lack the cognitive-functional ability to make a particular decision because they need assistance to exercise their borderline decision-making abilities and cannot be provided with that assistance (due to undue influence or other vitiating factor) without judicial intervention. The Court of Appeal's decision was not meant to apply to those who are unquestionably competent but have made an involuntary decision due to coercion or undue influence. Accordingly, the inherent jurisdiction only permits judicial intervention in the most extreme circumstances in which it is not otherwise possible to enable an adult with borderline or insufficient decision-making abilities to make an autonomous decision. It follows that the inherent jurisdiction cannot be used to prevent a vulnerable adult from exercising her will. In *Redcar & Cleveland BC v PR* [2019] EWHC 2305, at para 43, Cobb J thus held that it was "illogical" to conclude that a vulnerable adult needed the protection of the court and yet could be ordered to "refrain from doing something which she wanted to do, backed with the punitive force of an injunction". None of the cases cited to this court involved the inherent jurisdiction being used to override the consent or refusal of a competent adult to medical treatment.

49. Thirdly, it was submitted that, even if the court's powers are limited where a competent child consents to medically appropriate treatment, this is not the case where a competent child refuses life-sustaining treatment. I fully appreciate the intuitive appeal of this view, but do not accept that a child's wishes must be given non-determinate weight where those wishes are the product of profound understanding and full reflection. In my view, once a judge has properly concluded that a mature child is competent to refuse life-sustaining treatment, it is not the role of that judge to then override that decision. In the rare case where a child is competent to refuse life-sustaining treatment, their welfare interests with regard to the administration of such treatment are coterminous with their autonomy interests.

Application of the law to C

50. Apollo J reached the very clear conclusion that C was competent:

> "The transplant team consider C to understand what is proposed and the implications of her refusal. This conclusion is supported by a consultant child psychiatrist who said in her evidence:
>
> 'C is exceptionally mature and insightful for her age. She suffers from no mental illness or impairment. She has very carefully considered the proposed CLKT [combined liver and kidney transplantation] and the impact of her

> decision on both herself and her parents. After much discussion and reflection, she has concluded that she does not want to undergo invasive procedures of this type and simply wants to be allowed to die. She says that she had only supported the cryopreservation of her body because she had wanted to give some comfort to her parents and thought it extremely unlikely to result in her reanimation.'
>
> C has similarly struck me as exceptionally intelligent and fully able to understand what is proposed. I can therefore see no alternative to the conclusion that she is competent to make this decision. In my view, she satisfies the criteria in *Gillick* and cannot be regarded as unable to make a decision under the criteria in section 3 of the 2005 Act."

51. Counsel for the NHS Trust did not challenge this conclusion before this court or the Court of Appeal below. For the purposes of this appeal, it is accepted that C is currently regarded as competent to refuse the proposed treatment.
52. Apollo J gave considerable weight to C's wishes and feelings but nonetheless concluded that the transplant was in her best interests:

> "In weighing the competing factors, I have concluded that the balance comes down in favour of overriding C's wishes. I have attached significant weight to the wishes of this impressive young woman. In my judgment, however, those wishes are simply not determinate as to her best interests. The clear clinical evidence is that without this operation C will die and that death will be very painful and distressing. I believe C to be sincere when she says that if her wishes were to be overridden by this court, she would fully comply with all clinical guidance to maximise the likelihood that the transplantation will be successful."

53. The Court of Appeal reached a different conclusion to Apollo J on the lawfulness of what is proposed only because C was considered to be an adult. I will therefore now consider C's age.

Cryonics and legal age

54. While biology comprises combinations and continuums of states and processes, the law requires threshold determinations. The vastly different legal status of the living and dead human body renders this a profoundly significant legal threshold. It requires a line to be drawn on the spectrum between bodies that have operational hearts and brains and bodies for which there has been total and apparently irreversible cessation of all vital biological functions. Cryonic reanimation challenges scientific understanding of the irreversibility of some biological processes.
55. The only cryonics case considered by the courts of this country was an application to the Family Division brought prior to the death of a 14-year-old girl: *Re JS (Disposal of Body)* [2016] EWHC 2859 (Fam). JS's mother sought to obtain sole responsibility for making post-mortem decisions with regard to the disposal of her daughter's body. The case with which this appeal is concerned is very different.
56. There is no doubt that C was a living person up to the point of her cryopreservation (the cryopreservation date) and has been a living person since the date at which she was reanimated (the reanimation date). No argument otherwise has been put before this court. C now has a fully functional cardiovascular system and

brain and is therefore unequivocally a living human person. Unlike a dead person, C is capable of being assaulted or murdered. What is contested is her legal age. The courts below regarded a determination of her age relevant to the legal weight to be attached to her refusal of what would otherwise be an assault. Since C was properly regarded as competent to make that decision by Apollo J, I take a different view. Nonetheless, her legal age is also important to her other legal rights. By way of example, C wishes to vote in the upcoming UK Parliamentary election and she must be at least 18 years old to be eligible to do so (Representation of the People Act 1983, s 1(1)).

57. Determining C's age requires consideration of the legal effect of the three-year period in which C's body was cryopreserved (the cryopreservation period). Four options were put to this court:

    (a) C was legally alive during the cryopreservation period, which is to be regarded as equivalent to unconsciousness. Her legal age is therefore 18.
    (b) C was not legally alive during the cryopreservation period, but once reanimation occurs her legal personhood is to be regarded as having continued during that period for the purpose of determining her age. Her legal age is therefore 18.
    (c) C was not legally alive during the cryopreservation period, but her life continued from the time of her reanimation. Her legal age is therefore to be calculated by subtracting the cryopreservation period: she is 15 years old.
    (d) C was not legally alive during the cryopreservation period and the reanimation date marks the moment that a new legal person (with the name and memories of the previous person) came into existence. The reanimation date is, in effect, a new legal date of birth. Her legal age is therefore four months.

58. Apollo J considered position (c) to correctly state the law. Hercules LJ, giving the judgment of the Court of Appeal, held that Apollo J was wrong to hold that C is legally 15:

> "In both law and ordinary language a person's age is the period that has elapsed since the date of their birth. C remains alive over 18 years after the date of her birth and so must be considered to have attained the age of majority under section 1 of the Family Law Reform Act 1969. Her birth certificate remains accurate and provides the basis for calculating her age for all legal purposes. While neither the common law nor legislation anticipated C's situation, it would involve the usurpation of a legislative function for this court to re-write the law to exclude the period of cryopreservation when calculating C's age."

59. In my view, the Court of Appeal's approach equivocates between positions (a) and (b). Neither are tenable. With respect to Hercules LJ, the law is to be interpreted in terms of its underlying principles and, as I will explain below, those principles require her legal age to be calculated by excluding the period of her cryopreservation (position (c)).

60. Position (a) requires the period of cryopreservation, during which there were no signs of life, to be regarded as equivalent to unconscious life. This would involve redefinition of death in law. It would undermine attempts to certify death in other cases, save perhaps where the brain is destroyed beyond any possibility of repair in the distant future following a period of cryopreservation. Decisive determinations

of death are, however, required for many legal purposes. Redefining a frozen body with (what is then regarded as) the irreversible cessation of the brain stem as not legally dead could not be supported by any legal principle capable of being discerned from the existing law. It would indeed be contrary to one of the principles that explain and justify the provisions of the Human Tissue Act 2004. The 2004 Act provides that it is lawful, where appropriate consent has been obtained, to remove, retain and use tissue from the body of a deceased person for various purposes, including transplantation (s 1 and Sch 1 Pt 1 para 7). This implies that death encompasses the situation where the human body is still capable of providing organs for transplantation. Heart and lung transplants, which are unequivocally lawful under the 2004 Act, require the deceased donor to have a beating heart.

61. Position (b) accepts that C was dead during the period of cryopreservation but then requires this determination to be set aside on an ad hoc basis. This differs from position (a) only in that it does not require a general redefinition of death, only the retrospective recharacterisation of C's position during the period of her cryopreservation. However, this approach requires more than the combination of C currently being alive and age ordinarily being determined by reference to the date that has elapsed from birth. In the absence of a justificatory legal principle, discerned from the existing law, it involves departure from the proper role of the court. It involves something akin to the exercise of a legislative power for a retrospective exception to be made for C.

62. Position (d) would be the most radical of the four options. It would regard "C before cryopreservation" as a separate legal person from "C now". "C now" would be only four months old. In my view, the parties to this appeal, Apollo J and the Court of Appeal were right to dismiss this option. I can discern no legal principle that would support such a radical departure from law applying to all other living humans. It would place "C after reanimation" in a legal limbo. Her parents would no longer be her legal parents, and she would have no means of registering the start of her legal life in this jurisdiction recognised by the Births and Deaths Registration Act 1953.

63. This leaves position (c), according to which C was not legally alive during the cryopreservation period but her life continued from the time of her reanimation. Her legal age is therefore to be calculated by subtracting the cryopreservation period from the time that has expired since her birth, making her 15 (nearly 16) years old. This was the view of Apollo J, which Counsel for the NHS Trust submits was correct.

64. The argument for position C is that it coheres with principles that explain and justify the age distinctions drawn in the 1969 Act, 2005 Act and other legislation. I have discerned from the 1969 and 2005 Acts the principles that capacity tracks competence and attaining the ages of 16 and 18 give rise to evidential presumptions about competence (see, especially, para 23).

65. Eighteen is the legal age of majority (the 1969 Act, s 1) and the age for eligibility for various other rights. Two rights, raised by Counsel in their submissions, will serve as illustrative examples here: the right to vote in UK Parliamentary elections (Representation of the People Act 1983, s 1(1)) and the right to marry (Marriage and Civil Partnership (Minimum Age) Act 2022, s 1). At or above the age of 18,

a person cannot vote if they are subject to "any legal incapacity to vote" (1983 Act, s 1(1)(b)) and cannot marry if they are shown to lack capacity under the test in the 2005 Act. The effect of the 1983 and 2022 Acts is therefore to presume that adults are competent to vote or marry.

66. Nonetheless, Parliament decided not to allow those under 18 to vote or marry, even if they can be shown to be competent and there are no other defects in their consent. These legislative exceptions to the principle that capacity tracks competence are explained and justified on the basis that Parliament considers the burdens of ensuring competence and other consent conditions to outweigh the justification for bestowing these rights on children. Competence is decision and time specific and those confirming eligibility to vote or marry are, unlike healthcare professionals, not well placed to make this assessment. Nor are they well placed to assess the likelihood that the individual's will have been coerced or overborne, which is a particular issue in light of potential cultural pressures on some young persons to marry. Individual assessment would therefore be an administratively burdensome and particularly complicated condition for eligibility to vote or marry. It is the role of Parliament, rather than the courts, to determine when the burdens and complications are such that the right in question should not be granted to those under a certain age. It is also the role of Parliament to determine which age provides a suitable indication of whether a person is likely to have the relevant cognitive-functional abilities to exercise the right in question. Parliament has, as befits its constitutional role, made that determination in relation to eligibility to vote and marry. These determinations explain and justify these focused statutory exceptions to the principle that capacity tracks competence.

67. On this analysis, age is used by Parliament to trigger legal presumptions, rights and obligations on the basis that the selected age is regarded as suitably indicative of likely possession of the required cognitive-functional attributes. If this analysis is sound, it has implications for the determination of legal age in the exceptional case where a person has been legally dead, cryopreserved and then reanimated. In this exceptional situation, there is a gap between the time since birth and the time in which the body has been alive and developing. In C's case, her age is only linked to the time she has spent alive and developing if it is calculated by excluding the three years her body spent in a cryonic state.

68. This analysis supports Apollo J's conclusion that C is legally 15 years old over the Court of Appeal's conclusion that C is legally 18. Counsel for C contends that the Court of Appeal's view is to be preferred, because regarding C as a child involves departing from established medical, societal and legal practice and deprives her of the rights possessed by others who were born 18 years ago, including the right to vote in UK elections. However, legal principle requires departure from the standard method for calculating legal age in this truly exceptional situation and no binding rule or legal principle requires otherwise.

69. The calculation of the age of C must be the same as if would be for any other person whose body has been in a cryonic state, rather than the same as for those whose bodies have continued to age and develop. While C was 15 at the time of her cryopreservation and was cryopreserved for three years, the appropriate legal principle would apply even if these figures were reversed. If the figures had been reversed, so that C was 3 years old when preserved and had spent 15 years in a

cryonic state, the Court of Appeal's reasoning would still hold her to be 18 years old. Only option (c) retains the link between developmental age and legal age.

Conclusion

70. For reasons that I have articulated, in my view, Apollo J and the Court of Appeal were both correct on one of the two central legal points. Apollo J was correct to conclude that C is legally only 15. Hercules LJ was correct to conclude that C was entitled to refuse life-sustaining treatment.
71. I therefore, in part, allow this appeal from the decision of the Court of Appeal.
72. If I may, I would like to end this judgment by expressing my full sympathy to C and her family. The legal conclusions I have reached above mean that, while ever there remains no doubt as to C's competence to understand what is proposed, she is entitled to refuse medical treatment, including potentially life-sustaining transplantation. For my part, however, I very much hope that C changes her mind.

PART III

Conclusion

7

Legal Theory at the Frontiers of Biomedicine

7.1. Introduction

This book defends and applies an unusual legal theory. It is argued in chapter 2 that *contextual legal idealism* is implied by the attempt to understand the enterprise of regulating human conduct. This amounts to the claim that legislators and judges should apply a universal moral principle (the PGC) to the context in which they are operating, including its institutional, social and technological features. This book's four case studies seek to show how they would apply this theory to reach and support legal outcomes addressed to technological developments.

Brownsword identifies three ways of framing regulatory engagement with new technologies.[1] Law 1.0 adopts a doctrinal or coherentist mindset. What matters is the integrity and internal consistency of legal doctrine, so new technologies are to fit with existing legal principle. This is the method of traditional legal scholarship. Law 2.0 adopts a regulatory-instrumentalist mindset. What matters is that the law is instrumentally effective, so we are to regulate new technologies ex ante to best achieve specified objectives. Law 3.0 adopts a technological mindset. Instead of regulating by rules, technologies are to be utilised to preclude or at least channel certain behaviour.[2] Such responses take the form of products, places or processes and reduce or remove the need to have formal legal rules prohibiting the technologically regulated behaviour. Examples include embedded restrictions in digital products or, perhaps in the future, genome edits to restrict the ability to act in certain ways. Contextual idealism uses the PGC to bridge the directional tension between these mindsets. Accordingly, the PGC is to provide the overall principle governing doctrinal coherence, govern the goals for effective regulation and govern the identification of situations where technological management may be implemented or continued.

The courts provide a forum that is well suited for Law 1.0 conversations and the legislature provides a forum that is well suited for Law 2.0 conversations,

[1] See Brownsword 2021 and 2022.
[2] Discussed in 2.3.3.

but neither forum may ignore the other mindset. The appeal courts must adopt features of the regulatory-instrumentalist mindset when choosing between competing coherentist accounts or when blocking a direction of doctrinal travel to prevent a clear violation of the PGC. Conversely, the legislature must attend to the Law 1.0 mindset by ensuring that legislation fits with or coherently revises the overall web of legal principle and must attend to the options and restrictions presented by Law 3.0. Neither forum can attend to all features of these three regulatory mindsets. They represent only part of the regulatory picture in which regulators can be public, private or technological.

Biomedical and other technologies often highlight the limits of formal law. This is by no means a new phenomenon. Consider the impact of the creation of Dolly the sheep back in 1997.[3] This development raised questions about the application of this new cloning technique to humans. The United Kingdom seemed to have anticipated such questions because it had enacted detailed legislation, supported by a statutory licensing authority.[4] Indeed, that licensing authority declared that applying the Dolly technique to humans would require a licence, and it would grant no such licence.[5] But, a few years later, this view was successfully contested in the High Court.[6] Legislation was then rushed through Parliament to prohibit the creation of a cloned human in this way, coming into force just over *two weeks* after the decision of the High Court.[7] The law then completed a full circle when the Court of Appeal overruled the High Court in the following month and that decision was affirmed by the House of Lords just over a year later.[8] A new technology had thus challenged the remit of carefully crafted legislation and evoked an expedited back-and-forth between the courts and Parliament. The take-home message about the potential and limits of regulation by legislation and the common law has lost none of its relevance in the quarter of a century since the announcement of Dolly's creation. This book has examined four areas where developments in biomedicine would require regulatory reform of the formal rules and rulings.

Many biomedical developments are capable of being addressed by relying on existing legal rules, by judicial discernment and extension of legal principles from existing legal rules or by the operation of existing regulatory discretion. But there are many hurdles. There is, for example, often judicial resistance to departing from the confines of the facts of previously decided cases[9] or from strict literal

[3] See Wilmut et al 1997. See also the discussion in 1.1 and Pattinson 2015.

[4] The Human Fertilisation and Embryology Act 1990 and the Human Fertilisation and Embryology Authority, respectively.

[5] See HGAC & HFEA 1998a, para 2 and 1998b, para 3.4.

[6] *R (Bruno Quintavalle) v Secretary of State for Health* [2001] EWHC 918 (15 November 2001).

[7] Human Reproductive Cloning Act 2001 (royal assent and commencement on 4 December 2001).

[8] [2002] EWCA Civ 29 (18 January 2002) and [2003] UKHL 13 (13 March 2003). See the discussion in Pattinson 2005.

[9] Often the application of the legal test is said to be fact specific (eg most cases applying the best interest test) or the instant case is said to be unique (eg *Re A Children) (Conjoined Twins: Surgical Separation)* Fam 147, 155, 239 and 255).

interpretation of statutory provisions.[10] There are also limits to any method of judicial reasoning that holds to an element of fit with existing rules and principles, because even when developments at the frontiers of biomedicine highlight fault lines in historical compromises and assumptions, the required judicial innovation is often perceived to necessitate the exercise of authority that is more appropriate for the legislature. The legislature is not, however, free from the need to fit its innovations with the existing law. Legislative chambers that jettison established rules can cause legal chaos and evoke additional, difficult to predict, problems. Proposers of legislation therefore need to make careful decisions as to which of the extant rules and principles are to be jettisoned, modified or retained. This book has attempted to show how a committed Gewirthian would address the practicalities of operating within an existing legal system. Domestic legal systems do not, however, operate in global isolation. This chapter will consider the global context (7.2), before summarising the lessons learned from the analysis of the four case studies (7.3).

7.2. The World in which We Live

Have a go at writing down answers to these questions:

1. In all *low-income countries* across the world today, how many girls finish primary school?
   (a) 20%.
   (b) 40%.
   (c) 60%.
2. Where do the majority of the world's population live?
   (a) Low-income countries.
   (b) Middle-income countries.
   (c) High-income countries.
3. How many of the world's one-year-old children today have been vaccinated against some disease?
   (a) 20%.
   (b) 50%.
   (c) 80%.

The point of this exercise is to draw attention to outdated or otherwise mistaken assumptions often made about the world, such as those displayed by division of the world into two halves: the haves and have nots; the first and third world;

[10] See eg the High Courts (both overruled on appeal) in *R (Quintavalle) v Secretary of State for Health* [2001] EWHC 918 (Admin) and *R (Quintavalle) v Human Fertilisation and Embryology Authority* [2002] EWHC 3000 (Admin).

developed and developing countries; the global north and the global south. Hans Rosling, working with his son and daughter-in-law, presented these and similar questions to thousands of people.[11] They discovered that most people answer incorrectly because they are operating on a binary division of the world that hasn't been meaningful since the 1960s. Rosling and co-authors put forward a four-level model based on income per person and calculated that of the seven billion people in the world, the vast majority live in middle-income countries. One billion live at level 1, which they define as living on the equivalent of less than $2 per day, thereby likely to cook on an open fire, spend most of their day travelling to fetch water and sleep on a dirt floor. Two billion live at level 2, three billion at level 3 and one billion at level 4 (very probably including you). In other words, they categorise three-quarters of the world's population as middle-income. Did you select (b) as your answer to question 2? Did you select (c) in response to the other two questions? Most do not. On average only 13% get question 3 correct.[12] In fact, Rosling's answer for question 3 is now too low – more recent figures indicate that 86% of all infants born in the world are vaccinated every year.[13] The statistics indicate that the world's population has greater access to education and healthcare resources than most of us would have predicted and the proportion of those able to afford new inventions and interventions is increasing.

Even on a statistically informed view of the world, however, there are profound socio-economic disparities between different groups of humans and there will therefore be radically divergent opportunities presented by future biomedical developments. This book is focused on possible developments in a country that has greater potential to benefit than many others. Chapter 3 considered justice objections to genome editing, concerned with the probability of inequitable access to the benefits of the technology, but there the focus was on equity for humans within this jurisdiction, rather than for the world.[14] Some consideration was given to wider justice concerns in chapter 6 with regard to access to cryonic preservation and reanimation technologies.[15] Otherwise, this book has given little attention to alternative uses of resources, investment and technologies directed to addressing more immediate, and often more important, global needs.

A fully contextual approach would not be restricted to one jurisdiction, one type of human endeavour or even one species. The global effects of human actions can be (spatially and temporally) dispersed, so that many present and future others are affected in different ways.[16] Control can be fragmented, so that global effects

[11] See Rosling et al 2018, ch 1 (from which the three questions above and the statistics in this paragraph are quoted).

[12] Rosling et al 2018 reported the following percentage of correct answers per country: 21% in Sweden, 17% in the US, 15% in Canada and the UK, and 6% in Japan, Germany and France.

[13] See WHO 2020, 6.

[14] See 3.5.4.

[15] See 6.6.1.

[16] See Wardrope 2020, who discusses health justice in the Anthropocene from a communitarian perspective influenced by virtue-ethics.

are the cumulative consequence of many acts. Global institutions can hinder recognition and responses to morally relevant factors. Consequently, this book only scratches the surface of contextual legal idealism.

It was argued in chapter 1 that the trajectory of positive law in the United Kingdom has been towards a secular rights-based approach.[17] But there are powerful counter-pressures towards alternative moral approaches. Cultural moralities evolve and are influenced by powerful groups and individuals. It was argued in chapter 2 that judges and legislators are required to select the most appropriate path in a context where they will often lack the power and insight to choose the most direct path for identifying and protecting the generic rights of agents.[18] The global context presents significant additional forces and power structures, which require further trade-offs.

Existing power structures hinder the global application of universal moral values. Adherence to universal generic rights requires global enforcement mechanisms and democratic structures. Democratic structures are required to address the problems of moral complexity outlined in chapter 2, where a substantive answer cannot be deductively derived as a direct application of the PGC.[19] Crucially, the electorate ought to include anyone whose basic generic needs are likely to be negatively affected by the decisions of political leaders in response to these problems of moral complexity. Yet, in practice, the electorate comprises those who happen to be citizens or residents of a particular jurisdiction, and sometimes only a subcategory of those individuals.[20] There is no global citizenship giving rise to universal suffrage for electing global leaders to deal with cross-jurisdictional impacts.[21]

In the decades after the Second World War, many international treaties and declarations have proclaimed the universality of human rights and democracy, but for all this, 'sovereign equality of States' endures as 'a linchpin of international law'.[22] Not unreasonably, individual states are keen to protect themselves from other, often more powerful, countries. More recent political events and movements suggest that nationalism now grips the political imagination of a large part of the populace of the most economically and militarily powerful countries. Nationalism sometimes has instrumental value, particularly where it assists a populace to defend itself from the unjustified aggression of another nation, but it has no intrinsic value and more often operates as a rejection of the universality of human rights. The appropriate response to the global context needs to be multifaceted and dynamic, and above all aimed at achieving the incremental realisation of the PGC. That project is for other books.

[17] See 1.3.1 and 1.3.2.
[18] See 2.4ff.
[19] See 2.3.2 for discussion of the problem of value calculation and the problem of variable identification.
[20] Prisoners, for example, are denied suffrage in many jurisdictions.
[21] The closest structure of this type is probably the process for electing members of the European Parliament within the European Union.
[22] Hernández 2022, 22. It is recognised as a core principle in art 2(1) of the UN Charter.

7.3. Technologies at the Frontiers of Biomedicine

This book's four case studies focus on potential technological developments enabling the creation, enhancement and extension of human life. The envisaged developments are often capable of addressing more than one of these three themes. Developments in human genome editing could, for example, enable the *creation* of human life from gamete-precursors, gametes or embryos that would otherwise not survive, or bestow future human children with *enhanced* traits or *extended* lifespans.

Selectivity was required in the identification of this book's topics and the details of the future scenarios imagined as triggers for judicial or legislative responses. Some of these scenarios are closer to plausible predictions of future developments in biomedicine than others, and some have received greater attention from commentators than others. Chapter 3, on heritable genome editing, envisaged refinements to the extant ability to edit the genes of embryos. Most analyses of the technology have focused on its potential application to genetic diseases, whereas my three focal traits were immunity to coronaviruses, superhuman vision and selected eye colour.[23] Chapter 4, on human ectogestation, extrapolated from the experiments conducted on lamb fetuses. Others have considered a similar potential future, but primarily for other purposes, such as highlighting the inadequacies of the existing law and professional guidance.[24] Chapter 5, on cybernetic biohacking, envisages a combination of incremental developments to existing brain-implantation technology and to biohacking practices. It also envisages less likely effects of brain-implantation technology in terms of vast improvements to the memory creation abilities of modified individuals.[25] There is little overlap between the literature on brain-implantation technology and biohacking.[26] Chapter 6, on cryonic reanimation, involves imagining giant leaps in the technology for reanimating frozen corpses. The existing literature has not focused on how the law would address a reanimated person's age and status. The scenarios imagined in chapters 3 to 6 are unique and thereby raise issues for which the existing law has no automatic answer.

The case studies culminate in Explanatory Notes to two Bills and judgments in two appeal court cases.

The two Bills – the Human Fertilisation and Embryology (Heritable Genome Editing) Bill in chapter 3 and the Non-Medical Implantation Bill in chapter 5 – apply contextual legal idealism to the envisaged developments by utilising the United Kingdom's legislative system. The resultant Bills incrementally develop the existing law, rather than seek its wholesale replacement, because they are offered

[23] Cf eg NCOB 2018 and NAM et al 2020.
[24] Cf eg Alghrani & Brazier 2011, esp 81–82 and Romanis 2020a.
[25] See scenario two in 5.4.
[26] See eg Goering et al 2021, who focus on the involvement of large global research groups and commercial industries in the development and application of neurotechnologies.

as responses to narrow imagined scenarios and radical legal change is more likely to have unanticipated negative consequences.

The Explanatory Notes presuppose four types of background reforms to the existing legislative process: (1) reform of the process of public engagement and consultation, (2) reform of the process by which amendment legislation is published in its final consolidated form, (3) reform of the process by which the principles underlying the legislation are articulated and (4) reform of the utilisation of powers to enact secondary legislation and byelaws.

The first, perhaps the most significant, background reform is cited in the Explanatory Notes to the two Bills as the *Policy on Public Engagement and Consultation*. Increased participatory democracy is required to connect the legislative process to its justification as an indirect application of the PGC. This requires reinforcement of free speech and engagement of participatory structures to assist Parliament to identify overlooked assumptions and perspectives. The details of how this is to be achieved must be left to other works. For present purposes, let it suffice to remind ourselves that grounding contextual legal idealism in the PGC constrains the goals and means of participatory democracy. For example, the procedure for public participation needs to be sensitive to the tendency of passion and rhetoric to shape public discourse, for complex social phenomena to be presented as amenable to single-issue solutions and for powerful groups to influence public discourse in a way that is designed to prioritise their values or interests. The matters on which the public is consulted must therefore be carefully specified and communicated.

For public engagement to be meaningful, the issues on which views are sought cannot remain unaffected by those views. Recent governmental consultations have revealed widespread public opposition to some articulated policies and their rationales, which ministers have readily dismissed. In April 2022, for example, the government reported that 96% of respondents (53,426) to the question 'Do you think Channel 4 should be privatised?' answered 'No'.[27] Yet, the Culture Secretary Nadine Dorries responded to a select committee question by dismissing these responses as 'politically motivated'.[28]

The second reform seeks to increase transparency by modifying the system by which new legislation is published online. The Explanatory Notes refer to this as the *Policy on Public Availability of Acts of Parliament*. As explained in 3.6.1, the current system results in a significant lag in the time taken for amended legislation to appear online in its final form. Until this happens, those wishing to read the amended legislation in its final form will often need to rely on commercial databases. Themis Walpole's government would seek to ensure that it is possible to download a PDF of the amended legislation, as it will be when it comes into effect, no later than two weeks after it receives Royal Assent.

[27] Department for Digital, Culture, Media and Sport 2022, para 21.

[28] See youtu.be/mKWXU01jf3Y. Nadine Dorries initially mistakenly stated that 96% answered this question positively.

The third reform is to the template for structuring legislation, so that all new legislation begins with an explicit statement of its overarching principles. This is a departure from common practice where the purpose of a Bill is usually left to the preceding White Paper, its long title, the Explanatory Notes and statements to Parliament. A recent exception has been the Bill of Rights Bill (*sic*), which was introduced into the House of Commons on 22 June 2022. Section 1 of that Bill outlines its purpose. This accords with the approach taken to the hypothetical Bills described in chapters 3 and 5, both of which were written before that Bill was issued. What I propose is that such an approach is consistently adopted. This reform seeks to ensure that all future legislative interpretation is aided by a parliamentarily approved declaration of the Act's principles, in a similar way to the recitals of EU legislation and what is proposed for the Bill of Rights.

The final reform is to the process for monitoring the impact of legislation. Where legislation regulates technologies that are expected to develop further and could have unpredictable social consequences, consideration needs to be given to establishing supplemental regulatory and informational structures. Both of my Bills delegate functions to a regulatory body and provide for regulations/byelaws. The Human Fertilisation and Embryology (Heritable Genome Editing) Bill provides for regulation-making powers. A provision of the Bill requires the regulatory authority to submit an annual report to the House of Commons on heritable genome editing and its social effects. The Non-Medical Implantation Bill contains a provision requiring the regulatory committee it establishes to publish an annual report, and the Bill extends the byelaw powers of local authorities. These structures reduce the need for Parliament to engage in crystal ball gazing and ensure that suitable information is available to monitor the impact of the legislation. Such structures are not unique to these imagined Bills, but Parliament will need to ensure that the relevant reports are given proper scrutiny, assisted by the overarching principles provided by the third reform.

The two cases – *Re B* in chapter 4 and *Re C* in chapter 6 – apply a method within contextual legal idealism that I have elsewhere called modified law as integrity.[29] This involves judges discerning and applying legal principles according to fit and justification, with the PGC as the overarching principle. I have elsewhere shown how landmark cases in medical law could have been decided in ways that give effect to this method and, in chapters 4 and 6 of this book, I have shown how this method could be applied to the envisaged future scenarios. My scenarios highlight many assumptions and compromises underpinning the existing law. Chapter 4 focuses on the law's assumption of reproduction by gestation *in utero* leading to the birth of a human no longer in need of placental support. This chapter's hypothetical case, *Re B*, uses the purposive approach to statutory interpretation as a tool of modified law as integrity. Chapter 6 focuses on the law's assumption of a link between the time that has elapsed since birth and developmental and age-related

[29] See Pattinson 2018, esp ch 1.

attributes. This chapter's hypothetical case, *Re C*, is focused on using modified law as integrity to shape the common law response to a new legal situation. In both cases, Lady Athena discerns principles that can explain and justify the law and its response to these potential gaps.

The imagined future scenarios thereby both shape and limit this book's coverage. Its limits are well illustrated by the examination of cybernetic biohacking in chapter 5 by focusing on the imagined conviction of a tattooist and body-piercer for assisting biohackers to implant brain sensors and brain-device upgrades. This focus means that the resultant Bill is directed to non-medical implantation, even though I suggest in that chapter that the current criminal law on bodily harm needs wholesale review and reform. It follows that this book addresses only a subset of the issues raised by its topics.

7.4. Conclusion

Not all regulatory responses could or should involve judicial decisions or legislative intervention. It is to be expected that the trialling of a new regulatory approach, which must operate as a limitation to all major regulatory reforms, could reveal the need for a less legalistic regulatory response. To repeat the central message of contextual legal idealism: context is crucial when seeking to apply legally valid rules, rulings and regulatory structures to (embodied and socially, geographically and temporally situated) human beings.

BIBLIOGRAPHY

Aguilera-Castrejon, Alejandro, Oldak, Bernardo, Shani, Tom, et al (2021) 'Ex Utero Mouse Embryogenesis from Pre-Gastrulation to Late Organogenesis' 593 *Nature* 119–124.

Ahmad, Kaashif A, Frey, Charlotte S, Fierro, Mario A, et al (2017) 'Two-Year Neurodevelopmental Outcome of an Infant Born at 21 Weeks, 4 Days' Gestation' 140(6) *Pediatrics* e20170103: doi.org/10.1542/peds.2017-0103.

Alghrani, Amel (2009) 'The Human Fertilisation and Embryology Act 2008: A Missed Opportunity?' 35 *Journal of Medical Ethics* 718–719.

Alghrani, Amel (2018) *Regulating Assisted Reproductive Technologies: New Horizons* (Cambridge University Press).

Alghrani, Amel and Brazier, Margaret (2011) "What is it? Re-positioning the Fetus in the Context of Research?' 70(1) *Cambridge Law Journal* 51–82.

Alldridge, Peter (1996) 'Consent to Medical and Surgical Treatment – The Law Commission's Recommendations' 4(2) *Medical Law Review* 129–143.

AMRC (Academy of Medical Royal Colleges) (2008) *A Code of Practice for the Diagnosis of Confirmation of Death.*

Andorno, Roberto, Baylis, Françoise, Darnovsky, Marcy, et al (2020) 'Geneva Statement on Heritable Human Genome Editing: The Need for Course Correction' 38(4) *Trends in Biotechnology* 351–354.

Anscombe, GEM (1958) 'Modern Moral Philosophy' 33 *Philosophy* 1–19.

Appelbaum, Paul S, Roth, Loren H and Lidz, Charles (1982) 'The Therapeutic Misconception: Informed Consent in Psychiatric Research' 5 *International Journal of Law and Psychiatry* 319–329.

Aristotle (BCE) *Nicomachean Ethics,* translated by Roger Crisp (Cambridge University Press, 2000).

Baker, Dennis J (2014) 'Should Unnecessary Harmful Nontherapeutic Cosmetic Surgery be Criminalized?' 17(4) *New Criminal Law Review* 587–630.

Bauhn, Per (2016) 'The Gewirthian Duty to Rescue' in P Bauhn (ed) *Gewirthian Perspectives on Human Rights* (Routledge), 212–226.

Bayne, Tim and Levy, Neil (2005) 'Amputees by Choice: Body Integrity Identity Disorder and the Ethics of Amputation' 22(1) *Journal of Applied Philosophy* 75–86.

Baylis, Françoise (2020) 'To Publish or Not to Publish' 38 *Nature Biotechnology* 271.

BBC (1998) 'Technology Gets Under the Skin', 25 August, *BBC News*: news.bbc.co.uk/1/hi/sci/tech/158007.stm.

BBC (2004) 'Baby Born from 21-year-old Sperm', 25 May, *BBC News:* news.bbc.co.uk/1/hi/health/3742319.stm.

BBC (2013a) 'Living Ohio Man Donald Miller Ruled "Legally Dead"', 11 October, *BBC News:* www.bbc.co.uk/news/world-us-canada-24486718.

BBC (2013b) 'Dick Cheney: Heart Implant Attack Was Credible', 21 October, *BBC News:* www.bbc.co.uk/news/technology-24608435.

BBC (2014) 'First Womb-Transplant Baby Born', 4 October, *BBC News:* www.bbc.co.uk/news/health-29485996.

BBC (2017) 'Meet the Cyborgs: Five People Who Have Modified Their Bodies with Tech', *BBC Radio 4:* www.bbc.co.uk/programmes/articles/1g2gNvk4Gc4MwYqhtQ8KNlf.

BBC (2019) 'What Does the UK Think is Right and Wrong? The BBC Reveals a Snapshot of Morality in 2019', 21 November, *BBC News*: www.bbc.co.uk/mediacentre/latestnews/2019/year-of-beliefs-morality-ethics-survey-2019.

Bainbridge, David (2018) *Intellectual Property* (10th edn, Pearson).

Beal, James (2016) 'The Big Freeze: 100 More Brits Sign Up to Controversial Cryogenics Institute where 14-year-old Brit girl is Being Frozen for £37k in Hope of Being Brought to Life Again', 18 November, *The Sun*.

Beauchamp, Tom L and Childress, James F (2019) *Principles of Biomedical Ethics* (8th edn, Oxford University Press).

Bentham, Jeremy (1775) *A Fragment on Government*, in JH Burns and HLA Hart (eds) *The Collected Works of Jeremy Bentham: A Comment on the Commentaries and A Fragment on Government* (Oxford University Press, 1977), 393–421.

Berges, Sandrine (2015) *A Feminist Perspective on Virtue Ethics* (Palgrave Macmillan).

Berkowitz, Jonathan M and Snyder, Jack W (1998) 'Racism and Sexism in Medically Assisted Conception' 12(1) *Bioethics* 25–44.

Besser-Jones, Lorraine and Slote, Michael (eds) (2015) *The Routledge Companion to Virtue Ethics* (Routledge).

Beveridge, William (1942) *Social Insurance and Allied Services* (Cmd 6404) (HMSO).

Beyleveld, Deryck (1991) *The Dialectical Necessity of Morality: An Analysis and Defense of Alan Gewirth's Argument to the Principle of Generic Consistency* (University of Chicago Press).

Beyleveld, Deryck (1996) 'Legal Theory and Dialectically Contingent Justifications for the Principle of Generic Consistency' 9 *Ratio Juris* 15–41.

Beyleveld, Deryck (1997) 'Ethical Issues in the Forensic Application of DNA Analysis' 88 *Forensic Science International* 3–15.

Beyleveld, Deryck (2000) 'Is Embryo Research and Preimplantation Genetic Diagnosis Ethical?' 113(1–3) *Forensic Science International* 461–476.

Beyleveld, Deryck (2012) 'The Principle of Generic Consistency as the Supreme Principle of Human Rights' 13 *Human Rights Review* 1–18.

Beyleveld, Deryck (2013) 'Williams' False Dilemma: How to Give Categorically Binding Impartial Reasons to Real Agents' 10(2) *Journal of Moral Philosophy* 204–226.

Beyleveld, Deryck (2015) 'Korsgaard v Gewirth on Universalisation: Why Gewirthians are Kantians and Kantians Ought to be Gewirthians' 12 *Journal of Moral Philosophy* 573–597.

Beyleveld, Deryck (2017a) 'What Is Gewirth and What Is Beyleveld? A Retrospect with Comments on the Contributions' in Patrick Capps and Shaun D Pattinson (eds) *Ethical Rationalism and the Law* (Hart Publishing, 2017), 233–255.

Beyleveld, Deryck (2017b) 'The Sheffield Natural Law School' in Mortimer Sellers and Stephen Kirste (eds) *Encyclopedia of the Philosophy of Law and Social Philosophy* (Springer) 1–8.

Beyleveld, Deryck (2017c) 'Transcendental Arguments for a Categorical Imperative as Arguments from Agential Self-understanding' in Jens Peter Brune, Robert Stern and Micha H Werner (eds) *Transcendental Arguments in Moral Theory* (De Gruyter), 141–159.

Beyleveld, Deryck and Bos, Gerhard (2009) 'The Foundational Role of the Principle of Instrumental Reason in Gewirth's Argument for the Principle of Generic Consistency: A Reply to Andrew Chitty' 20 *King's Law Journal* 1–20.

Beyleveld, Deryck and Brownsword, Roger (1986) *Law as a Moral Judgment* (Sweet & Maxwell; reprinted Sheffield Academic Press, 1994).

Beyleveld, Deryck and Brownsword, Roger (1993) *Mice, Morality, and Patents* (Common Law Institute of Intellectual Property).

Beyleveld, Deryck and Brownsword, Roger (2001) *Human Dignity in Bioethics and Biolaw* (Oxford University Press).

Beyleveld, Deryck and Brownsword, Roger (2006) 'Principle, Proceduralism and Precaution in a Community of Rights' 19(2) *Ratio Juris* 141–168.

Beyleveld, Deryck and Pattinson, Shaun D (2000) 'Precautionary Reasoning as a Link to Moral Action' in Michael Boylan (ed) *Medical Ethics* (Prentice-Hall), 39–53.

Beyleveld, Deryck and Pattinson, Shaun D (2004) 'Individual Rights, Social Justice and the Allocation of Advances in Biotechnology' in Michael Boylan (ed) *Public Health Policy and Ethics* (The Hague, Kluwer International), 59–72.

Beyleveld, Deryck and Pattinson, Shaun D (2010) 'Defending Moral Precaution as a Solution to the Problem of Other Minds' 23(2) *Ratio Juris* 258–273.

Beyleveld, Deryck, Quarrell, Oliver, and Toddington, Stuart (1998) 'Generic Consistency in the Reproductive Enterprise' 3(2&3) *Medical Law International* 135–158.

Bibbings, Lois and Alldridge, Peter (1993) 'Sexual Expression, Body Alteration and the Defence of Consent' 20 *Journal of Law and Society* 356–370.

Bilger, Micaiah (2020) 'Born at 21 Weeks, Youngest Surviving Premature Baby in the World Now Heading Home', 24 June, *LifeNews.com*: www.lifenews.com/2020/06/24/born-at-21-weeks-youngest-surviving-premature-baby-in-the-world-now-heading-home.

Blackshaw, Bruce P and Rodger, Daniel (2019) 'Ectogenesis and the Case against the Right to the Death of the Foetus' 33(1) *Bioethics* 76–81.

Bostrom, Nick and Ord, Toby (2006) 'The Reversal Test: Eliminating Status Quo Bias in Ap-plied Ethics' 116 *Ethics* 656–679.

Brahmabhatt, Rupendra (2021) 'Cryonics Clinics: Where People Sleep and Wake Up in the Future' *Interesting Engineering*, 9 November: interestingengineering.com/culture/cryonics-clinics-where-people-sleep-and-wake-up-in-the-future.

Brännström, Mats (2017) 'Uterus Transplantation and Beyond' 28(5) *Journal of Materials Science: Materials in Medicine*, article number 70: doi.org/10.1007/s10856-017-5872-0.

Brännström, Mats, Johannesson, Liza, Bokström, Hans, et al (2015) 'Livebirth After Uterus Transplantation' 385 *The Lancet* 607–616.

Braveman, Paula and Gruskin, Sofia (2003) 'Defining Equity in Health' 57(4) *Journal of Epidemiology and Community Health* 254–258.

Brazier, Margaret and Fovargue, Sara (2017) 'Transforming Wrong into Right: What Is 'Proper Medical Treatment?'" in Sara Fovargue and Alexandra Mullock (eds) *The Legitimacy of Medical Treatment: What Role for the Medical Exception?* (London: Routledge), 12–31.

Britannica (The Editors of Encyclopaedia) (2016) 'Fetus', 14 June 2016, *Encyclopedia Britannica*: www.britannica.com/science/fetus.

Brown, Stephen (2016) 'A Dialectically Necessary Approach to the Sociological Understanding of Power and Real Interests' in Per Bauhn (ed) *Gewirthian Perspectives on Human Rights* (Routledge), 82–95.

Brownsword, Roger (2004) 'What the World Needs Now: Techno-Regulation, Human Rights and Human Dignity' in Roger Brownsword (ed), *Global Governance and the Quest for Justice: Volume IV. Human Rights* (Hart 2004), 203–234.

Brownsword, Roger (2017) '*Law as a Moral Judgement*, the Domain of Jurisprudence, and Technological Regulation' in Patrick Capps and Shaun D Pattinson (eds), *Ethical Rationalism and the Law* (Hart 2017), 109–130.

Brownsword, Roger (2021) *Law 3.0: Rules, Regulation and Technology* (Routledge).

Brownsword, Roger (2022) 'Thinking Outside the Box: Graeme Laurie's Legacy to Medical Jurisprudence' in Edward Dove and Niamh Nic Shuibhne (eds) *Law and Legacy in Medical Jurisprudence: Essays in Honour of Graeme Laurie* (Cambridge University Press), 62–93.

Brownsword, Roger and Wale, Jeff (2018) 'Testing Times Ahead: Non-Invasive Prenatal Testing and the Kind of Community We Want to Be' 81(4) *Modern Law Review* 646–672.

Buchanan, Allen, Brock, Dan W, Daniels, Norman and Wilkler, Daniel (2000) *From Chance to Choice: Genetics and Justice* (Cambridge University Press).

Burns, JH (2005) 'Happiness and Utility: Jeremy Bentham's Equation' 17(1) *Utilitas* 46–61.

Carey, Nessa (2019) *Hacking the Code of Life: How Gene Editing Will Rewrite Our Futures* (Icon Books).

Cavaliere, Giulia (2020) 'Ectogenesis and Gender-based Oppression: Resisting the Ideal of Assimilation' 34(7) *Bioethics* 727–734.

Chambers, Clare (2019) 'Choice and Female Genital Cosmetic Surgery' in Sarah M Creighton and Lih-Mei Liao, *Female Genital Cosmetic Surgery: Solution to What Problem?* (Cambridge University Press), 72–79.

Chan, Sarah and Harris, John (2006) *The Nuffield Council on Bioethics: An Ethical Review of Publications* (NCOB).

Chen, Chiann-Mun (Sheny) and Chisholm, Andrew (2017) 'Human Development Between 14 and 28 Days' in Nuffield Council on Bioethics (eds) *Human Embryo Culture* (Nuffield Council on Bioethics, 2017), 48–49.

Chen, Christopher (1986) 'Pregnancy After Human Oocyte Cryopreservation' 327 *Lancet* 884–886.

Chen Ci-Di, Zeldich, Ellan, Li, Yuexuan, et al (2018) 'Activation of the Anti-Aging and Cognition-Enhancing Gene Klotho by CRISPR-dCas9 Transcriptional Effector Complex' 64 *Journal of Molecular Neuroscience* 175–184.

Chitty, Andrew (2008) 'Protagonist and Subject in Gewirth's Argument for Human Rights' 19 *King's Law Journal* 1–26.

Chrisafis, Angelique (2006) 'Freezer Failure Ends Couple's Hopes of Life After Death' 17 March, *The Guardian.*

Clausen, Jens (2010) 'Ethical Brain Stimulation – Neuroethics of Deep Brain Stimulation in Research and Clinical Practice' 32 *European Journal of Neuroscience* 1152–1162.

CLRC (Criminal Law Revision Committee) (1980) *Fourteenth Report: Offences Against the Person* (Cmnd 7844).

Clynes, Manfred E and Kline, Nathan S (1960) 'Cyborgs and Space' (September) *Astronautics* 26–76.

Coggon, John (2007) 'Varied and Principled Understandings of Autonomy in English Law: Justifiable Inconsistency or Blinkered Moralism?' 15 *Health Care Analysis* 235–255.

Coggon, John (2012) *What Makes Health Public? A Critical Evaluation of Moral, Legal, and Political Claims in Public Health* (Cambridge University Press).

Cohen, GA (2003) 'Facts and Principles' 31(3) *Philosophy & Public Affairs* 211–245.

Coleman, Jules L (1982) 'Negative and Positive Positivism' 11(1) *The Journal of Legal Studies* 139–164.

Connor, Steven (1998) 'Professor has World's First Silicon Chip Implant', 26 August, *The Independent.*

Conway, Heather (2016) *The Law and the Dead* (Routledge).

Conway, Heather (2018) 'Frozen Corpses and Feuding Parents: Re JS (Disposal of Body) 81(1) *Modern Law Review* 132–153.

Cornock, Marc and Montgomery, Heather (2011) 'Children's Rights in and out of the Womb' (2011) 19 *International Journal of Children's Rights* 3–19.

Costeloe Kate L, Hennessy Enid, Haider Sadia, at al (2012) 'Short Term Outcomes after Extreme Preterm Birth in England: Comparison of Two Birth Cohorts in 1995 and 2006 (EPICure Studies)' 345 *British Medical Journal* e7976: www.bmj.com/content/345/bmj.e7976.

Couzin-Frankel, Jennifer (2017) 'Fluid-filled "Biobag" Allows Premature Lambs to Develop Outside the Womb' 25 April, *Science*: www.sciencemag.org/news/2017/04/fluid-filled-biobag-allows-premature-lambs-develop-outside-womb.

CPS (2013) 'CPS Statement on Abortion Related Case' Press Release, 5/9/13.

Cyranoski, David (2018) 'First CRISPR Babies: Six Questions That Remain', 30 Nov 2018, *Nature*: www.nature.com/articles/d41586-018-07607-3.

Cyranoski, David (2020) 'What CRISPR-baby Prison Sentences Mean for Research' 3 Jan, *Nature*: www.nature.com/articles/d41586-020-00001-y.

Davey, Tina and Mead, David (2022) 'Whose Right Is It Anyway? The Duties Owed to a Deceased and to Surviving Family Members When Dealing with a Corpse: Brennan v City of Bradford Metropolitan District Council and Leeds Teaching Hospitals NHS Trust [2021] 1 WLUK 429' 30(1) *Medical Law Review* 137–149.

Davis, Dena S (1997) 'Genetic Dilemmas and the Child's Right to An Open Future' 28 *Rutgers Law Journal* 549–592.

Daley, Suzanne (2002) 'France Orders Removal of Couple's Frozen Bodies from Chateau', 14 March, *New York Times.*

de Beer, Jeremy and Jain, Vipal (2018) 'Inclusive Innovation in Biohacker Spaces: The Role of Systems and Networks Technology' 8(2) *Innovation Management Review* 27–37.

De Bie, Felix R, Kim, Sarah D, Bose, Sourav K, et al (2022) 'Ethics Considerations Regarding Artificial Womb Technology for the Fetonate' *American Journal of Bioethics:* doi.org/10.1080/15265161.2022.2048738.

Deglincerti, Alessia, Croft, Gist F, Pietila, Lauren Z, et al (2016) 'Self-Organization of the In Vitro Attached Human Embryo' 533 *Nature* 251–254.
De Melo-Martín, Inmaculada (2004) 'On Our Obligation to Select the Best Children: A Reply to Savulescu' 18(1) *Bioethics* 72–83.
Department for Digital, Culture, Media and Sport (2022) *Consultation Outcome: Government Response to the Consultation on a Potential Change of Ownership of Channel 4 Television Corporation*, 22 April.
Devlin, Hannan (2017) 'Artificial Womb for Premature Babies Successful in Animal Trials', 25 April, *The Guardian*.
DH (Department of Health) (2004) Regulation of Cosmetic Piercing and Skin-Colouring Businesses: Guidance on Section 120 and Schedule 6.
DH (2014) Mitochondrial Donation: Government Response to the Consultation on Draft Regulations to Permit the Use of New Treatment Techniques to Prevent the Transmission of a Serious Mitochondrial Disease from Mother to Child.
DHSC (Department of Health and Social Care) (2021) Abortion Statistics, England and Wales: 2020. www.gov.uk/government/statistics/abortion-statistics-for-england-and-wales-2020/abortion-statistics-england-and-wales-2020.
DHSC (2022) Abortion Statistics, England and Wales: 2021. www.gov.uk/government/statistics/abortion-statistics-for-england-and-wales-2021/abortion-statistics-england-and-wales-2021.
DHSS (Department of Health and Social Security) (1983) Health Services Management Ownership of Implants and Removal of Cardiac Pacemakers After Death HN(83)641.
Dicey, AV (1915) *Introduction to the Study of the Law of the Constitution* (8th edn, Macmillan).
Djuwantono, Tono, Wirakusumah, Firman F, Achmad, Tri H, et al (2011) 'A Comparison of Cryopreservation Methods: Slow-Cooling vs Rapid-Cooling Based on Cell Viability, Oxidative Stress, Apoptosis, and CD34+ Enumeration of Human Umbilical Cord Blood Mononucleated Cells' 4 *BMC Research Notes*: doi.org/10.1186/1756-0500-4-371.
Dobson, Sarah-Jane (2021) 'The Legislation and Regulation of Medical Devices' in Peter Feldschreiber (eds) *The Law and Regulation of Medicines and Medical Devices* (2nd edn, Oxford University Press), 177–194.
Donnez, Jacques and Dolmans, Marie-Madeleine (2017) 'Fertility Preservation in Women' 377(17) *New England Journal of Medicine* 1657–1665.
Donnez J, Dolmans MM, Demylle D, et al (2004) 'Livebirth After Orthotopic Transplantation of Cryopreserved Ovarian Tissue' 364 *Lancet* 1405–1410.
Douglas, Benedict (2018) 'Too Attentive to our Duty: The Fundamental Conflict Underlying Human Rights Protection in the UK' (2018) 38(3) *Legal Studies* 360–378.
Douglas, Gillian (1992) 'The Retreat from Gillick' 55 *Modern Law Review* 569–576.
Downey, Laura and Quigley, Muireann (2021) 'Software as a Medical Device: A Bad Regulatory Fit?' *Everyday Cyborgs 2.0*, 15 March: blog.bham.ac.uk/everydaycyborgs/2021/03/15/software-as-a-medical-device-a-bad-regulatory-fit.
Doyle, Arthur Conan (1905) *The Return of Sherlock Holmes* (Georges Newnes).
Dubal, Dena B, Yokoyama Jennifer S (2014) 'Life Extension Factor Klotho Enhances Cognition' 7(4) *Cell Reports* 1065–1076.
Dukeminier, Jesse Jr (1970) 'Supplying Organs for Transplantation' 68(5) *Michigan Law Review* 811–866.
Duxbury, Neil (2009) *The Nature and Authority of Precedent* (Cambridge University Press).
Dworkin, Gerald (1988) *The Theory and Practice of Autonomy* (Cambridge University Press).
Dworkin, Ronald (1977) *Taking Rights Seriously* (Duckworth).
Dworkin, Ronald (1986) *Law's Empire* (Hart Publishing).
EGE (European Group on Ethics in Science and New Technologies) (2021) *Ethics of Genome Editing* (European Commission).
Eijkholt, Marleen (2011) 'Procreative Autonomy and the Human Fertilisation and Embryology Act 2008: Does a Coherent Conception Underpin UK Law?' 11 *Medical Law International* 93–126.

Elliott, Tracey (2009) 'Body Dysmorphic Disorder, Radical Surgery and the Limits of Consent' 17(2) *Medical Law Review* 149–182.

Enoch, David (2006) 'Agency, Schmagency: Why Normativity Won't Come from What is Constitutive of Action' 115 *Philosophical Review* 169–198.

European Commission (2020) *MDCG 2019-16: Guidance on Cybersecurity for Medical Devices* (7 January).

Fahy, Gregory M, Wowk, Brian, Pagotan, Roberto, et al (2009) 'Physical and Biological Aspects of Renal Vitrification' 5(3) *Organogenesis* 167–175.

Fanelli, Adele, Ferlauto, Laura, Zollinger, Elodie Geneviève, et al (2021) 'Transient Neurovascular Interface for Minimally Invasive Neural Recording and Stimulation' *Advanced Materials Technologies*: doi.org/10.1002/admt.202100176.

Feinberg, Joel (1980) 'The Child's Right to an Open Future' Reprinted in Joel Feinberg, *Freedom and Fulfillment: Philosophical Essays* (Princeton University Press, 1992), 76–97.

Ferlauto, Laura, Bagni, Paolo, Fanelli, Adele, et al (2021) 'All-polymeric Transient Neural Probe for Prolonged in-vivo Electrophysiological Recordings' *Biomaterials*: doi.org/10.1016/j.biomaterials.2021.120889.

Fernandez, Colin, Boyle, Sian and Bates, Daniel (2016) 'Frozen and Flown to US by a Bunch of "Dad's Army" Amateurs: The journey of a terminally-ill schoolgirl from London to a bleak industrial estate in Michigan' 19 November, *Daily Mail*.

Finnis, John (1993) 'Bland: Crossing the Rubicon?' 109 *Law Quarterly Review* 329–337.

Fisher, Jane RW and Hammarberg, Karin (2012) 'Psychological and Social Aspects of Infertility in Men: An Overview of the Evidence and Implications for Psychologically Informed Clinical Care and Future Research' 14(1) *Asian Journal of Andrology* 121–129.

Fogarty, Norah ME, McCarthy, Afshan, Snijders, Kirsten E, et al (2017) 'Genome Editing Reveals a Role for OCT4 in Human Embryogenesis' 550 *Nature* 67–73.

Foot, Philippa (1967) 'The Problem of Abortion and the Doctrine of Double Effect' 5 *Oxford Review* 5–15.

Fovargue, Sara and Mullock, Alexandra (2017) 'Introduction'" in Sarah Fovargue and Alexandra Mullock (eds) *The Legitimacy of Medical Treatment: What Role for the Medical Exception?* (London: Routledge), 1–11.

Fox, Marie (2009) 'The Human Fertilisation and Embryology Act 2008: Tinkering at the Margins' 17(3) *Feminist Legal Studies* 333–334.

Frank, RN, Puklin, JE, Stock, C and Canter, LA (2000) 'Race, Iris Color and Age-Related Macular Degeneration' 98 *Transactions of the American Ophiological Society* 109–117.

Frias, Lopez and Javier, Francisco (2016) 'The Defining Components of the Cyborg: Cyborg-Athletes, Fictional or Real?' 10(1) *Sport, Ethics and Philosophy* 97–111.

Fuller, Lon (1969) *The Morality of Law* (Yale University Press).

Fuller, Lon L (1978) 'The Forms and Limits of Adjudication' 92(2) *Harvard Law Review* 353–409.

Gasiunas, Giedrius, Barrangou, Rodolphe, Horvath, Philippe and Siksnys, Virginijus (2012) 'Cas9–crRNA Ribonucleoprotein Complex Mediates Specific DNA Cleavage for Adaptive Immunity in Bacteria' 109 *Proceedings of the National Academy of Sciences of the United States of America (PNAS)* 15539–15540.

Gauthier, David (1986) *Morals by Agreement* (Clarendon Press).

Gewirth, Alan (1978) *Reason and Morality* (University of Chicago Press).

Gewirth, Alan (1988) 'The Justification of Morality' 53 *Philosophical Studies* 245–262.

Gewirth, Alan (1991) 'Foreword' in Deryck Beyleveld, *The Dialectical Necessity of Morality: An Analysis and Defense of Alan Gewirth's Argument to the Principle of Generic Consistency* (University of Chicago Press, 1991), vii–xvii.

Gewirth, Alan (1996) *The Community of Rights* (University of Chicago Press).

Glass, Hannah, Costarino, Andrew T, Stayer, Stephen A, et al (2015) 'Outcomes for Extremely Premature Infants' 120(6) *Anesthesia & Analgesia* 1337–1351.

Goering, Sara, Klein, Eran, Sullivan, Laura Specker, et al (2021) 'Recommendations for Responsible Development and Application of Neurotechnologies' 14 *Neuroethics* 365–386.

Grace, John (1999) 'Should the Foetus Have Rights in Law?' 67(2) *Medico-Legal Journal* 57–67.

Green, Ronald (2007) *Babies by Design: The Ethics of Genetic Choice* (Yale University Press).

Gregory, Andrew (2022) 'People with Type 1 Diabetes in England to be given Skin Sensor to Monitor Blood Sugar' 31 March, *The Guardian*.

Griffths, Danielle and Mullock, Alexandra (2017) 'The Medical Exception and Cosmetic Surgery: Culpable Doctors and Harmful Enhancements?' in Sara Fovargue and Alexandra Mullock (eds) *The Legitimacy of Medical Treatment: What Role for the Medical Exception?* (London: Routledge), 105–123.

Gutierrez, Nicolas (2022) 'What's Next for the Gene-edited Children from CRISPR Trial in China?' 29 June, *New Scientist*.

Haddow, Gill, Harmon Shawn HE & Gilman, Leah (2016) 'Implantable Smart Technologies (IST): Defining the "Sting" in Data and Device' 24(3) *Health Care Analysis* 210–227.

Haddow, Gill, King, Emma, Kunkler, Ian and McLaren, Duncan (2015) 'Cyborgs in the Everyday: Masculinity and Biosensing Prostate Cancer' 24(4) *Science as Culture* 484–506.

Haldane, JBS (1923) *Daedalus, or Science and the Future* (Kegan Paul, Trench & Co).

Hamzelou, Jessica (2016) 'World's First Baby Born with New "3 Parent" Technique', 27 September, *New Scientist*.

Hamzelou, Jessica (2017) 'Artificial Womb Helps Premature Lamb Fetuses Grow for 4 Weeks', 25 April, *New Scientist*.

Hare, RM (1981) *Moral Thinking: Its Levels, Method and Point* (Clarendon Press).

Harris, John (1985) *The Value of Life: An Introduction to Medical Ethics* (Routledge).

Harris, John (1998) *Clones, Genes and Immortality: Ethics and the Genetic Revolution* (Oxford University Press).

Harris, John (2006) *Enhancing Evolution: The Ethical Case for Making Better People* (Princeton University Press).

Hart, HLA (1955) 'Are There Any Natural Rights?' 64(2) *Philosophical Review* 175–191.

Hart, HLA (2012) *The Concept of Law* (3rd edn, Clarendon Press) (First edition published in 1961).

Häyry, Matti (2001) *Playing Good: Essays on Bioethics* (Helsinki University Press).

Hendl, Tereza (2017) 'Queering the Odds: The Case Against "Family Balancing"' 10(2) *International Journal of Feminist Approaches to Bioethics* 4–30.

Hernández, Gleider (2022) *International Law* (2nd edn, Oxford University Press).

Hewson, Barbara (2013) '"Neither Midwives nor Rainmakers" – Why DL Is Wrong' *Public Law* 451–459.

HFEA (Human Fertilisation and Embryology Authority) (2019) *Code of Practice* (9th edn) (HFEA).

HFEA (2021) *Fertility Treatment 2019: Trends and Figures* (HFEA). (May 2021) www.hfea.gov.uk/about-us/publications/research-and-data/fertility-treatment-2019-trends-and-figures.

Hill, James F (1984) 'Are Marginal Agents "Our Recipients"?' in Edward Regis (ed) *Gewirth's Ethical Rationalism: Critical Essays with a Reply by Gewirth* (University of Chicago Press), 180–191.

Hohfeld, Wesley Newcomb (1923) *Fundamental Legal Conceptions: As Applied in Judicial Reasoning and Other Legal Essays* (ed Walter Wheeler Cook) (Yale University Press).

Holm, Søren and Coggon, John (2008) 'A Cautionary Note Against 'Precautionary Reasoning' in Action Guiding Morality' 22(2) *Ratio Juris* 295–309.

HGAC (Human Genetics Advisory Commission) & HFEA (Human Fertilisation and Embryology Authority (1998a) *Cloning Issues in Reproduction, Science and Medicine: A Consultation Document* (HMSO).

HGAC & HFEA (1998b) *Cloning Issues in Reproduction, Science, and Medicine* (HMSO).

HM Passport Office (2019) *Guidance: Birth Certificates and the Full Birth Certificate Policy*, 30 October: www.gov.uk/government/publications/birth-certificates-and-the-full-birth-certificate-policy/birth-certificates-and-the-full-birth-certificate-policy.

Hull, Michael (1992) *Infertility Treatment: Needs and Effectiveness. A Report from the University of Bristol Department of Obstetrics and Gynaecology* (Serond Laboratories).

Hume, David (1739–1740) *A Treatise of Human Nature.*

Hursthouse, Rosalind (1991) 'Virtue Theory and Abortion' 20(3) *Philosophy and Public Affairs* 223–246.

Hursthouse, Rosalind (2016) 'Virtue Ethics' *Stanford Encyclopedia of Philosophy*, first published 18 July 2003; substantive revision 8 December 2016: plato.stanford.edu/entries/ethics-virtue.

Huxley, Aldous (1932) *Brave New World* (Chatto & Windus).

Huxtable, Richard (2018) 'Cryonics in the Courtroom: Which Interests? Whose Interests?' 26(3) *Medical Law Review* 476–499.

IBC (International Bioethics Committee) (2015) *Report of the IBC on Updating Its Reflection on the Human Genome and Human Rights*, 2 October, Paris. SHS/YES/IBC-22/15/2 REV.2.

IHGSC (International Human Genome Sequencing Consortium) (2004) 'Finishing the Euchromatic Sequence of the Human Genome' 431 *Nature* 931–945.

ISSCR (International Society for Stem Cell Research) (2021) *ICCR Guidelines for Stem Cell Research and Clinical Translation* (version 1.0, May 2021).

Ivers, Kathryn (1995) 'Towards a Bilingual Education Policy in the Mainstreaming of Deaf Children' 26 *Columbia Human Rights Law Review* 439–482.

Jasanoff, Sheila (2016) *The Ethics of Invention: Technology and the Human Future* (WW Norton & Co).

Jinek, Martin, Chylinski, Krzysztof, Fonfara, Ines, et al (2012) 'A Programmable Dual-RNA-Guided DNA Endonuclease in Adaptive Bacterial Immunity' 337 *Science* 816–821.

Jones, Imogen (2017) 'A Grave Offence: Corpse Desecration and the Criminal Law' 37(4) *Legal Studies* 599–620.

Jones, Imogen and Quigley, Muireann (2016) 'Preventing Lawful and Decent Burial: Resurrecting Dead Offences' 36(2) *Legal Studies* 354–374.

Jordan, Gabriele, Deeb, Samir, Bosten, Jenny M and Mollon, JD (2010) 'The Dimensionality of Color Vision in Carriers of Anomalous Trichromacy' 10(12) *Journal of Vision:* doi.org/10.1167/10.8.12.

Juengst, Eric T, Henderson, Gail E, Walker, Rebecca L, et al (2018) 'Is Enhancement the Price of Prevention in Human Gene Editing?' 1(6) *The CRISPR Journal* 351–354.

Kaczor, Christopher (2018) 'Ectogenesis and a Right to the Death of the Prenatal Human Being: A Reply to Räsänen' 32(9) *Bioethics* 634–638.

Kant, Immanuel (1785) *Groundwork of the Metaphysic of Morals* [vol 4 in the Academy edition], translated by HJ Paton, *The Moral Law* (Hutchinson, 1972).

Kass, Leon R (1988) *Toward a More Natural Science: Biology and Human Affairs* (Free Press).

Kawamura, Kazuhiro, Cheng Yuan, Suzuki Nao, et al (2013) 'Hippo Signaling Disruption and Akt Stimulation of Ovarian Follicles for Infertility Treatment' 110(43) *Proceedings of the National Academy of Sciences of the United States of America* 17474–17479.

Kendal, Evie (2015) *Equal Opportunity and the Case for State Sponsored Ectogenesis* (Palgrave Macmillan).

Kennedy, Ian (1992) 'Consent to Treatment: The Capable Person' in Clare Dyer (ed) *Doctors Patients and the Law* (Blackwell), ch 3.

Keown, John (1997) 'Restoring Moral and Intellectual Shape to the Law after Bland' 113 *Law Quarterly Review* 482–503.

Keown, John (2018) *Euthanasia, Ethics and Public Policy: An Argument Against Euthanasia* (2nd edn) (Cambridge University Press).

Khan, Sikandar Hayat (2019) 'Genome-Editing Technologies: Concept, Pros, and Cons of Various Genome-Editing Techniques and Bioethical Concerns for Clinical Application' 16 *Molecular Therapy: Nucleic Acids* 326–334.

Kingma, Elselijn and Finn, Suki (2020) 'Neonatal Incubator or Artificial Womb? Distinguishing Ectogenestation and Ectogenesis Using the Metaphysics of Pregnancy' 34(4) *Bioethics* 354–363.

Kleeman, Jenny (2020) '"Parents Can Look at their Foetus in Real Time": Are Artificial Wombs the Future?', 27 June, *The Guardian.*

Kumar, Mritunjay, Chawla, Rajiv and Goyal, Manish (2015) 'Topical Anesthesia' 31(4) *Journal of Anaesthesiology, Clinical Pharmacology* 450–456.

Kurosu, Hiroshi, Yamamoto Masaya, Clark, Jeremy D, et al (2005) 'Suppression of Aging in Mice by the Hormone Klotho' 309(5742) *Science* 1829–1833.

Laird, Karl (2018) '*R v BM*' 10 *Criminal Law Review* 847–850.

Lander, Eric S (2015) 'Brave New Genome' 373 *New England Journal of Medicine* 5–8.

Lander, Eric, Baylis, Françoise, Zhang, Feng, et al (2019) 'Adopt A Moratorium on Heritable Genome Editing' 567 *Nature* 165–168.

Latham, Katherine (2022) 'The Microchip Implants That Let You Pay with Your Hand', 11 April, *BBC News*: www.bbc.co.uk/news/business-61008730.

Laurie, GT, Harmon, SHE and Porter, G (2016) *Mason & McCall Smith's Law and Medical Ethics* (10th edn) (Oxford University Press).

Laurie, GT, Harmon, SHE and Dove, ES (2019) *Mason & McCall Smith's Law and Medical Ethics* (11th edn) (Oxford University Press).

Law Commission (1992) *Legislating the Criminal Code: Offences against the Person and General Principles. A Consultation Paper.* Consultation Paper No 122 (HMSO).

Law Commission (1995) *Consent in the Criminal Law: A Consultation Paper*. Consultation Paper No 139 (HMSO).

Lawrence, David R and Brazier, Margaret (2018) 'Legally Human? "Novel Beings" and English Law' 26(2) *Medical Law Review* 309–327.

Lawton, Graham (2021) 'First Universal Coronavirus Vaccine Will Start Human Trials this Year' 3323 (24 February), *New Scientist.*

Lee, Jihun Leung, Vincent, Lee, Ah-Hyoung, et al (2021) 'Neural Recording and Stimulation Using Wireless Networks of Microimplants' 4 *Nature Electronics* 604–614.

Lee, Stephanie (2017) 'This Guy Says He's the First Person to Attempt Editing His DNA with CRISPR' 14 October, *BuzzFeed News:* www.buzzfeednews.com/article/stephaniemlee/this-biohacker-wants-to-edit-his-own-dna.

Leonel, Ellen Cristina Rivas, Lucci, Carolina M and Amorim, Christiani A (2019) 'Cryopreservation of Human Ovarian Tissue: A Review' 46(3) *Transfusion Mdicine and Hemotherapy* 173–181.

Lewens, Tim (2018) 'Blurring the Germline: Genome Editing and Transgenerational Epigenetic Inheritance' *Bioethics:* doi.org/10.1111/bioe.12606.

Lewis, Penney (2011) 'Legal Change on Contraceptive Sterilisation' 32(3) *Journal of Legal History* 295–317.

Lewis, Penney (2012) 'The Medical Exception' 65(1) *Current Legal Problems* 355–376.

Liang, Puping, Xu, Yanwen, Zhang, Xiya, et al (2015) 'CRISPR/Cas9-mediated Gene Editing in Human Tripronuclear Zygotes' 6(5) *Protein & Cell* 363–372.

Lobo, Ingrid (2008) 'Pleiotropy: One Gene Can Affect Multiple Traits' 1(1) *Nature Education* 10.

Locke, John (1690) *An Essay Concerning Human Understanding*. Reprinted in R Woolhouse (ed) (Penguin Classics, 1997).

Lucy, William (2022) 'The Death of Law: Another Obituary' 81(1) *Cambridge Law Review* 109–138.

McCarthy, David (2001) 'Why Sex Selection Should Be Legal' 27 *Journal of Medical Ethics* 302–307.

MacCormick, Neil (1977) 'Rights in Legislation' in PMS Hacker and J Raz (eds) *Law, Morality and Society: Essays in Honour of HLA Hart* (Clarendon Press), 189–209.

McGrath, James and Solter, Davor (1984) 'Inability of Mouse Blastomere Nuclei Transferred to Enucleated Zygotes to Support Development In Vitro' 226 *Science* 1317–1319.

MacKay, Kathryn (2020) 'The "Tyranny of Reproduction": Could Ectogenesis Further Women's Liberation?' 34(4) *Bioethics* 346–353.

Macintosh, Keegan and Wong, Carrie (2018) 'A New Chapter for Cryonics in British Columbia' 39(6) *Cryonics* 8–10.

Macintosh, Kerry Lynn (2018) *Enhanced Beings: Human Germline Modification and the Law* (Cambridge University Press).

McIntyre, Robert L and Fahy, Gregory M (2015) 'Aldehyde-stabilized Cryopreservation' 71(3) *Cryobiology* 448–458.

Mameli, M (2007) 'Reproductive Cloning, Genetic Engineering and the Autonomy of the Child' 33 *Journal of Medical Ethics* 87–93.

Marco-Jiménez, Francisco, Garcia-Domingueza, Ximo, Jimenez-Trigosa, Estrella, et al (2015) Vitrification of Kidney Precursors as a New Source for Organ Transplantation' 70(3) *Cryobiology* 278–282.

Marshall, Barry and Adams, Paul C (2008) '*Helicobacter pylori*: A Nobel Pursuit?' 22(11) *Canadian Journal of Gastroenterology* 895–896.

Marx, Karl (1891) *Critique of the Gotha Programme* (Dodo Press, 2009).

Matthews, Paul (1983) 'Whose Body? People as Property' 36 *Current Legal Problems* 193–239.

Mehler, Katrin, Oberthuer, André, Keller, Titus, et al (2016) 'Survival Among Infants Born at 22 or 23 Weeks' Gestation Following Active Prenatal and Postnatal Care' 170(7) *JAMA Pediatrics* 671–677.

Menning, Barbara Eck (1977) *Infertility: A Guide for the Childless Couple* (Prentice Hall).

Menning, Barbara Eck (1980) 'The Emotional Needs of Infertile Couples' 34(4) *Fertility and Sterility* 313–319.

Meisel, Ari R (2014) *Intro to Biohacking: Be Smarter, Stronger, and Happier* (Create Space Independent Publishing).

MHRA (Medicines and Healthcare products Regulatory Agency) (2011) *Leaving Hospital with a Medical Device*, 21 July.

MHRA (2014) *Guidance on Off-Label Use of a Medical Device* (18 December): www.gov.uk/government/publications/medical-devices-off-label-use/off-label-use-of-a-medical-device.

MHRA (2020a) *Guidance on Exceptional Use of Non-UKCA Marked Medical Devices* (31 December): www.gov.uk/guidance/exceptional-use-of-non-ukca-marked-medical-devices.

MHRA (2020b) *Custom-Made Devices in Great Britain* (31 December): www.gov.uk/government/publications/custom-made-medical-devices/custom-made-devices-in-great-britain.

MHRA (2020c) *Medical Devices: Conformity Assessment and the UKCA Mark* (31 December): www.gov.uk/guidance/medical-devices-conformity-assessment-and-the-ukca-mark.

MHRA (2020d) *Approved Bodies for Medical Devices* (31 December): www.gov.uk/government/publications/approved-bodies-for-medical-devices/approved-bodies-for-medical-devices.

MHRA (2021a) *Register Medical Devices to Place on the Market* (updated 1 Jan): www.gov.uk/guidance/register-medical-devices-to-place-on-the-market.

MHRA (2021b) *Guidance on Legislation: Clinical Investigations of Medical Devices – Guidance for Investigators* (March 2021): assets.publishing.service.gov.uk/government/uploads/system/uploads/attachment_data/file/989421/Information_for_clinical_investigators_-_May_2021.pdf.

MHRA (2021c) *Clinical Investigations of Medical Devices – Guidance for Manufacturers* (May): assets.publishing.service.gov.uk/government/uploads/system/uploads/attachment_data/file/989420/Guidance_for_mfrs_on_clinical_investigations-May_2021.pdf.

Michalowski, Sabine (1999) 'Court-Authorised Caesarean Sections – The End of a Trend? – *Re MB (An Adult: Medical Treatment)*' 62(1) *Modern Law Review* 115–127.

Mill, John Stuart (1859) *On Liberty* (John W Parker & Son).

Miller, Franklin G and Brody, Howard (2002) 'What Makes Placebo-Controlled Trials Unethical?' 2(2) *American Journal of Bioethics* 3–9.

Minerva, Francesca (2021) 'Should We Freeze Our Bodies for Future Resuscitation?' in David Edmonds (ed) *Future Mortality* (Oxford University Press, 2021), 235–242.

Minerva, Francesca and Sandberg, Anders (2017) 'Euthanasia and Cryothanasia' 31(7) *Bioethics* 526–533.

Ministry of Justice (2021) *Human Rights Act Reform: A Modern Bill of Rights. A Consultation to Reform the Human Rights Act 1998* (CP 588) (HMSO).

Moen, Ole Martin (2015) 'The Case for Cryonics' (2015) 41(8) *Journal of Medical Ethics* 677–681.

Morgan, Derek (1998) 'Foetal Sex Identification, Abortion and the Law' 18 *Family Law* 355.

Moore, Tamanna, Hennessy, Enid M, Myles, Jonathan, et al (2012) 'Neurological and Developmental Outcome in Extremely Preterm Children Born in England in 1995 and 2006: The ePICure Studies' 345 *British Medical Journal* e7961: doi: 10.1136/bmj.e7961.

Morton, James (1992) 'Obituary: Lord Devlin', 11 August, *The Independent.*

Mukaida, Tetsunori and Oka, Chikahiro (2012) 'Vitrification of Oocytes, Embryos and Blastocysts' 26(6) *Best Practice & Research Clinical Obstetrics & Gynaecology* 789–803.

Mullally, Siobhán (2006) *Gender, Culture and Human Rights* (Hart).

Mullender, Richard (1996) 'Judicial Review and the Rule of Law' 112 *Law Quarterly Review* 182–186.

Mullin, Emily (2000) 'The Price of DNA Sequencing Dropped From $2.7 Billion to $300 in Less Than 20 Years' *One Zero*, 18 February: onezero.medium.com/the-price-of-dna-sequencing-dropped-from-2-7-billion-to-300-in-less-than-20-years-f5e07c2f18b4.

Musunuru, Kiran (2019) 'Opinion: We Need to Know What Happened to CRISPR Twins Lulu and Nana' *MIT Technology Review* (3 December 2019): www.technologyreview.com/2019/12/03/65024/crispr-baby-twins-lulu-and-nana-what-happened.

Nagy, Zsolt Peter, Shapiro, Daniel and Chang, Ching-Chien (2020) 'Vitrification of the Human Embryo: A More Efficient and Safer *In Vitro* Fertilization Treatment' 113(2) *Fertility and Sterility* 241–247.

NAM (National Academy of Medicine), National Academy of Sciences and the Royal Society (2020) *Heritable Human Genome Editing* (The National Academies Press).

NASEM (National Academies of Sciences, Engineering, and Medicine) (2017) *Human Genome Editing: Science, Ethics, and Governance* (The National Academies Press).

NCOB (Nuffield Council on Bioethics) (1999) *Genetically Modified Crops: The Ethical and Social Issues* (NCOB).

NCOB (2005) *The Ethics of Research Involving Animals* (NCOB).

NCOB (2006) *Critical Care Decisions in Fetal and Neonatal Medicine* (NCOB).

NCOB (2012) *Novel Techniques for the Prevention of Mitochondrial DNA Disorders: An Ethical Review* (NCOB).

NCOB (2013) *Novel Neurotechnologies: Intervening in the Brain* (NCOB).

NCOB (2015) *Children and Clinical Research: Ethical Issues* (NCOB).

NCOB (2017) *Non-Invasive Prenatal Testing: Ethical Issues* (NCOB).

NCOB (2018) *Genome Editing and Human Reproduction: Social and Ethical Issues.* (NCOB).

NCOB (2019) *Bioethics Briefing Note: Medical Implants* (NCOB). www.nuffieldbioethics.org/publications/medical-implants.

Neal, Mary (2021) '"Not Nothing"? The Late Term Foetus in the Court of Protection', *Open Justice: Court of Protection Project*, 3 June: openjusticecourtofprotection.org/2021/06/03/not-nothing-the-late-term-foetus-in-the-court-of-protection.

Nelson, Bob, Bly, Kenneth and Magana, Sally (2014) *Freezing People Is (Not) Easy: My Adventures in Cryonics* (Lyons Press).

Nelson, Robert F and Stanley, Sandra (1968) *We Froze the First Man* (Dell Books).

Newman, John C, Milman, Sofiya, et al (2016) 'Strategies and Challenges in Clinical Trials Targeting Human Aging' 71(1)) *The Journals of Gerontology: Series A* 1424.

NHGR (National Human Genome Research Institute) (2019) 'DNA Sequencing Costs: Data', 30 October: www.genome.gov/about-genomics/fact-sheets/DNA-Sequencing-Costs-Data.

Niemann, Heiner and Seamark, Bob (2021) 'Blastoids: A New Model for Human Blastocyst Development' 6 *Signal Transduction and Targeted Therapy*, Article number 239: doi.org/10.1038/s41392-021-00663-8.

Normile, Dennis (2018) 'CRISPR Bombshell: Chinese Researcher Claims to Have Created Gene-Edited Twins', 26 November, *Science.*

Normile, Dennis (2019) 'Chinese Scientist Who Produced Genetically Altered Babies Sentenced to 3 Years in Jail', 30 December, *Science.*

Nurk, Sergey, Koren, Sergey, Rhie, Arang, et al (2022) 'The Complete Sequence of a Human Genome' 376 *Science* 44–53.

Nussbaum, Martha C (2000) *Women and Human Development: The Capabilities Approach* (Cambridge University Press).

Nussbaum, Martha C (2006) *Frontiers of Justice: Disability, Nationality, Species Membership* (Harvard University Press).
Office of the Parliamentary Council (2015) *Explanatory Notes Pilot: Office of the Parliamentary Counsel Response to Consultation* (April 2015).
Ó Néill, Clayton (2018) *Religion, Medicine and the Law* (Routledge).
O'Neill, Onora (1998) 'Consistency in Action' in James Rachels (ed) *Ethical Theory* (Oxford University Press), 504–529.
OpenMind BBAV (2021) 'Technology Under Your Skin: 3 Challenges of Microchip Implants', 5 April: www.bbvaopenmind.com/en/technology/innovation/technology-under-your-skin.
Parfit, Derek (1984) *Reason and Persons* (Clarendon Press; reprinted with corrections in 1987).
Partridge, Emily A, Davey, Marcus G, Hornick, Matthew A, et al (2017) 'An Extra-Uterine System to Physiologically Support the Extreme Premature Lamb' 8 *Nature Communications*: doi.org/10.1038/ncomms15112.
Pascal, Blaise (1670) *Pensées*, translated by AJ Krailsheimer (1966, Penguin).
Pashaeya, Yana (2021) 'A Divorced Couple is Fighting Over Frozen Dead Bodies', 21 September, *Slate*.
Pattinson, Shaun D (2000) 'Regulating Germ-Line Gene Therapy to Avoid Sliding Down the Slippery Slope' 4(3&4) *Medical Law International* 213–222.
Pattinson, Shaun D (2002) *Influencing Traits Before Birth* (Ashgate).
Pattinson, Shaun D (2003) 'Paying Living Organ Providers' 3 *Web Journal of Current Legal Issues*.
Pattinson, Shaun D (2005) 'Some Problems Challenging the UK's Human Fertilisation and Embryology Authority' 24 *Medicine and Law* 391–401.
Pattinson, Shaun D (2006) *Medical Law and Ethics* (1st edn, Sweet & Maxwell).
Pattinson, Shaun D (2008) 'Organ Trading, Tourism and Trafficking Within Europe' 27 *Medicine and Law* 191–201.
Pattinson, Shaun D (2009) 'Consent and Informational Responsibility' 35(3) *Journal of Medical Ethics* 176–179.
Pattinson, Shaun D (2011) 'Directed Donation and Ownership of Human Organs' 31(3) *Legal Studies* 392–410.
Pattinson, Shaun D (2014) *Medical Law and Ethics* (4th edn, Sweet & Maxwell).
Pattinson, Shaun D (2015) 'Contemporaneous and Advance Requests: The Fight for Rights at the End of Life' in Jonathan Herring and Jesse Wall (eds) *Landmark Cases in Medical Law* (Hart Publishing), 255–269.
Pattinson, Shaun D (2017) 'Advance Refusals and the Personal Identity Objection' in Patrick Capps and Shaun D Pattinson (eds) *Ethical Rationalism and the Law* (Hart Publishing), 91–108.
Pattinson, Shaun D (2018) *Revisiting Landmark Cases in Medical Law* (Routledge).
Pattinson, Shaun D (2020) *Medical Law and Ethics* (6th edn, Sweet & Maxwell).
Pegg, Samantha (2019) 'Not So Clear Cut: The Lawfulness of Body Modifications' 7 *Criminal Law Review* 579–598.
Pei, Wen-Di, Zhang, Yan, Yin, Tai-Lang and Yu, Yang (2019) 'Epigenome Editing by CRISPR/Cas9 in Clinical Settings: Possibilities and Challenges' *Briefings in Functional Genomics* 1–14.
Perry, R Michael (1992) 'Suspension Failures: Lessons from the Early Days' February, *Cryonics*. Available at www.alcor.org/library/suspension-failures-lessons-from-the-early-years.
Pluhar, Evelyn B (1995) *Beyond Prejudice: The Moral Significance of Human and Nonhuman Animals* (Duke University Press).
Pommer, Robert W (1993) '*Donaldson v Van de Kamp*: Cryonics, Assisted Suicide, and the Challenges of Medical Science' 9 *Journal of Contemporary Health Law and Policy* 589–604.
President's Council on Bioethics (2003) *Beyond Therapy: Biotechnology and the Pursuit of Happiness*.
Public Health England, Chartered Institute of Environmental Health, Health and Safety Laboratory and Tattooing and Piercing Industry Union (2013) *Tattooing and Body Piercing Guidance*: www.cieh.org/media/2004/tattooing-and-body-piercing-guidance-toolkit-july-2013.pdf.
Purshouse, Craig (2018) 'Utilitarianism as Tort Theory: Countering the Caricature' (2018) 38(1) *Legal Studies* 24–41.

Quigley, Muireann and Ayihongbe, Semande (2018) 'Everyday Cyborgs: On Integrated Persons and Integrated Goods' 26(2) *Medical Law Review* 276–308.

Quigley, Muireann and Downey, Laura (2022) 'Integrating the Biological and the Technological: Time to Move Beyond Law's Binaries?' in Edward Dove and Niamh Nic Shuibhne (eds) *Law and Legacy in Medical Jurisprudence: Essays in Honour of Graeme Laurie* (Cambridge University Press), 279–306.

Rachels, James (1979) 'Killing and Starving to Death' 54 *Philosophy* 159–171.

Räsänen, Joona (2017) 'Ectogenesis, Abortion and a Right to the Death of the Fetus' 31(9) *Bioethics* 697–702.

Rawls, John (1999) *A Theory of Justice: Revised Edition* (Oxford University Press) (First edition published in 1971).

RCS (Royal College of Surgeons) (2003) *Facial Transplantation: Working Party Report* (1st edn, RCS).

RCS (2006) *Facial Transplantation: Working Party Report* (2nd edn, RCS).

Reardon, Sara (2017) 'Genetic Details of Controversial "Three-Parent Baby" Revealed' 544 *Nature* 17–18.

Regalado, Antonio (2022) 'The Creator of the CRISPR Babies Has Been Released from a Chinese Prison' 4 April, *MIT Technology Review:* www.technologyreview.com/2022/04/04/1048829/he-jiankui-prison-free-crispr-babies.

Regan, Tom (2003) *Animal Rights, Human Wrongs: An Introduction to Moral Philosophy* (Rowman & Littlefield).

Ridley, Matt (2020) *How Innovation Works: And Why it Flourishes in Freedom* (Harper Collins).

Roberts, Joseph TF, Moore, Victoria and Quigley, Muireann (2021) 'Prescribing Unapproved Medical Devices? The Case of DIY Artificial Pancreas Systems' 21(1) *Medical Law International* 42–68.

Robertson, John A (1983) 'Procreative Liberty and the Control of Conception, Pregnancy and Childbirth' 69 *Virginia Law Review* 405–464.

Robeyns, Ingrid (2008) 'Ideal Theory in Theory and Practice' 34(3) *Social Theory and Practice* 341–362.

Robson, David (2014) 'The Women with Superhuman Vision', 5 September, *BBC*: www.bbc.com/future/article/20140905-the-women-with-super-human-vision.

Romanis, Elizabeth Chloe (2018) 'Artificial Womb Technology and the Frontiers of Human Reproduction: Conceptual Differences and Potential Implications' 44(11) *Journal of Medical Ethics* 751–755.

Romanis, Elizabeth Chloe (2020a) 'Challenging the "Born Alive" Threshold: Fetal Surgery, Artificial Wombs, and the English Approach to Legal Personhood' 28(1) *Medical Law Review* 93–123.

Romanis, Elizabeth Chloe (2020b) 'Artificial Womb Technology and Clinical Translation: Innovation Treatment or Medical Research' 34(4) *Bioethics* 392–402.

Romanis, Elizabeth Chloe (2020c) 'Artificial Womb Technology and the Choice to Gestate Ex Utero: Is Partial Ectogenesis the Business of the Criminal Law?' 28(3) *Medical Law Review* 342–374.

Rorty, Richard (1993) 'Human Rights, Rationality, and Sentimentality' in Stephen Shute and Susan Hurley (eds) *On Human Rights: The Oxford Amnesty Lectures 1993* (Basic Books), 112–134.

Rosling, Hans, Rosling, Ola and Rosling Rönnlund, Anna (2018) *Factfulness: Ten Reasons We're Wrong About the World – And Why Things Are Better Than You Think* (Sceptre).

Russlan, Jim (2020) *Biohacking Guide: Learn How to Implement Biohacks into Your Daily Life To Be Healthier, Feel Better and Achieve More* (Independently published).

Resuscitation Council (UK), British Cardiovascular Society and National Council for Palliative Care (2015) *Cardiovascular Implanted Electronic Devices in People towards the End of Life, During Cardiopulmonary Resuscitation and After Death*: www.resus.org.uk/sites/default/files/2020-05/CIEDs%20-%20guidance.pdf.

Sample, Ian (2018) 'Stephen Hawking, Science's Brightest Star, Dies Aged 76' 14 March, *The Guardian*.

Samuelson, William and Zeckhauser, Richard (1988) 'Status Quo Bias in Decision Making' 1 *Journal of Risk and Uncertainty* 7–59.

Sankey, Diana and Brooks, Thom (2017) 'Beyond Reason: The Legal Importance of Emotions' in Patrick Capps and Shaun D Pattinson (eds) *Ethical Rationalism and the Law* (Hart Publishing, 2017), 131–148.

Savulescu, Julian (1999) 'Sex Selection: The Case For' 171 *Medical Journal of Australia* 373–375.
Savulescu, Julian (2001) 'Procreative Beneficence: Why We Should Select the Best Children' (2001) 15(5/6) *Bioethics* 413–426.
Schillo, R Sandra and Robinson, Ryan M (2017) 'Inclusive Innovation in Developed Countries: The Who, What, Why, and How' 7(7) *Innovation Management Review* 34–46.
Schmidt, Harald and Schwartz, Jason L (2016) 'The Missions of National Commissions: Mapping the Forms and Functions of Bioethics Advisory Bodies' (2016) 26(4) *Kennedy Institute of Ethics Journal* 431–456.
Schwartz, Joe (2017) 'Thomas Donaldson and Cryonics' www.mcgill.ca/oss/article/aging-controversial-science-health-quirky-science-technology/thomas-donaldson-and-cryonics.
Scott, Rosamund (2004) 'The English Fetus and the Right to Life' (2004) 11 *European Journal of Health Law* 347–364.
Scott, Rosamund and Wilkinson, Stephen (2017) 'Germline Genetic Modification and Identity: The Mitochondrial and Nuclear Genomes' 37(4) *Oxford Journal of Legal Studies* 886–915.
Scutti, Susan (2016) 'Meet the Baby Who Was Born Twice' 20 October, *CCN*: edition.cnn.com/2016/10/20/health/baby-born-twice-fetal-surgery.
Shahbazi, Marta N, Jedrusik, Agnieszka, Vuotisto, Sanna, et al (2016) 'Self-Organization of the Human Embryo in the Absence of Maternal Tissues' 18(6) *Nature Cell Biology* 700–708.
Shakespeare, Tom and Hull, Richard J (2018) 'Termination of Pregnancy After Non-Invasive Prenatal Testing (NIPT): Ethical Considerations' 6(2) *Journal of Practical Ethics* 36–54.
Shaw, David (2009) 'Cryoethics: Seeking Life after Death' 23(9) *Bioethics* 515–521.
Sherman, JK (1964) 'Low Temperature Research on Spermatozoa and Eggs' 1(2) *Cryobiology* 103–129.
Sherman, JK and Bunge, RG (1953) 'Observations on Preservation of Human Spermatozoa at Low Temperatures. Experimental Biology and Medicine' 82(4) *Experimental Biology and Medicine* 686–688.
Simcoe, Mark, Valdes, Ana, Liu, Fan, et al (2021) 'Genome-wide Association Study in Almost 195,000 Individuals Identifies 50 Previously Unidentified Genetic Loci for Eye Color' 7(11) *Science Advances*: doi.org/10.1126/sciadv.abd1239.
Simonstein, Frida (2006) 'Artificial Reproduction Technologies (RTs) – All the Way to the Artificial Womb?' 9 *Medicine, Health Care and Philosophy* 359–365.
Singer, Peter (1994) *Rethinking Life and Death: The Collapse of Our Traditional Ethics* (Oxford University Press).
Singer, Peter and Wells, Deane (1984) *The Reproductive Revolution: New Ways of Making Babies* (Oxford University Press).
Skegg, Peter (1984) *Law, Ethics and Medicine: Studies in Medical Law* (Clarendon Press).
Smith, George P II (1983) 'Intimations of Immortality: Clones, Cyrons and the Law' 6(1) *University of New South Wales Law Journal* 119–132.
Spriggs, Merle (2002) 'Lesbian Couple Create a Child Who Is Deaf Like Them' 28 *Journal of Medical Ethics* 283.
Starr, Michelle (2017) 'Cool Dude James Bedford Has Been Cryonically Frozen for 50 Years', 11 January, *CNET*: www.cnet.com/science/cool-dude-james-bedford-has-been-cryonically-frozen-for-50-years.
Stauch, Mark, Wheat, Kay and Tingle, John (1998) *Sourcebook on Medical Law* (1st edn, Routledge-Cavendish).
Stefano, Lydia, Mills, Catherine, Watkins, Andrew and Wilkinson, Dominic (2020) 'Ectogestation Ethics: The Implications of Artificially Extending Gestation for Viability, Newborn Resuscitation and Abortion' 34(4) *Bioethics* 371–384.
Stephen, Leslie (1882) *Science of Ethics* (1st edn) (reprinted by Cambridge University Press, 2012).
Stix, Madeleine (2016) 'World's First Cyborg Wants to Hack Your Body' 7 January, *CCN*: edition.cnn.com/2014/09/02/tech/innovation/cyborg-neil-harbisson-implant-antenna.
Stoller, Sarah E (2008) 'Why We Are Not Morally Required to Select the Best Children: A Response to Savulescu' 22(7) *Bioethics* 364–369.
Suda I, Kito K, Adachi C (1966) 'Viability of Long Term Frozen Cat Brain *In Vitro*' 212 *Nature* 268–270.

Suda I, Kito K, Adachi C (1974) 'Bioelectric Discharges of Isolated Cat Brain After Revival From Years Of Frozen Storage' 70 *Brain Research* 527–531.

Suzuki, Nao, Yoshioka, Nobuhito, Takae, Seido, et al (2015) 'Successful Fertility Preservation following Ovarian Tissue Vitrification in Patients with Primary Ovarian Insufficiency' 30(3) *Human Reproduction* 608–615.

Taylor-Phillips, Sian, Freeman, Karloline, Geppert, Julia, et al (2016) 'Accuracy of Non-Invasive Prenatal Testing Using Cellfree DNA for Detection of Down, Edwards and Patau Syndromes: Asystematic Review and Meta-analysis' 6 *BMJ Open* e010002. doi.org/10.1136/bmjopen-2015-010002.

Thomson, Helen (2019) 'Exclusive: Humans Placed in Suspended Animation for the First Time', 20 November, *The New Scientist*.

Thomson, Judith Jarvis (1971) 'A Defence of Abortion' 1 *Philosophy and Public Affairs* 47–66.

Thurston, Alan J (2007) 'Paré and Prosthetics: The Early History of Artificial Limbs' 77(12) *ANZ Journal of Surgery* 1114–1119.

Time (1981) 'Law: The Rip Van Winkle Wrinkle' 117(25) *Time* 71.

Tyner, Stuart D, Venkatachalam, Sundaresan, Choi, Jene, et al (2002) 'Mutant Mice that Display Early Ageing-Associated Phenotypes' 415 *Nature* 45–53.

Usuda, Haruo, Watanabe, Shimpei, SaitoMiura, Yuichiro, et al (2017) 'Successful Maintenance of Key Physiological Parameters in Preterm Lambs Treated with Ex Vivo Uterine Environment Therapy for a Period of 1 Week' 217(4) *American Journal of Obstetrics & Gynecology* 457.e1–13: doi.org/10.1016/j.ajog.2017.05.046.

Usuda, Haruo, Watanabe, Shimpei, Saito, Masatoshi, et al (2019) 'Successful Use of an Artificial Placenta to Support Extremely Preterm Ovine Fetuses at the Border of Viability' 221(1) *American Journal of Obstetrics & Gynecology* 69.e1–17: doi.org/10.1016/j.ajog.2019.03.001.

Valentini, Laura (2012) 'Ideal v Non-ideal Theory: A Conceptual Map' 7(9) *Philosophy Compass* 654–664.

Wakefield, Jane (2021) 'Elon Musk's Neuralink "Shows Monkey playing Pong with Mind"', 9 April, *BBC News*: www.bbc.co.uk/news/technology-56688812.

Waldron, Jeremy (2009) 'Judges as Moral Reasoners' 7(1) *International Journal of Constitutional Law* 2–24.

Wale, Jeffrey I (2015) 'Don't Forget the Legal Framework: The Public Provision of Non-Invasive Prenatal Testing in England and Wales' 15(4) *Medical Law International* 15 (4) 203–215.

Wardrope, Alistair (2020) 'Health Justice in the Anthropocene: Medical Ethics and the Land Ethic' 46 *Journal of Medical Ethics* 791–796.

Warnock, Mary et al (1984) *The Report of the Committee of Inquiry into Human Fertilisation and Embryology* (Cmnd 9314) (HMSO).

Watson, James D and Crick, Francis HC (1953) 'A Structure for Deoxy-Ribo Nucleic Acid' 171 Nature 737–738.

Watson, James D, Berry, Andrew and Davies, Kevin (2017) *DNA: The Story of the Genetic Revolution* (Arrow Books).

Weizmann Institute of Science (2021) 'Advanced Mouse Embryos Grown Outside the Uterus', 18 March, *ScienceDaily*: www.sciencedaily.com/releases/2021/03/210318084759.htm.

WHO (World Health Organization) (2012) *Safe Abortion: Technical and Policy Guidance for Health Systems* (2nd edn, WHO).

WHO (2020) *Immunization Agenda 2030: A Global Strategy to Leave No One Behind* (WHO).

Wilks-Heeg, Stuart, Blick, Andrew and Crone, Stephen (2013) 'The Unreformed House of Lords is Already the Largest Parliamentary Chamber of Any Democracy' 10 August, *LSE Blog:* blogs.lse.ac.uk/politicsandpolicy/the-unreformed-house-of-lords-is-already-the-largest-parliamentary-chamber-of-any-democracy.

Williams, Glanville (1990) 'Force, Injury and Serious Injury' 140 *New Law Journal* 1227–1229.

Williams, Glanville (1994) 'The Fetus and the "Right to Life"' 53(1) *Cambridge Law Journal* 71–88.

Wilmut, I, Schnieke, AE, McWhir, A, et al (1997) 'Viable Offspring Derived from Fetal and Adult Mammalian Cells' 385 *Nature* 810–813.

Wilson, Peter (2021) 'The Cryonics Industry Would Like to Give You the Past Year, and Many More, Back', 29 June, *New York Times*.

Wise, Jacqui (2018) 'Baby is Born after Uterus Transplantation from Dead Donor' 361 *British Medical Journal* k5135: doi.org/10.1136/bmj.k5135.

Zeilmaker, GH, Alberda, AT, van Gent, Imprintetta, et al (1984) 'Two Pregnancies Following Transfer of Intact Frozen-Thawed Embryos' 42(2) *Fertility and Sterility* 293–296.

Zernicka-Goetz, Magdalena (2017) 'A Need to Expand Our Knowledge of Early Development' in Nuffield Council on Bioethics, *Human Embryo Culture* (Nuffield Council on Bioethics, 2017), 50–55.

INDEX

www.ingramcontent.com/pod-product-compliance
Ingram Content Group UK Ltd.
Pitfield, Milton Keynes, MK11 3LW, UK
UKHW030010020225
454486UK00005B/181

9 781509 966745